Using

Access 97

Using

Access 97

Kevin Marlowe

que®

Using Access 97

Library of Congress Catalog No.: 97-69802

ISBN: 0-7897-1439-6

00 99 98   6 5 4 3 2 1

Interpretation of the printing code: the rightmost double-digit number is the year of the book's printing; the rightmost single-digit number, the number of the book's printing. For example, a printing code of 98-1 shows that the first printing of the book occurred in 1998.

Screen reproductions in this book were created using Collage Plus from Inner Media, Inc., Hollis, NH.

Contents at a Glance

Table of Contents

III | Database Applications: Advanced Topics

Credits

Senior Vice President of Publishing
Richard K. Swadley

Publisher
Joseph B. Wikert

Executive Editor
Rosemarie Graham

Manager of Publishing Operations
Linda H. Buehler

General Manager
Joe Muldoon

Director of Editorial Services
Lisa Wilson

Managing Editor
Patrick Kanouse

Acquisitions Editor
Lisa Swayne

Senior Product Director
Lisa D. Wagner

Product Director
Melanie Palaisa

Production Editor
Linda Seifert

Product Marketing Manager
Kourtnaye Sturgeon

Assistant Product Marketing Manager
Gretchen Schlesinger

Technical Editor
David Garratt

Acquisitions Coordinator
Michelle R. Newcomb

Software Relations Coordinator
Susan D. Gallagher

Editorial Assistant
Virginia Stoller

Book Designer
Ruth Harvey
Kim Scott

Cover Designer
Sandra Schroeder

Production Team
Marcia Deboy
Trey Frank
Christy Lemasters
Paul Wilson
Donna Wright

Indexer
Tim Tate

Composed in *Century Old Style* and *ITC Franklin Gothic* by Que Corporation.

This book is dedicated to my parents, who taught me how to read, to write, and so many other things. Thanks for showing me how to reach for the brass rings when they come by and for giving me the tools to hang on.

About the Author

Kevin Marlowe is a systems analyst with Computer Sciences Corporation at NASA's Langley Research Center in Hampton, Virginia. A graduate of the University of Virginia and Old Dominion University with more than ten years' experience in information systems, his current work focuses on the management of scientific data with Access databases and the application of computing technology to scientific problems. In his spare time, he serves as an officer in the U.S. Navy Reserve and consults on office automation solutions. His interests include user interface design, the use of PCs in the technical community, gardening, and fathering. His wife and favorite computer user, Jill, is a NASA aerospace engineer. They live with their two children, future rocket scientists, in Yorktown, Virginia.

Acknowledgments

I'd like to thank the people who took my words on disk and turned them into words on paper: Lisa Swayne, Melanie Palaisa, and the staff at Que—true professionals.

Thanks also to my agent, Laura Belt for bringing this opportunity my way and making it worth my while. What's next?

Finally, as always, thanks to my wonderful wife and kids, who serve as constant reminders of all that's good in the world. Who could ask for more?

We'd Like to Hear from You!

Que Corporation has a long-standing reputation for high-quality books and products. To ensure your continued satisfaction, we also understand the importance of customer service and support.

Tech Support

If you need assistance with the information in this book or with a CD/disk accompanying the book, please access Macmillan Computer Publishing's online Knowledge Base at:

http://www.superlibrary.com/general/support

If you do not find the answer to your questions on our Web site, you may contact Macmillan Technical Support by phone at **317/581-3833** or via e-mail at **support@mcp.com**.

Also be sure to visit Que's Desktop Applications and Operating Systems team Web resource center for all the latest information, enhancements, errata, downloads, and more. It's located at:

http://www.quecorp.com/

Orders, Catalogs, and Customer Service

To order other Que or Macmillan Computer Publishing books, catalogs, or products, please contact our Customer Service Department:

Phone: 800/428-5331
Fax: 800/835-3202
International Fax: 317/228-4400

Or visit our online bookstore:

http://www.mcp.com/

Comments and Suggestions

We want you to let us know what you like or dislike most about this book or other Que products. Your comments will help us to continue publishing the best books available on computer topics in today's market.

Melanie Palaisa, Product Director
Que Corporation
201 West 103rd Street, 4B
Indianapolis, Indiana 46290 USA
Fax: 317/581-4663
E-mail: mpalaisa@mcp.com

Please be sure to include the book's title and author as well as your name and phone or fax number. We will carefully review your comments and share them with the author. Please note that due to the high volume of mail we receive, we may not be able to reply to every message.

Thank you for choosing Que!

Introduction

When you install Access 97 on your PC, you'll notice that its associated icon is a stylized, old-fashioned key. That's an apt representation of what you'll find when you fire up the program—a device that unlocks a door, behind which lies a potentially unlimited amount of data in the form of numbers, text, pictures, and even sounds and links to other sources of data. Your mouse and keyboard become the key you will use to unlock nearly any kind of information you want to keep. You will use that key to obtain access to data or processes, and by building better and stronger keys, you will add value to the data you store.

This book tells you exactly what you need to know to create powerful, flexible databases using Access 97, a component feature of Microsoft Office 97, Professional Edition (and also available separately). I'm not going to dwell on the fringe features that you'll never use; think of this book as your desktop companion to getting the job done right the first time. If there's a feature in Access that you're unlikely ever to need, you can expect that it will be dealt a glancing blow in this book. On the other hand, skills that are critical to the creation or management of top-notch databases will get all of the attention they deserve. ■

Audience

To use this book effectively, you should be familiar with the day-to-day operation of your IBM-compatible personal computer running either Microsoft Windows 95 or Windows NT (version 3.51 or later). Terms like *Windows Explorer, Clipboard,* and *minimize* should be familiar to you, and you should have an idea of how to use the Control Panel and right mouse button. The general look and feel of Microsoft Office applications should be comfortable to you, except for the annoying Office Assistants, which should be as uncomfortable to you as they are to everyone else who has ever used them. If you're an Office guru, there's meat in here for you, too—details of Access-specific VBA calls, ODBC configuration, and many of the topics that must be mastered to complete the Microsoft Certified Professional program.

Goals of This Book

This book (and the *Using* series) is designed to force-feed your brain the knowledge you need to become as accomplished a user as you desire. If all you're interested in is understanding the potential uses of a database, you'll find that information in the first few chapters. If you have a specific use for an Access database in mind, the first two-thirds of this book contains enough details and examples to enable you to create a database application. The final third of this book concentrates on the technical details that can turn an effective database application into a polished, professional product, with no fluff. And if you want to know *all* there is to know about Access...well, you can read *Special Edition Using Access 97* cover to cover.

There are a couple of additional features that make the *Using* series, and this book in particular, the perfect guides for doing real work with Office applications. The first is the extensive index in the back of this book. How many times have you looked for a specific topic in a technical book, only to find that it was indexed under a different name? Are they windows or dialog boxes? Is that control a combo box or a pull-down list? Are you interested in table relationships or in referential integrity?

We've tried to anticipate this kind of problem by building a special index to this book that attempts to guess every kind of synonym and related topic imaginable to lower your frustration level. When you're working on a deadline, who needs the frustration?

How This Book Is Organized

After this introduction, *Using Access 97* goes full-throttle to reach cruising altitude as quickly as possible:

Part I: Learning Access Database Basics

You'll find standard introductory material in the first few chapters: database design basics, using tables to store data, creating forms to enter and view data in your database. After your database is created, you can learn about using queries and reports to extract data.

Part II: Creating Database Applications

This part of the book teaches you how to build macros to automate repetitive tasks, and how to create Web pages to make your data available over the Internet. You'll also learn the basics for improving database performance and programming with modules and VBA.

Part III: Database Applications: Advanced Topics

For the adventurous, we work on advanced programming techniques and database security; we'll look at database replication across networks and ways to manipulate Windows and external applications to do our bidding. Finally, we'll discuss distributing your database, with or without the Microsoft Office 97, Developer's Edition.

Office 97 Online Resource Center

Check out Que's special Office 97 Resource Center Web site at **http://www.quecorp.com**.

We'll be presenting more topics on Access and the other Office applications there, and we'll cover new ideas and product enhancements to Access as they're available. We recognize that you're busy, and we'll keep the content of those pages dynamic and engaging with the goal of helping you use your Microsoft Office 97 package as effectively as possible.

What's New in Access 97?

Access 97 represents an incremental improvement over Access 95, which incorporated most of the benefits of the 32-bit Windows 95 architecture. Access 95 was kind of a short-lived product, however; only about a year separated its release and the release of Access 97. The quick release of Access 97 was a real boon to developers, however, as Access 95 was a buggy, temperamental product that tended to corrupt databases beyond repair. Access 97 seems to be much more stable, maybe even as stable as Access 2.0. Some people say that Microsoft gets it right for every other release, and the pattern seems to be holding with Access.

The differences between Access 97 and Access 95 are, for the most part, hidden in the details. Many large, user interface modifications and paradigm shifts were incorporated in Access 95 and Access 97's new features are less obvious to the uninitiated. These new features include:

- **More efficient memory use**.   Access 97 doesn't load code until it's actually needed, easing memory bloat and speeding up application startup (at a minimal cost to runtime performance). Microsoft insists that the new "Lightweight Forms," which don't have any code attached to them at all, further increase performance, but independent tests have failed to corroborate that claim.

- **Hyperlinks connect you to the Internet**.   A new data type, Hyperlink, is provided to provide navigation features between your database and the Internet. You could include a customer's e-mail address as a hyperlink in your database, for example, and clicking on it in a form would open up an e-mail window on a properly configured machine.

- **A new database engine**.   The heart of Access 97 is the Jet 3.5 database engine, which includes moderate performance increases over the Jet 3.0 engine in Access 95, and considerable performance increases over the engines in Access 1.0 and 2.0. The author's experience with large databases has generally shown that the same application runs faster under Access 97 on Windows NT 4.0 than did the same application under Access 2.0 on Windows 3.1 on the same machine.

■ **Real tabs**.   There were a lot of form and report enhancements in Access 95 that carry over to Access 97, but the real bonus in Access 97 is integrated Tab control. This control, heavily used in standard Windows dialog boxes, was only available as a third-party product in Access 2.0 and only available with the Developer's Kit for Access 95. It's included in every copy of Access 97.

■ **Module-building enhancements**.   Access includes wizard-like features that suggest appropriate completions for built-in functions and properties *as you type them* in the Code Builder window. It's often enough to remember the name of a built-in function; as you start typing it, Access shows you all of the possible parameters for it and their data types.

Of course, the new features of Access 97 that are most useful to you are dependent on how you use Access. For a detailed list of the new features in Access 97 (and in Access 95), see the topic "What's New about Access 97?" in Access help.

Notations Used in This Book

The following special features are provided in this book to assist readers.

 Tips are intended to help you use Access more effectively by recommending (or clarifying) techniques that may not be apparent from the context. For example, a tip might tell you to avoid using drawing objects in Web pages, because the Save As HTML Wizard tends to delete such objects. You might figure this out for yourself, but you can avoid some grief by reading the tip.

N O T E   When a tip is of a more general nature, or isn't critical to the specific task being discussed, it may be placed in an unobtrusive note for your reading pleasure. ■

CAUTION

Cautions exist to warn you of potentially dire consequences of certain actions. For example, using the `Set Warnings False` statement in VBA can result in critical error messages not being shown to the user, possibly causing a loss of data or your application to crash. This kind of information will typically be found in a caution.

To try and save you from the frustration of paging back and forth to the index when you want to find out all there is to know about a given topic, we've included cross-references throughout the book that will help you follow a topic from chapter to chapter.

▶ **See** "Using Design View," **p. 23**

Learning Access Database Basics

Designing Databases

Just as the best houses are built on strong foundations, so are the best databases designed around some tried-and-true theory. This chapter isn't a graduate course in database performance and organization. Some basic database concepts will go a long way toward making your Access databases more efficient and maintainable, and after a few tries they'll become rote. ■

Learn the differences between databases and spreadsheets

All too often, people use spread-sheets to store large volumes of data because the row/column format is easy and familiar. Sometimes, that's appropriate. You'll learn when it's not, and how to convert spread-sheets to database tables.

Discover the features of Access

Access databases are made up of several components: tables, forms, queries, reports, macros, and mod-ules. You'll see how they differ and how to create and edit each type of component.

Create a simple database

The best way to get comfortable with the product is to get your hands dirty and try it. This chapter gets you started before referring you to later chapters for details.

The Differences Between Databases and Spreadsheets

Most computer-savvy people know what a spreadsheet is. It's an intuitive way to present data: neat columns and rows, totals at the bottom, titles across the top. It turns out that this representation of data is correct for databases, too; the objects that Excel calls *spreadsheets* (or *worksheets*) are called *tables* in most database programs. *Rows* become *records*; *columns* become *fields*. It is possible to build a database that accurately reproduces the look and feel of a spreadsheet—in fact, that's how most databases begin.

Where databases excel (no pun intended) and spreadsheets fall by the wayside is in the implementation of *relationships*. In a database, key elements of data in one table (a spreadsheet) are related to identical elements in other tables (or spreadsheets). This linking of tables allows databases to do many more tasks than most run-of-the-mill spreadsheets, like ensure the correctness (or integrity) of data entered and permit data changed in one table to change data in a related one. If your data doesn't fit easily into a simple two-dimensional grid, maybe it's time to consider using Access instead of Excel.

Spreadsheets aren't all bad, though—they are expert at crunching data to arrive at results, usually represented by a formula or a graph. While Access can perform enough calculations for most applications, it's not the tool to use to compute a loan amortization.

To make an intelligent decision about whether a spreadsheet or a database is appropriate for a given application, it may help to consider a typical use for an office spreadsheet and see how it might be better served by a database instead.

Pushing the Limits of Spreadsheets

Consider an inventory of office computers, entered into a spreadsheet by the developer of the spreadsheet and modified by several other people over time. It might look like Figure 1.1.

FIG. 1.1

An office inventory spreadsheet.

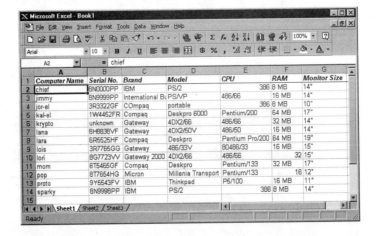

Because data can clearly include text as well as numbers, some of the spreadsheet cells contain text information, like brand names, and part numbers. Even though Excel is a number-cruncher *par excellence*, it wouldn't make any sense to perform calculations on these "fields," like summing them; they are there just to be stored and retrieved. A quick look at the spreadsheet tells you exactly what you need to know about a given piece of equipment. But there are problems brewing here. If you look closely at the spreadsheet in Figure 1.1, you may notice the following:

- *There's no consistency to the manufacturer names used.* Sometimes it's IBM, and sometimes it's International Business Machines. How are you going to run a report of all IBM machines when you call them something different in different rows?

- *A similar problem exists with the software records.* The designer of this spreadsheet created space for 10 installed software applications, but is Microsoft Office one application or five? Sometimes it's entered as MS Office, sometimes as Word/Excel/PowerPoint, and so on. Good luck pulling out the Microsoft software records!

- *The spreadsheet is pretty limited in functionality.* What if you wanted to store a picture of each machine in its row? For that matter, what if you wanted to attach a scanned image of a repair order or attach the e-mail that authorized its purchase? There's only so much that a spreadsheet can do, and that limit is quickly reached.

It's certainly possible to create a database with all of the same problems you see here, but it's actually pretty hard to do that. Where spreadsheets are superior collators and calculators of data, databases are the preeminent organizers and verifiers. If the main thrust behind your use of a computer program to store your data isn't the calculation of results, you should probably be thinking "database" instead of "spreadsheet."

There are certainly some things that spreadsheets do better than databases. Don't even try to do detailed financial analysis with a database! You may, however, consider using a database to store raw financial data and export relevant records to Excel when you need to crunch the numbers. For quick and dirty charts, nothing beats a spreadsheet, although a database makes it easier to create charts based on only certain subsets of your data (like a criteria query in Excel). Learning when to use a spreadsheet and when to use a database for a given task is a matter of practice and experience; if you know how to use a database, though, you'll be in a better position to make the right decision.

How a Database Organizes Data

The standard representation of data in a database looks the same as it does in a spreadsheet—a two-dimensional array of rows and columns. In fact, there are several database elements that are similar in appearance and use to a spreadsheet. Some of these are summarized in Table 1.1.

Table 1.1 Spreadsheet versus Database Terminology

Spreadsheet Name	Database Name
Worksheet, Spreadsheet	Table
Row	Record
Column	Field
Cell	(no equivalent)
(no equivalent)	Key Field
Workbook	Database
Macro	Macro
Form	Form, Report
Query	Query
Control	Control
Pivot Table	Crosstab Query

Of course, there's more to each kind of application than the table shows, but you get the idea. A key difference between the two is that it's highly unlikely that you'll ever see two identical records in any database table. This is because most well-designed databases require that the data in at least one field in every table will be guaranteed unique among all of the records. In a spreadsheet, this would be like guaranteeing that at least one column in a worksheet will have a different value in every row. This sometimes happens by chance, but a good database will force it to be true. This special field is called a *key*, and it is indeed the key to the ability of a database program to validate data and maintain what's called *data integrity*.

In the previous example, each row in the office inventory spreadsheet is uniquely identified by a computer name. It wouldn't make sense to have two computers with the same name, so we can assume that the computer name acts as a key. If we were to import this spreadsheet into a database program like Access, there would be no problem converting this spreadsheet into a table; the field "Computer Name" would become a key field, and each row of the spreadsheet would become a record in the table, as in Figure 1.2.

Unfortunately, a database table used in the same way as a spreadsheet is no better than a spreadsheet for most applications. We still can't extract all of the IBM machines, for example, because they were entered differently. Furthermore, it's harder to work with this spreadsheet in its table form because many of its fields are forced off the edge of the screen. But we're not through yet—we need to make some changes to the structure of this table to make the value of using a database apparent.

Microsoft Excel, and most spreadsheet applications, permit you to organize several separate worksheets into a *workbook*. You typically use different worksheets to break a large, monolithic spreadsheet into manageable pieces, but there's usually not anything relating one worksheet to another. It's convenient to organize a database in the same way; you organize fields into subject areas or categories of data and put them in separate tables for clarity and ease of use. Unlike worksheets, though, you carry the field containing the key into all of the smaller tables to maintain the relationship between all of the tables. This practice gives birth to the name *relational database*, which is what Access is.

FIG. 1.2

The office inventory spreadsheet imported into Access as a single table.

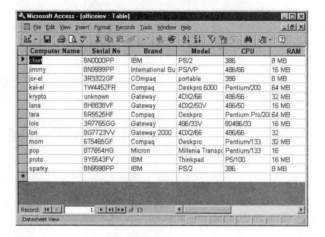

Computer Name	Serial No	Brand	Model	CPU	RAM
chief	6N0000PP	IBM	PS/2	386	8 MB
jimmy	8N9999PP	International Bu	PS/VP	486/66	16 MB
jor-el	3R3322GF	COmpaq	portable	386	8 MB
kal-el	1W4452FR	Compaq	Deskpro 6000	Pentium/200	64 MB
krypto	unknown	Gateway	4DX2/66	486/66	32 MB
lana	8H8838VF	Gateway	4DX2/50V	486/50	16 MB
lara	6R5525HF	Compaq	Deskpro	Pentium Pro/20	64 MB
lois	3R7765GG	Gateway	486/33V	80486/33	16 MB
lori	8G7723VV	Gateway 2000	4DX2/66	486/66	32
mom	6T5465GF	Compaq	Deskpro	Pentium/133	32 MB
pop	8T7654HG	Micron	Millenia Transpc	Pentium/133	16
proto	9Y5543FV	IBM	Thinkpad	P5/100	16 MB
sparky	8N9998PP	IBM	PS/2	386	8 MB

Restructuring Data into Related Tables

You can apply these concepts to the table shown in Figure 1.2 by breaking it down into three smaller tables:

■ The *administration table* contains information about the computer model and serial number.

■ The *hardware table* includes details about the CPU and RAM in each machine.

■ The *software table* stores the installed software list.

To maintain the relationships between the tables, you need to make sure that they all have something in common—like the key field discussed earlier. The Computer Name field is maintained in all three tables, and the result looks like Figure 1.3.

This is better, but Access has no way of knowing that the three small tables are related. You can use Access' Relationships window to connect the key fields of all three tables, which links them inextricably together (see Figure 1.4).

▶ **See** "Understanding Table Relationships," **p. 36**

By drawing two lines, you've added a lot of structure to this spreadsheet:

■ Creating the relationship between all of the tables ensures that a computer with one name in one table is always referred to in the same way in all of the tables (this is *referential integrity*).

FIG. 1.3

The office inventory spreadsheet as three related tables.

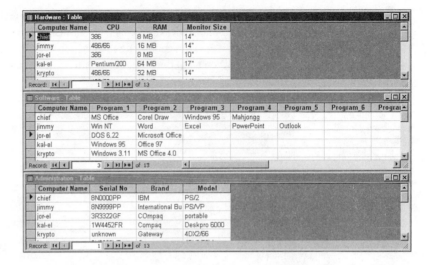

- Because the Computer Name field is a key field, you know that no two machines can have the same name.

- The relationship between all of the tables allows you to treat all of them as if they were one table, or to extract certain information from all or some of them.

FIG. 1.4

The Relationships window, with the three tables in the office inventory linked together.

Tables organize data into subject areas or categories

Fields in the table

These lines show that the tables are related through the key field called Computer Name

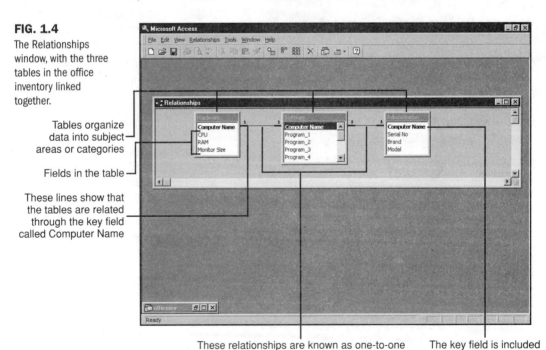

These relationships are known as one-to-one relationships. There are two other relationship types, as discussed in Chapter 2.

The key field is included in all the tables involved in the relationship

In a few simple steps, you've changed a doomed spreadsheet into a database. This should have been a database in the first place, and the panic caused by the data problems could have been prevented.

Starting Access

When you start Access for the first time, it fills the screen, and you're asked if you want to create a new database or open an existing one. Most of the examples in this book, use the Northwind Traders sample database that ships with Access.

If you're following along, you can click the OK button at this point and Access displays a File Selection dialog box. Find the Northwind database on your hard disk (usually \Program Files\Microsoft Office\Office\Samples\Northwind.mdb) and select it. You'll see a splash screen, which you can happily close (click the Close button in the top-right corner).

TIP If you can't find Northwind on your disk, you may not have installed it. Insert your Access or Office Pro CD, run Setup, and ensure that you've installed the Sample Databases under Access.

The Database Window

The screen in front of you should look something like Figure 1.5. This view of the desktop is called the *Database view*; it includes the Database menu bar, the Database toolbar, and the Database window in the middle of the desktop. The horizontal bar at the bottom of the screen is called the *status bar*.

FIG. 1.5

The Database window is the primary tool you'll use to create and manipulate databases.

TIP You can't open more than one database in Access at one time. You can, however, open more than one copy of Access and open different databases in each of them.

Most of the icons and menu options should be familiar to you if you've used other Office applications. The real work in Access is performed in the Database window, which you use to select and create objects of the six major types that Access supports. They are:

- **Tables**   The spreadsheets of the database that arrange data in rows and columns on the screen. Internally, tables store data as records, which correspond roughly to the rows displayed in Table view. Tables are discussed in Chapter 2.

- **Queries**   Requests for tables to extract or organize data in a certain way, and then to display it. Queries are usually designed using an easy-to-understand graphical interface, and are stored in the standard Structured Query Language (SQL). For more information about queries, see Chapter 4.

- **Forms**   Provide a nice front-end to enter data into the database or to view it on-screen. Access forms are used as the primary user interface in database applications by hiding the uglier tables from view. There's more about forms in Chapter 3.

- **Reports**   Extract data from tables, often using queries, and format it for presentation on paper. You can't enter data using reports (use forms for that). Report design is discussed in Chapter 6.

- **Macros**   Contain collections of commands that Access follows to produce a certain result, like opening a form or running a query. Macros are used to create custom menus and to execute simple commands when programming seems too complicated. We'll look at macros in Chapter 7.

- **Modules**   Contain one or more subroutines or functions written in *Visual Basic for Applications (VBA)*, the common programming language used in all Microsoft Office applications. VBA code can be used to make the database do anything it's capable of doing, from shutting itself down to reconciling a day's ATM transactions. The bulk of this book from Chapter 10 on concerns using modules.

To create or view an object of any of these types, click the appropriate tab at the top of the Database window. A list of all existing objects of the selected type will appear; you can then select any of these objects and use the buttons on the side of the Database window to:

- Open it (which means "view it" for forms, tables, and reports, and run a macro or query)
- Design it (edit the selected object)
- Create a new object of the current type

Creating New Objects

Most of the object types visible in the Database window have a bewildering myriad of options available for creating new instances of similar objects. For example, if you select the Forms tab, then click the New button, you'll be asked if you want to create a new form in Design view, with the Form Wizard, by using three different types of AutoForms, or the Chart Wizard or Pivot Table Wizard. Finally, you're asked where the data for the form is coming from.

Unless you know what each of these options does, the only safe bets are the first two: Design view, which gives you a blank canvas to work on, and the Form Wizard, which walks you through the steps of creating the object you've specified. You could easily design an entire application by never using anything but Design view.

N O T E There are no wizards for modules and macros. You're automatically taken to their respective design environments, called the *Macro Builder* and *Module Builder* windows. ▪

To get a feel for how Access works, let's create a simple table.

1. Close Northwind (if you have it open) and open a blank database.

2. Go to the Tables window by clicking the Tables tab, click the New button, and select the Table Wizard as your method for creating the table. The Table Wizard is shown briefly again in Chapter 2.

3. Access comes with almost two dozen built-in databases, so choose a table from the Sample Table list concerning a topic that interests you to store data.

4. In the Sample Fields list, click the field(s) you want in the table. After each selection, click the button with the single arrow-head pointing to the right to move the field to the Fields window in the My New Table list. If you prefer, you can click the double-headed arrow to move all the sample fields into this list.

5. After you've selected several fields, click Next and enter a name for your table.

6. Finally, click Finish.

7. When your new table is displayed, click the Close button at the upper-right corner to return to the Database window. Your new table is listed under the Table tab.

Creating simple forms is just as easy. To create a simple data entry form:

1. From the Database window, select the Forms tab, then click the New button.

2. In the New Form dialog that appears, choose the Form Wizard.

3. Before clicking Next to continue, click the down arrow (called a combo box) next to the empty text field at the bottom of the New Form dialog. You'll see a list of all the tables and queries currently defined; select the table you just created. Now click the Next button.

4. The next window of the Form Wizard asks which fields in your table you want on the form. Choose several by selecting them individually and clicking the right arrow button to move them to the "Selected Fields" pane one at a time. Experiment with the arrow buttons and see what effect they have on the fields selected. Finally, click Next.

5. You'll be given four options that specify how the data fields in your form will be laid out. Select Columnar for now and click Next to continue.

6. Ten styles are displayed, corresponding to colors and text styles for your form. Select each style in turn to see how they look, and click Next when you've settled on one.

7. Click Finish to save your form and display it, complete with data.

You can use the form to enter and view data in your table if you like. In Chapter 3, you'll get detailed instructions on how to use the Form Wizard and Design view to create tables and forms from scratch.

▶ **See** "Storing Your Data," **p. 21**

▶ **See** "Entering Data in the Database with Forms," **p. 49**

Designing a Database

It's possible to design an awful database that reproduces all of the errors of the worst spreadsheet, but it's very hard to do. There are several things that you can do to help ensure that your database is efficient and functional:

- *Understand your data.* If you're designing for your own use, figure out what all of the data elements are and what kinds of information they need to track before you create a table to store them. If the data is numeric, what format does it follow? If it's text, is it long (greater than 255 characters) or short? Is it none of the above, like a picture or a document?

- *Use all of the features of Access.* Design tables with keys, and establish relationships between those keys. Create queries to see if you can easily extract the data from the tables you've designed. Design forms to see if you can easily enter and view the data in your tables.

- *Keep it simple.* Make your tables small and easy to understand. Use descriptive names for objects and variables, following a naming scheme if you can. Choose your keys carefully, selecting the smallest element of data that uniquely identifies a record.

- *Enlist others to help.* You'll be amazed at the data elements that others will think are critical which you didn't even list. If you're designing a database for someone with a different level of computer knowledge than yourself, expect questions about parts of your design that seem intuitive to you.

Entire careers are made around the "correct" and efficient design of databases. Fortunately, it's possible to create very efficient and technically correct databases from scratch with only a little practice; you should expect to make mistakes along the way and to have to go back and change things many times before you get it right.

Using the Database Wizard to Create Tables

If the database you're about to create is simple and straightforward, and you find yourself thinking "Someone must have set up one of these before," and you're probably right. In those cases, you might consider starting with the Database Wizard. The Database Wizard presents you with a set of database templates that describe some commonly used types of databases, and you can either use them as is or customize them to your liking.

To use the Database Wizard:

1. Start Access. If Access is already running, select File, then New from the menu.

2. When the Microsoft Access dialog box appears, select the Database Wizard, and click OK.

3. In the New dialog box, select the Databases tab. You'll see 22 predesigned databases (see Figure 1.6). The General tab contains only one option, a blank database, for which the wizard isn't useful.

4. Select any of these by double-clicking the appropriate icon. Unlike the preview windows in Microsoft Word or Excel, the Preview window doesn't show a useful preview of the database.

N O T E You'll see several different file extensions while working with Access that may not be familiar. A few of the more common include:

.mdb Microsoft Access database

.ldb Access database index file, automatically generated

.mda Access system database (stores security information)

.mde Access compiled application database (non-editable)

.mdz Access database template

FIG. 1.6
The Database Wizard shows a list of predesigned databases from which to choose.

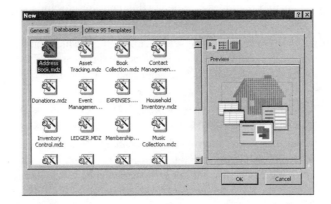

5. After you select a sample database, the File New Database dialog box appears and you'll be prompted for a file name for your new copy of the database. Choose a name and location for the database file, and click Create.

T I P If you've used wizards in other Office applications, this wizard will be very familiar and comfortable to you. You'll notice the same Next, Back, and Finish buttons at the bottom of each wizard screen which allow you to move forward when you've completed the information in the current screen, or to move back to a previous screen if you need to change previously completed information. You can end the wizard by clicking the Cancel button. If you click the Finish button, the wizard creates the database with all the current settings.

6. Next, you'll see a series of wizard screens that ask you questions about how you want your database to work. The first screen describes the application you've chosen and provides a list of the kinds of information it will track. Click Next to move to the next screen.

7. The second Wizard screen displays the tables in the database. If you select a table from list, its fields are displayed in the right window. A check mark next to the field indicates it will appear in the table. If you click the field to remove the check mark, the field will not

be made a part of the table. Scroll through the list of fields for each table to make sure the ones you want are included in the table. On this second screen, depending on which template you chose, you'll see different dialog boxes and different questions; these typically include questions about which fields you want various tables to contain and whether you want sample data written to your database. Click Next to move to the next wizard screen.

 Checking "Include Sample Data" can be useful for beginners, or if you want to see how the application works. After you are finished looking at the sample data, all the sample records can easily be deleted.

8. The third and fourth wizard screens allow you to select the color scheme and font styles for the database's forms and printed reports. As you select each style, a sample is displayed on-screen. You can change the look of the report here but you can't change what kind of information is included in the report or how the information is organized. Choose a style on each screen and click Next.

9. The last wizard screen lets you select a name under which the database can be saved to disk, and what to call the database (this can be different from the file name). It's a good idea to use short, simple names for your disk files, and descriptive names for your databases. By default, Access doesn't use short, descriptive names. The database name will be displayed while you're working in the database, but users will never see the file name you choose. Click Finish.

10. The database will start, and you'll be presented with the main form of the application that was just designed for you, called the *Main Switchboard*. The Database window, which contains the tables, forms, and reports that make up your database, is automatically minimized in the lower left corner of the screen.

 The database Wizard creates several professionally designed objects for your database, but that doesn't mean you have to like them. Any of them can be modified in their respective Design Views by selecting the object you want to change in the Database window (you'll have to restore it to normal size first) and selecting Design. Chapters 2 through 8 and Chapter 10 discuss the details of customizing database objects of all types.

This is an incredibly easy way to get started, and the results are quite professional. If one of these predesigned databases can fulfill your needs, then you've just gotten most of your Access purchase price back in productivity gains. Using Access in this way is just like buying a suite of off-the-shelf databases from your local software store, and it may well suffice.

To discover how to create tables from scratch or to modify the tables the wizard generated for you, you'll want to read on. Chapter 2 describes how to work with tables, which do most of the work of a database. If you used the Database Wizard to create your tables, you can edit and modify them to your liking using the techniques in the next chapter. ●

Storing Your Data

Tables are the building blocks of databases. They do the hard work of organizing and storing your data so you can enter more or retrieve it later. It's possible to have a database without queries, forms, macros, modules, or reports, but you've got to have tables. Access makes entering data into tables as easy as entering data into spreadsheets, and provides tools to handle the hard work of defining the characteristics of data stored in tables and the relationships tables have to one another. ■

Learn what tables are and explore Access data types

You can't have a database without tables. This chapter discusses how to create and edit them.

Learn about keys and indices

The power of a relational database derives from key fields, which are guaranteed to contain unique data. Key fields are closely related to indexed fields.

Get comfortable with table relationships

If keys are defined in database tables, relationships can be inferred between them. This gives separate tables the capability to work together as a complete system.

Get comfortable with normalization

Normalization is the practice of constructing your database so data isn't duplicated unless it's in a key. This makes for efficient structure and readies your database for the later addition of more tables.

Learn how to use the Table Analyzer Wizard

Access contains a program that will "read" the structure of individual tables in your database and recommend changes.

Creating Tables

Database tables store your data and make it available to all of the other objects in a database application for manipulation, display, and reporting. It's sufficiently easy to create and modify Access tables so that you don't need to try to get it right the first time; you can work within Table Design view as easily as you can sketch tables with a pen on a napkin.

There are several ways to build tables in Access. The simplest and most versatile is Design view, which gives you a blank grid in which you define data fields and specify options for those fields. Design view is discussed later, because it's probably where you'll do most of your table design work. However, Access also provides several wizards to ease the task of defining tables. If one of these wizards satisfies your requirements, you'll save a little time.

To create a new table using any of these methods:

1. From the Database window, select the Tables tab to view the Tables pane.
2. Click the New button.
3. Select the table creation option you want from the list presented. Access includes the following table creation options and wizards:

   - **Datasheet view**.   A blank spreadsheet into which you enter data values. Access guesses at the data types if you haven't already defined them in Design view.
   - **Design view**.   A blank grid into which you select data definitions from a list. You don't actually enter any data in this view.
   - **Table Wizard**.   Drawing from a list of a couple dozen predefined databases, Access walks you through the process of selecting fields and establishing keys and relationships.
   - **Import Table**.   Used to import a data table in another file, created in Access or another recognized database application.
   - **Link Table**.   Like Import Table, but the external data remains in the external file.

▶ **See** "Importing and Exporting Data," **p. 42**

Datasheet view is most useful when you've already designed your tables and want to enter data directly into them. It's more convenient to use either the Table Wizard or Design view to create new tables.

Design view is probably where you'll create your database tables and edit the structure of your tables. For details, see the section that follows "Using Design View."

You'll find the Table Wizard very straightforward and easy to use, if limited. If the application you're developing is similar to one of the predefined databases, this may be a good place to start. You can then use Design view to edit the selections the Table Wizard makes for you.

You'll almost never use the Import Table or Link Table options from here, because they're easier to use from the menu.

Using Design View

When you create a new table in Design view, you're presented with a grid that looks like Figure 2.1, except that yours will appear empty.

FIG. 2.1

A filled-in table definition (Northwind.Customers) in Design view.

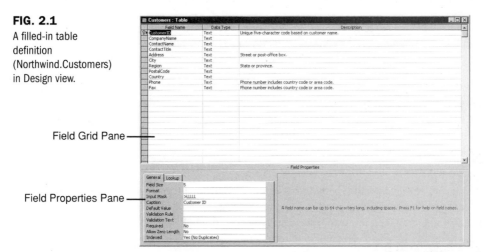

Field Grid Pane

Field Properties Pane

The grid at the top of the window, called the *Field Grid pane*, is where you'll enter the names and specify the types of the fields that will make up your table. The pane at the bottom, called the *Field Properties pane*, allows you to modify the properties of each field in the table. As you enter the data types of fields in the Data Type column in the Field Grid pane, you'll see the list of properties in the Table Properties pane change.

To create a new field in your table:

1. Type a name in the Field Names column.
2. Select a data type in the Data Type column from the pull-down combo box provided (see the next section, "Understanding Access Data Types," for details).
3. Enter a comment describing how the field is to be used in the Description column (optional).
4. Tab or click the next row's Field Name to start entering another field.

Access field names are limited to 64 characters, including numbers and most punctuation (look up "object naming rules" in Access help for more details). If you're going to refer to this field frequently in forms or other Access objects, consider keeping the name short and avoiding the use of spaces to make the task of typing the name easier.

▶ **See** "Common Uses for Forms," **p. 50**

The number of fields you can enter in a single table is large, but most tables become unmanageable after about 30 fields. If your table seems to need more fields, you might consider other ways of building the table to simplify it, or breaking it up into several smaller tables.

Part

I

Ch

2

NOTE A common error in defining fields to store information by date is the definition of separate fields for each month in the year or each day of the month. A table containing the fields product_name, product_sales_jan, product_sales_feb, and so on (13 fields) would be better structured as product_name, sales_month, and sales_amt (three fields). ■

To edit a field in an existing table, or one you've entered erroneously in a new table, simply select it and change the appropriate field name, data type, or property.

CAUTION

Be careful when changing the data type of fields that already have data stored in them; if the new format uses less internal storage than the old one did (as when changing a floating-point number to an integer), you may lose some precision or your data may be truncated to fit the new format. Access will warn you if this is about to happen.

To save your work, close the Design view window by clicking the Close button in the upper-right corner. Access will save your changes in the original table if you're editing an existing one, or prompt you for a name for your new table. As with fields, table names can be as many as 64 characters long and can contain letters, Ïumbers, spaces, and most punctuation. Keep the names short to make typing easier later.

CAUTION

After you save a modified table, you can't undo your changes. Make sure that you've made changes you intend to keep before exiting Design view and saving your work. Also, make frequent backups.

Understanding Access Data Types

It wouldn't make sense to store a sentence in a field designated for numbers, and you couldn't store an image in a field intended for a date. The type of data that you select for each field determines how Access will store it. Therefore, selecting the correct data type for each field is particularly critical to obtaining the correct information from your database.

Access provides nine different types for data as described in Table 2.1.

Table 2.1   Access Data Types

Data Type	Description
Text	A set of up to 50 characters (including numbers and punctuation)
Memo	Like text, but of essentially unlimited length
Number	An integer or floating-point number

Data Type	Description
Date/Time	A date or time in one of seven different formats, ranging from hh:mm to day/month/year, hh:mm:ss
Currency	A number, but comma separators and two decimal points are automatically assumed, and negative numbers appear in parentheses
AutoNumber	An integer that automatically increments as records are added to a table
Yes/No	A boolean type, used to store simple True/False, On/Off, or Yes/No values
OLE Object	A miscellaneous object, like an image or sound; usually not text or numbers
Hyperlink	A reference to an external document that, when selected, opens that document in its appropriate view

N O T E One additional data type is available: The Lookup Wizard data type prompts to retrieve a value(s) from another table or query, and sets the data type for the field in question to the data type of the result. You can use any standard Select query, in SQL or created with the Query Builder, to make a value in a Lookup field appear to be something it's not. For example, Northwind uses a Lookup to make the numeric field [EmployeeID] in the Orders table appear as the name of the employee (from the Employees table) when the Orders table is displayed in Datasheet view. ▪

▶ **See** "Select Queries," **p. 72**

For most general-purpose fields, you'll use the Text or Number data types. It's reasonable to expect that 90 percent of all of your fields will be one or the other of these "basic" data types. If you're working with relatively large pieces of textual data, like entire documents (or even individual paragraphs), you'll want to use the Memo data type.

 If you have the least suspicion that the contents of a field may exceed 255 characters, use Memo type instead of Text. Access truncates your data at the 256th character if you use the default Text type, and various errors and annoying warnings result.

The Currency, Date/Time, and Yes/No data types are extensions to the basic types mentioned earlier. You could use Number instead of Currency, Number (or Text) instead of Date/Time, and Number or Text instead of Yes/No. These data types are provided for your convenience and make programming Access applications and designing forms easier. If your data is one of these types, it may help later to use these specific types rather than sticking with the generic number or text types.

The AutoNumber type is especially useful in applications where you're assigning serial numbers, order IDs, or the like. If you need to be sure that no two records share the same ID, use AutoNumber, and make Access do the work for you. If you assign a field the type AutoNumber, it appears in Datasheet view as in Figure 2.2.

FIG. 2.2

The AutoNumber data type guarantees unique integer IDs for each record.

The data type of the currently selected record is AutoNumber...

...and the attributes relevant to an AutoNumber field appear in the Field Properties pane

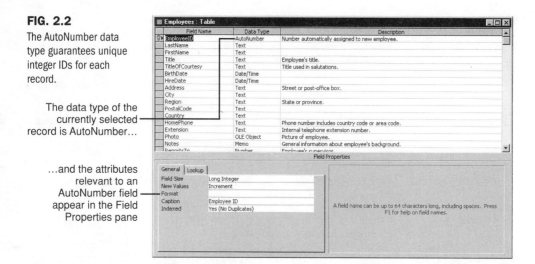

Even if you delete some data later, Access picks up numbering where you left off. If you start numbering at a number other than 1, Access continues from the highest ID entered so far.

The AutoNumber data type is especially useful when you need to generate a unique key field for data that isn't otherwise guaranteed unique, as in Figure 2.2. In this example, there's no reason why you could assume that any of the fields shown should be unique, so it's convenient to let Access assign unique numbers that you can use as references later—or even use as keys to link to other tables (see the section "Understanding Table Relationships" later in this chapter).

If you specify a field in one table to be type AutoNumber with the intention of linking it to another table, remember to make the key field in the other table of type Number (Long Integer), or the relationship will not work.

An *OLE object* is, in short, a file. In other databases, this type is sometimes called *BLOB*, or *Binary Large Database Object*; it is intended to store large pieces of data that are typically (but not necessarily) stored in files on a disk. Once you've created a table that includes a field of type OLE Object, you can select the empty field in Datasheet view (or on a form), and select the Insert, Object command from the menu. A listing of the object types registered with your local copy of Windows will appear, looking something like the Insert Object dialog box shown in Figure 2.3.

The list of available objects in the Insert Object dialog box may appear somewhat different on your system, depending on what object-creating applications you have installed. If you select the Create from File radio button, you can select the file you want to store in the database. You'll be asked to decide whether you want to Link it; selecting this option reduces your database size but requires the file to remain on the disk. An embedded (as opposed to linked) file object can be deleted after embedding, and it will remain stored safely in the database.

FIG. 2.3

The Insert Object dialog box, where you can select a type of object to create, or the file name of an existing binary object (BLOB).

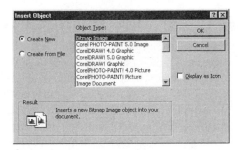

If you prefer to create a new object from scratch, you can choose any of the object types shown in the Object Type list and the associated application will start.

N O T E The data that you store in an OLE Object field won't necessarily be displayed either in Datasheet view or in a form. Because Access treats all OLE objects the same, it has no way of knowing how to display the object you've embedded; you'll need to use a custom control for special handling of your BLOB when showing it to users in your database application.

Lastly, the Hyperlink data type is new in Access 97. It permits the storage of data that is intended to supply only an address to a remote document. When a user selects that address in Datasheet view or on a form, the appropriate application to read that type of document will start, and the document will be displayed. In the most common case, this data type is used to link sites on the World Wide Web (as *Uniform Resource Locators*, or *URLs*) to your database, allowing potential users to see whatever it is on a Web site that is somehow pertinent to the current record.

N O T E URLs are addresses that specify the location of a specific document on a specific computer on the Internet. Most URLs are of the form:

http://computername/documentname

indicating that the address given references a page on the World Wide Web that can be viewed using a browser like Microsoft's Internet Explorer or Netscape's Navigator. Some URLs contain:

ftp://computername/filename

denoting a reference to a file for download, or **mailto://person** to send mail to a particular person.

Depending on the data type you select, certain options may become pertinent to the field you're describing. For example, if you mark a field as type Number, what kind of number is it? You'll see the options for the current data type displayed in the Field Properties pane of the Design view (refer to Figure 2.2).

Setting Field Property Options for Data Types

You can only change your data types and set the values of field properties while in Design view, and you use the Field Properties pane (see Figure 2.4) of the Design view window to do that. You'll see all the field attributes for the current data type listed on the General tab, and we'll discuss these attributes in the next few sections (the Lookup tab is covered later in the chapter in the section "Using Lookups in Tables"). These attributes change when you change the data type of a given field in a table. All data types share some options, or *attributes*, and most have several that can be configured. In general, the defaults that Access selects suffice for most data fields.

FIG. 2.4

The Field Properties pane for a field of type Number. All of the different properties panes look more or less the same, with different attributes to select and modify.

The selected data type

Attributes for the selected data type

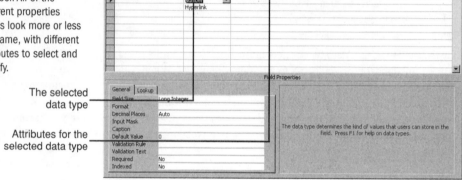

The attributes you'll change most often are the Field Size for numbers and text, and the Format for numbers and dates.

The Field Size Attribute

The data type Number supports six subtypes, denoted by entries in the Field Size attribute in the Field Properties pane of Design view. When you click the text box containing the current value of the Field Size attribute, a drop-down list appears. Click the small arrow to view the following options as shown in Table 2.2.

Table 2.2   Number Subtypes

Subtype Name	Description
Byte	Stores integers from 0 to 255, and each value takes up one byte on the disk; used only rarely for small positive numbers where disk space or system memory is an issue.

Subtype Name	Description
Integer	Whole numbers from –32,768 to 32,767, two bytes; used for most whole numbers in practice.
Long Integer	Whole numbers from about –2 billion to +2 billion, four bytes; used for very large numbers or, more commonly, to allow referential integrity links to fields of type AutoNumber.
Single	Just about any floating point (decimal) numbers to seven decimal places, four bytes; used for most numbers, including decimals.
Double	Incredibly large negative or positive floating point numbers to 15 decimal places, eight bytes; used rarely for very large decimal numbers or for calculations requiring extreme precision.
Replication ID	A special number used internally by Access to uniquely identify database objects (see Chapter 15), 16 bytes; used for table replication applications (see Chapter 14).

You should always use the smallest numeric data type that will absolutely handle all of the imaginable data your field may someday contain. Don't use Byte for a customer number, assuming you'll never have more than 255 customers, for example. Generally, you'll use Integer for whole numbers (Long Integer for scientific data) and Single for fractional numbers.

The only other data type with the Field Size attribute (except for AutoNumber's Replication ID subtype, which is discussed in Chapter 15) is Text, which defaults to 50 characters. Because Text is limited by Access to 255 characters maximum, you may be better off using 50 as a practical limit and using the Memo data type if your data is longer than 50 characters. If it can be longer than 50, it can probably be longer than 255, too.

The Format Attribute

Setting the format of your data affects the default appearance of the data on forms and reports. You can always change the format for a specific report or form, but you have a chance to make a decision about the preferred appearance by clicking the Format Attribute box, clicking the drop-down arrow button, and choosing the desired format from the list. Formats can be specified for all data types except OLE Object and AutoNumber, and the formatting rules are different for each data type.

You should understand the kinds of effects formatting can have on the appearance of your data. For example, the format options for numbers affect the number of decimal places shown, the appearance of exponents, and custom options for positive numbers, negative numbers, zero, and nulls (the absence of data). You can even specify the colors in which the data appears based on its value.

 The default decimal separator is a period (.), and the thousands separator is a comma (,). If you're formatting data for use where these defaults are not correct, you can change the settings for all of your Windows programs by changing the Regional Settings in the Control Panel.

For text (including the Text and Memo data types), the format settings affect the style of the text displayed, forcing it all to uppercase (format specifier >) or lowercase (<), or forcing it to appear in a standard format (like a phone number, format specifier (@@@) @@@-@@@@ in the U.S.). Remember that these settings only affect the display of the data, not the values themselves; this means that a phone number stored as **2024353342** would appear as (202) 435-3342 in the previous example, but data entered as **(202) 435-3342** would display as (202() 4) 35-3342. (This anomaly can be prevented by use of the Input Mask attribute for text and memos; see the online help for more information.)

Other Attributes

Here is a quick synopsis of the other attributes you'll find in the Field Properties pane of Design view:

- **Input Mask**. A pattern for data to be entered in this field. Using certain characters, you can force data entry to be of a certain length or contain certain characters.
- **Caption**. The field name that Access automatically assigns to this field when it is used on a form. This can be (and often is) overridden by the designer.
- **Default Value**. A value to use for this field in all new records.
- **Validation Rule**. A literal or expression that Access checks newly entered data against and rejects if it doesn't match. For example, if a field called Color can only contain primary colors, you might set the Validation Rule to Red;Yellow;Blue.
- **Validation Text**. The text that Access displays when someone enters invalid data (as determined by the Validation Rule) in a field.
- **Required**. Set to Yes if a valid entry in this field is required for a record to be saved in the database. Key fields (see the upcoming section "Understanding Table Relationships") are assumed to be required.
- **Allow Zero Length**. Set to Yes if zero-length strings ("") are allowable in this text or memo field.
- **Decimal Places**. An integer representing the number of decimal places to be displayed for numeric data types.
- **New Values**. The AutoNumber data type will automatically assign unique integers to each record; it will use sequential integers if this attribute is set to Increment, and random long integers if it's set to Random, which produces some pretty wild customer IDs.
- **Indexed**. Set to Yes to request that Access remember the location of records in the table based on this field, which is usually used for searching records. It would be reasonable to set a Customer Name field to Indexed, but probably not a Purchase Amount field. If you choose to index a field, you can also allow or prevent duplicates with this attribute, but that's often better done with relational integrity constraints (see the section "Understanding Table Relationships" later in the chapter).

Using these attributes, like so much in Access, is largely a matter of practice. Having a general idea of what options are available will come in handy when you need to know how to use one, though.

Data Type Attribute Summary

A summary of all of the Access 97 data types and the attributes available for each is shown in Table 2.3.

Table 2.3   Access Data Type Attributes

	Text	Memo	Number	Date/ Time	Currency	Auto- Number	Yes/ No	OLE Object	Hyperlink
Field Size	✓		✓			✓			
Format	✓	✓	✓	✓	✓	✓	✓	✓	
Input Mask	✓		✓	✓	✓				
Caption	✓	✓	✓	✓	✓	✓	✓	✓	✓
Default Value	✓	✓	✓	✓	✓		✓		✓
Validation Rule	✓	✓	✓	✓	✓		✓		✓
Validation text	✓	✓	✓	✓	✓		✓		✓
Required	✓	✓	✓	✓	✓		✓	✓	✓
Allow Zero Length	✓	✓							✓
Decimal Places			✓		✓				
New Values						✓			
Indexed	✓		✓	✓	✓	✓	✓		

You will probably use two or three (Format, Field Size, and either Required or Indexed) of these attributes 75 percent of the time.

CAUTION

Beware of data type conversion problems. For example, if you define a field to be of type Double and later change it to Single, you will lose about eight decimal places in precision. Likewise, changing a Text field to Memo after data has been entered isn't a problem, but changing a Memo to Text will truncate each entry at the number of characters specified in the Field Length attribute. Access will typically warn you of impending doom when you are about to destroy data, but Access warns about a lot of things that you will probably learn to ignore.

> **CAUTION**
>
> The Undo feature does not reverse the effects of a data type change. Use great care when changing field definitions from a more-precise type (Long Integer, Double, Memo) to a less-precise type (Integer, Byte, Single, Text).

Using Lookups in Tables

In the Field Properties area of Design view, there is another tab called the Lookup tab. Click it to bring it to the front. Setting Lookup options for a given field makes entering data in the table easier in Datasheet view. Instead of entering data in a blank cell, a user can activate a pull-down menu containing any number of possible entries for that cell, as defined by the table designer. This makes the Datasheet view of a table, in essence, an Access form; the field with the Lookup options set changes from a text box to a combo box. In fact, the settings and options for the Lookup box are the same as those for a generic combo box control.

> **N O T E** It is possible to obfuscate the design of a table with the Lookup options, and an example of this is helpfully provided in Northwind. In the Order Details table, the Product ID field (containing a number, the Product ID) appears to contain the text name of the product. This is accomplished by setting the RowSource property of the ProductID field to a query that displays the name of the product, instead of its ID. The real function of the field is masked further by using the Caption property to change the title appearing over the field in Datasheet view.
>
> Masquerading the data like this serves only to confuse the casual user and any designer who comes after you to work on your design. Lookup fields, when used to simplify data entry, can be a real boon. But they can really make database maintenance more difficult if used to hide the real nature of data.

The use of lookups and the effects they have on table design are discussed further in the section "Understanding Table Relationships" later in this chapter.

Understanding Primary Keys and Composite Keys

The terms *key* and *index* are often confused, probably because keys are usually indexed. They are similar in that both make the retrieval of data from a database table easier, but that's where the similarity ends. Keys are absolutely critical to the definition of any complex database, while indices are purely optional and exist for the convenience of the user.

Key fields, or *primary keys*, provide an unambiguous "handle" for a database engine, like Access, to use in working with a given table. The data in a key field must be unique across all records; if someone attempts to add a record with data in a key field that duplicates a record already in the table, Access will refuse to add it. Likewise, the addition of a record with no data in the key field will also be prevented. By forcing key fields to be unique among a given table, the database cannot possibly mistake one record for another.

Consider, for example, the table Customers in the Northwind database. The field CustomerID is a key field; this is apparent from the little key icon to the left of the CustomerID field in the Design view of the table (see Figure 2.5).

You set a field to be a key by opening the table in Design view, clicking in the square to the left of the field name, and then selecting the Primary Key button from the toolbar.

FIG. 2.5

The key field
CustomerID in the
Customers table, with
the key icon to the left
of its name.

The Primary Key button ──

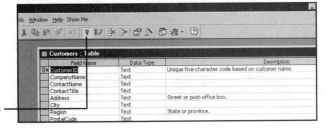

Let's take a look at the Customer table in Datasheet view to see what this primary key looks like. In the toolbar, click the down arrow next to the Table view button and select Datasheet view. You can see the gibberish customer identification codes that have been assigned to each customer (see Figure 2.6). They don't make a lot of sense, but as long as they're guaranteed to be unique, they'll work fine. These Customer IDs are necessary in this case because there is no way to guarantee that two customers won't have the same name. Maybe it's unlikely, but it's not impossible, and wouldn't it be embarrassing to send a bill to the wrong customer because you didn't know which "John Smith" it belonged to? The rest of the Northwind application uses the CustomerID field to uniquely identify records in the Customers table. You'll see how to verify that in the section "Understanding Table Relationships."

FIG. 2.6

The Customers table in
Datasheet view. The
CustomerIDs are not
intuitive, but they are
probably unique, unlike
the customer names.

Customer ID	Company Name	Contact Name	Contact Title	
ALFKI	Alfreds Futterkiste	Maria Anders	Sales Representative	Ober
ANATR	Ana Trujillo Emparedados y helados	Ana Trujillo	Owner	Avda.
ANTON	Antonio Moreno Taquería	Antonio Moreno	Owner	Mata
AROUT	Around the Horn	Thomas Hardy	Sales Representative	120 H
BERGS	Berglunds snabbköp	Christina Berglund	Order Administrator	Berg
BLAUS	Blauer See Delikatessen	Hanna Moos	Sales Representative	Forst
BLONP	Blondel père et fils	Frédérique Citeaux	Marketing Manager	24, p
BOLID	Bólido Comidas preparadas	Martín Sommer	Owner	C/ Ar
BONAP	Bon app'	Laurence Lebihan	Owner	12, ru
BOTTM	Bottom-Dollar Markets	Elizabeth Lincoln	Accounting Manager	23 Ts
BSBEV	B's Beverages	Victoria Ashworth	Sales Representative	Faun
CACTU	Cactus Comidas para llevar	Patricio Simpson	Sales Agent	Cerrit
CENTC	Centro comercial Moctezuma	Francisco Chang	Marketing Manager	Sierr:
CHOPS	Chop-suey Chinese	Yang Wang	Owner	Haup
COMMI	Comércio Mineiro	Pedro Afonso	Sales Associate	Av. d
CONSH	Consolidated Holdings	Elizabeth Brown	Sales Representative	Berk
DRACD	Drachenblut Delikatessen	Sven Ottlieb	Order Administrator	Wals
DUMON	Du monde entier	Janine Labrune	Owner	67, ru
EASTC	Eastern Connection	Ann Devon	Sales Agent	35 Ki
ERNSH	Ernst Handel	Roland Mendel	Sales Manager	Kirch
FAMIA	Familia Arquibaldo	Aria Cruz	Marketing Assistant	Rua (
FISSA	FISSA Fabrica Inter. Salchichas S.A.	Diego Roel	Accounting Manager	C/ Mc
FOLIG	Folies gourmandes	Martine Rancé	Assistant Sales Agent	184,

Record: 1 of 91

Keys need not be restricted to only one field in a table. In some cases, you may need two or more keys to ensure a unique identity for each record in your database. For an example, open the Order Details table in Northwind in Design view (from the Database window, select the Tables tab, then the Orders table, then the button marked Design). You'll see that two fields—Order ID and Product ID—are marked with the key icon; together, they comprise a *composite key*, where the combination of the two fields is guaranteed to be unique.

In this example, more than one product can be ordered on the same order form, so the Order ID is not unique. Likewise, different orders may contain the same Products. But a given product can only be ordered once on one order form, so the combination of Order ID and Product must be unique. Switch to Datasheet view to see how this composite key appears (see Figure 2.7). A report detailing sales will have no trouble determining which items are on which order, or which orders a given item is listed upon, because of this composite key.

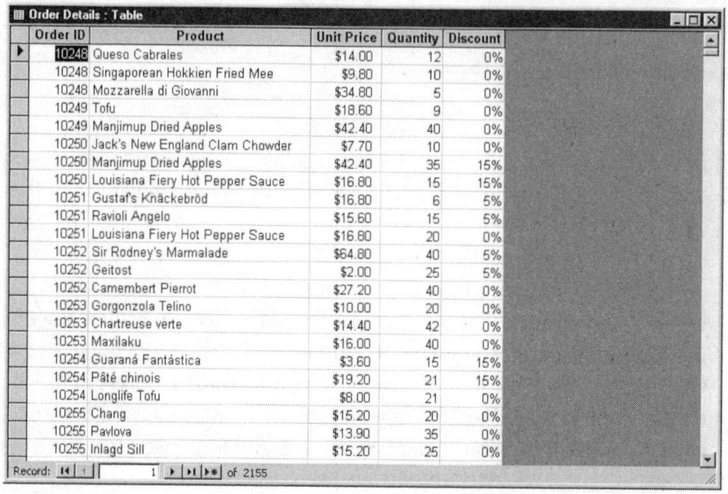

Order Details : Table

Order ID	Product	Unit Price	Quantity	Discount
10248	Queso Cabrales	$14.00	12	0%
10248	Singaporean Hokkien Fried Mee	$9.80	10	0%
10248	Mozzarella di Giovanni	$34.80	5	0%
10249	Tofu	$18.60	9	0%
10249	Manjimup Dried Apples	$42.40	40	0%
10250	Jack's New England Clam Chowder	$7.70	10	0%
10250	Manjimup Dried Apples	$42.40	35	15%
10250	Louisiana Fiery Hot Pepper Sauce	$16.80	15	15%
10251	Gustaf's Knäckebröd	$16.80	6	5%
10251	Ravioli Angelo	$15.60	15	5%
10251	Louisiana Fiery Hot Pepper Sauce	$16.80	20	0%
10252	Sir Rodney's Marmalade	$64.80	40	5%
10252	Geitost	$2.00	25	5%
10252	Camembert Pierrot	$27.20	40	0%
10253	Gorgonzola Telino	$10.00	20	0%
10253	Chartreuse verte	$14.40	42	0%
10253	Maxilaku	$16.00	40	0%
10254	Guaraná Fantástica	$3.60	15	15%
10254	Pâté chinois	$19.20	21	15%
10254	Longlife Tofu	$8.00	21	0%
10255	Chang	$15.20	20	0%
10255	Pavlova	$13.90	35	0%
10255	Inlagd Sill	$15.20	25	0%

Record: 1 of 2155

FIG. 2.7
The fields Order ID and Product comprise a composite key in Datasheet view. The combination of the data in the two fields must be unique.

Choosing appropriate keys for your tables is critical to the correct operation of your database. In general, all tables should have primary keys. A field with data type AutoNumber is an excellent candidate for a key, because AutoNumbers will never duplicate. If you can, use a field that makes sense to you (like a serial number, or Social Security number, or even a telephone number) as a key field to make it easier to reference later.

Using Indexes

An *index* in a database table is just like an index in a book. It's a cross-reference between data in certain fields and their locations in the table, and it makes the process of searching for records faster. There's no requirement that you manually mark any field(s) as indexes, and in many tables, you won't need to consider it. Consider using an index if the following conditions apply:

- Your table is very large (greater than 1,000 records).
- Your database is running on a not-so-speedy machine.
- You expect to search for data that's frequently not located in a key field.

Key fields are automatically indexed, and in most cases that will be sufficient. An example of when you might want to consider adding an index is shown in Northwind's Products table, which contains information about the 77 products that Northwind Traders sells. The primary key to this table is the field "Product ID," but isn't it equally (or more) likely that someone searching for product information will search by the product name? Similarly, users might want to search for all products from a given supplier, or within a certain category. Indexing these fields will make these searches faster.

Part
I
Ch
2

N O T E Creating an index in a table with only 77 records is an academic exercise; there won't be any noticeable performance gain from indexing a table this small. But maybe Northwind expects to branch out into online book sales, in which case their Products table will grow significantly.

To create an index:

1. In Design view, select the Indexes button on the Table Design toolbar. The Index dialog box appears (see Figure 2.8).

2. Enter the names of fields you want to index, and specify the sort order (Ascending or Descending).

Your key field will always appear in this box labeled Primary Key; you can add as many other indexes as you like. Note that indexes can be composite, just like keys; if the search criteria will normally contain more than one field, so should the index.

FIG. 2.8

The Indexes dialog box. The primary key is automatically indexed.

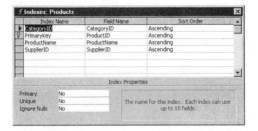

Here are some caveats about indexes:

- Don't delete the index automatically created for the primary key. Access will use the primary key for searches, even if the user never does.
- Indices can actually slow some kinds of operations, including those that add data to the table (because the index must be re-created). If you typically add one record at a time, that's not a problem, but you wouldn't want to index extra fields in a table that sees hundreds of records added at a time, because updating the index would slow the process to a crawl.

■ You can't index fields of type Memo, Hyperlink, or OLE Object.

To remove an index:

1. Select the index you want to remove by clicking in the gray box to the left of its name in the Indexes table.
2. Press the Delete key on the keyboard.

> **CAUTION**
>
> Don't remove the index from the primary key. Access uses that index to sort your data in the default order, which is defined by the primary key.

Understanding Table Relationships

The second-most-important thing about designing a database is to correctly define the relationships between its tables. (The number one thing is to remember where you saved the @%^$#* database file.) Without relationships, a database isn't much better than a spreadsheet, and most of the capability of the database engine is wasted. It is difficult to conceive of a useful, real-world database that does not include several table relationships.

The best way to understand how table relationships work is to look at an example and work backward to the general theory. In Northwind, there's an obvious relationship between the tables Orders, Products, and Order Details. In the event that you don't want to open them in Access, they're shown in Datasheet view in Figure 2.9.

N O T E   If you do want to open them in Access, double-click on each of the table names in the Database window to open them in Datasheet view (you may need to move them out of the way after opening them), minimize the Database window, and choose Window, Tile Horizontally. ■

In the table Products, each product has a unique ID number (Product ID) that represents it. In the table Orders, each order has a unique ID number (Order ID) that represents it. In Order Details, the two are put together: The Order ID and Product ID are matched to show which products were ordered on which invoice. There is a "one-to-many" relationship between Order ID in Orders and Order ID in Order Details (each order number can have several products associated with it), meaning that an order number that appears once in Orders can appear many times in Order Details. There is also a one-to-many relationship between Product ID in Products and Product ID in Order Details, meaning that a product that appears once in Products can appear many times in Order Details.

N O T E   There is some sleight of hand going on here. The designer(s) of the Northwind database used the ID numbers to match the keys in all three tables, but when you look at the data in Datasheet view, you see the product name in Order Details instead of the Product ID. If you switch to Design view, you'll see that it really is the Product ID that is in the table; the smoke and mirrors replacement of the product name for its ID is accomplished with the Lookup attributes of the Product

ID field (see the section "Using Lookups in Tables" earlier in the chapter). While this makes the datasheet look nice, it's really confusing for anyone who has to maintain the database and is generally a bad idea. Use forms (Chapter 4) to change the appearance of data and the Datasheet view of tables to look at the raw data. ▓

FIG. 2.9
Three interrelated tables in the Northwind database.

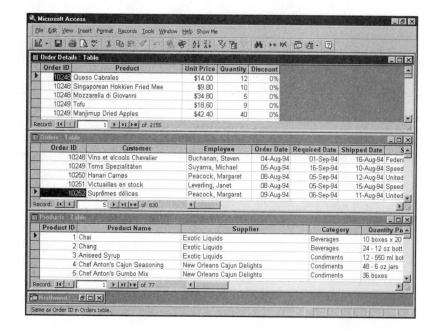

Access provides a dialog box for viewing and creating these relationships called the *Relationships window*.

To create relationships between tables,

1. Click the Tools menu and choose Relationships. If this is the first time you've opened the Relationships window, you will be overwhelmed by the number of boxes and lines that appear inside it. Don't be; press the Delete key on your keyboard eight or nine times until the window clears. You're only changing the display, not the database.

2. Click the Show Tables button on the toolbar (see Figure 2.10), select the table Order Details, click the Add button, then the Close button.

3. Click the Show Direct Relationships button on the toolbar, which should now be enabled. You should see something like Figure 2.10.

You'll notice that the primary keys in all three tables are shown in bold, and that there are lines between each of the keys in Orders and Products and the corresponding keys in Order Details. This line, which is created just by clicking the primary key in one table and dragging it onto the corresponding field in another table, shows clearly the relationships between the three tables.

FIG. 2.10

The relationships that the table "Order Details" participates in.

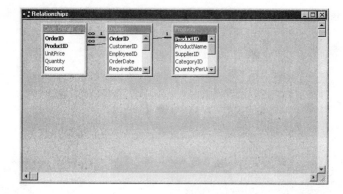

Also, the line running from Order Details to Products runs *behind* the Orders table. You can change the appearance of the tables in the Relationships window by dragging and resizing them as much as you like; sometimes, this results in lines crossing each other and disappearing behind tables. Once you get a design you like, you'll get an opportunity to save the arrangement when you close the Relationships window.

In this example, the fields Order ID in Orders and Product ID in the Products table are primary keys, with which you're already familiar. The fields Order ID and Product ID in the Order Details table are called *foreign keys*. Together, they form a composite primary key in the table Order Details, but by matching them to the corresponding primary keys in other tables, you set up a network of relationships that together ensure that the data in all of the tables is accurate. There's no way to enter an invalid Product ID in the Order Details table because the keys are linked. Likewise, there's no way to sell products on an invalid order, because every Order ID in Order Details must be linked back to the Orders table, complete with customer, salesperson, and so on.

 Foreign keys are as important as primary keys in the world of table relationships. For a relationship to work, you must ensure that your foreign keys (the primary keys in the table being connected to) are defined correctly, that the data types are appropriate, and that the key is complete. You will save yourself endless hours of torment if you ensure that your keys are selected correctly from the beginning.

There's a pattern here. You'll find that most well-designed databases use many small tables to track items that need to be referenced by other tables to get the real work of the system done. Typical things to use as keys in these "master" tables include employee numbers, supplier IDs, customer numbers, equipment serial numbers—things which are needed in many places in the database, but need to be maintained in one place to make sure there are no duplicates or transpositions. Other examples of this kind of use of table relationships in Northwind are listed in Table 2.4.

Table 2.4   Table Relationships in Northwind

Field	Primary Key in Table	Field Referenced in Table
Customer ID	Customers	Orders
Employee ID	Employees	Orders
Shipper ID	Shippers	Orders
Supplier ID	Suppliers	Products
Category ID	Categories	Products

You can view all of the active relationships in a database by clicking the Show All Relationships button while the Relationships window is open. If things get too busy, you can rearrange the tables displayed by dragging them around the Relationships window, or delete them (with the Delete key) to remove them from the display without affecting the actual relationships they're involved in.

Creating new relationships and editing existing ones is a skill that will prove critical to your building effective databases. You'll do all of your relationship work in the Relationships window, adding relationships between tables and deleting them as necessary.

To create a new relationship between two tables:

1. Open the Relationships window by choosing Tools from the menu, and then selecting Relationships.

2. If there are extraneous tables already visible in the window, remove them by selecting them and pressing the Delete key. You can clear the entire display by repeatedly pressing the Delete key. Note that removing tables from the Relationships window does not delete the relationships they participate in; it only affects the display. Deleting relationships is covered later in this section.

3. Add the tables you want to create relationships between by clicking the Show Table button, selecting the appropriate table name from the list that appears, and clicking Add. You can view as many tables as you like, but you can only create relationships between any two of them at a time.

4. The primary keys in each table appear in boldface. Click and hold on the name of the primary key in one of the tables and drag it over the name of the corresponding key in the other table. The Edit Relationships window appears as in Figure 2.11.

N O T E   Because all of the appropriate relationships are already defined in the Northwind database, you won't be able to create any new ones without deleting an existing one first. If you'd like to try this, back up your copy of Northwind first, then follow the instructions for deleting a relationship.

5. In the Edit Relationships window, you'll see the names of the fields you linked. Select the Enforce Referential Integrity box if appropriate (most of the time), and Cascade Update and Cascade Delete if necessary (almost never).

6. Select the Join Types button and modify the join type if necessary to specify how Access should match the data in the fields you linked. (Joins in tables are analogous to joins in queries and are discussed at length in Chapter 4, "Managing Data with Queries.")

7. Click OK to save your changes and close the Edit Relationships window.

▶ **See** "Understanding Referential Integrity," **p. 42**

▶ **See** "Cascading Updates and Deletes," **p. 42**

FIG. 2.11

The Edit Relationships window, where you detail the relationship between two tables.

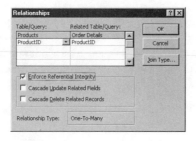

To edit an existing relationship:

1. Open the Relationships window and add the tables you want to modify.

2. Double-click the line between the two tables that denotes the relationship. You have to be careful to double-click the line without moving off of it.

3. The Edit Relationships window appears. Modify the relationship as appropriate.

4. Click OK to save your changes and close the Edit Relationships window.

To delete an existing relationship:

1. Open the Relationships window and add the tables you want to modify.

2. Click the line between the two tables that denotes the relationship to select it.

3. Press the Delete key to remove the relationship.

CAUTION

Note the difference between removing a table from the Relationships window (you select the table and press Delete) and removing a relationship (you select the relationship line and press Delete). The former only affects the display; the latter affects the integrity of the database. Be careful.

There are a few special cases to mention regarding establishing and modifying relationships:

■ You can't delete data in a table when data in another table depends on it because of a relationship. For example, you couldn't delete the name of a customer in the Customers table who had placed an order (stored in the Orders table), because the CustomerID field in Orders has data that depends on the Customer record being present in the Customers table.

- When creating a relationship, the table that you drag *from* is called the *primary table* in the relationship. If you are establishing referential integrity, your relationship must include at least all fields that make up the primary key in the primary table. You can establish a relationship encompassing more than one field by holding down the Ctrl key and clicking the name of each field you want to select, then dragging all of them to the secondary table. This technique is most useful when the primary table contains a composite key.

- The layout of the Relationships window is saved from Access session to session, and Access will usually prompt you to `Save changes to the layout of Relationships` whenever you try to exit the Relationships window after modifying something. You can save the layout if it's helpful, but many developers prefer to start with a clean Relationships window in every session.

The Referential Integrity and Cascade options are described in detail in the next sections.

Types of Relationships

There are three types of relationships that you can establish between tables:

- **One-to-many**.   The key in the primary table can appear many times in the secondary table.

- **One-to-one**.   The key in the primary table can only appear once in the secondary table.

- **Many-to-many**.   A *menage a trois* where two tables have one-to-many relationships with a third, thus establishing a many-to-many relationship between each other.

By far, the most common of these is the one-to-many relationship; in fact, all of the relationships in Northwind are one-to-many. This is a typical choice for the kind of relationship described, where one table contains values that are referenced by another table to ensure that there are no unintended duplicates or errors. Access creates one-to-many relationships by default when you drag a key field in a primary table onto a primary key in a second table.

One-to-one relationships are much less common; in general, if you can use a one-to-one relationship between two tables, you should consider combining the tables. This technique is most useful when you're trying to keep the number of fields in a table small for efficiency in reporting.

The classic example of a many-to-many relationship is for registration in classes. Student IDs make up the primary key in one table and Class IDs are primary in another. A third table uses one-to-many relationships with the first two to track which students are registered in which classes, thus establishing a many-to-many relationship between students and classes. You're unlikely to create one of these links intentionally, although they sometimes appear in large, highly interconnected databases.

Understanding Referential Integrity

Enabling referential integrity is like permitting your little sister to tattle on you. When referential integrity is established between two tables, you require that the values at either side of the link be absolutely the same. Most links should have referential integrity enabled to make sure that no erroneous data is entered; this helps preserve normalization and helps you sleep at night when users are banging on your database.

The times when you'll want to create a link without setting referential integrity are few; they might include the establishment of links between tables to find errors (that probably could have been prevented if referential integrity was established before the data was entered). You'll almost always want to enable referential integrity between tables where links exist.

Cascading Updates and Deletes

If you enable referential integrity, you can also enable "cascading" of delete and update operations from the same Edit Relationships window (see Figure 2.11). This means that a change made in the key in the linked-to table will automatically change the primary key in the linked-from table. For example, say you're using employee Social Security numbers as a primary key in your Employees table. One employee makes several sales, and related records are created in the Orders table referencing her SSN. But, wait—there's a mistake. You've somehow transposed two numbers in her SSN when you entered it into the Employees table. If you have referential integrity enabled and you try to change her SSN in the Employees table, you'll get an error message—there are related records in Orders, so you can't make this change. But if you have the Cascade Update Related Fields option selected, the updated SSN will trickle down to the Orders table as well, saving the day. Cascade Delete Related Records works in much the same way; if an employee quits, deleting his SSN in the Employees table will delete all related order records in Orders.

As you can imagine, these options can be incredibly dangerous if used inappropriately. Because the deletion of records is not generally reversible, you can create a real mess if you cascade an operation you don't want to. You should usually leave these options turned off (the default), unless it's appropriate to turn them on for a specific application.

Importing and Exporting Data

Sometimes you'll find that the data you want to use in your database has already been entered somewhere else—in a spreadsheet, in another database, or elsewhere. In many of these cases, you can directly import the data from the external source and into your tables, saving hours of work. Similarly, you may find it convenient to extract data from your Access tables and make it available to other database systems or applications.

In some cases, it's not even necessary to have Access tables designed before you import external data; Access will analyze the structure of the external file and, with a little prompting, create a table structure that's usually appropriate for it. Obviously, if you need detailed control of what you're importing, knowing the structure of the file helps immeasurably.

Access provides a wizard to help you through the process of importing. To start the Import Data Wizard:

1. Click the File menu, and then select Get External Data.

2. On the submenu that appears, you have two options:
   - Import (which copies the data you specify into your local copy of Access)
   - Link Tables (which leaves the data where it is and makes it available to you from within Access)

   Choose the desired option.

3. Depending on which option you chose in step 2, the Import or Link dialog box appears. These contain identical options. Select a file residing somewhere on your network, and Access will begin the process of integrating the remote data into your database.

If Access recognizes the external data source as having been created by a database application (typically Access, dBASE, Excel, or FoxPro), it will list the tables, queries, and more in the external database for you to select and import or link. The process of importing data from a recognized database application is practically foolproof; either the database format will be recognized or it won't.

If the file you select was not created by another database application (raw text files, comma-delimited text, or tab-delimited text), Access will automatically start the Import Text Wizard (see Figure 2.12). It will walk you through the process of identifying the field delimiters and ask whether you want to create a new table or append the imported data to an existing one.

FIG. 2.12

The Import Text Wizard guesses as to the field titles and data types based on the appearance of the data in a comma-delimited text file.

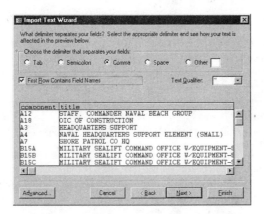

In some cases, you won't be able to make an external database program export data in a format Access can recognize. Windows provides a mechanism for permitting data sources of various types to talk to one another; this feature is called Open Database Connectivity, or ODBC. If the second database program is a native Windows program, you may be able to make it act as an ODBC data source, providing its data to any requesting application through Windows.

To set up an ODBC data source:

1. Open the Control Panel and double-click the ODBC applet (called 32-bit ODBC in Windows 95) to start the ODBC Data Source Administrator.

2. Choose the System DSN tab and click the Add button to add a system data source.

3. Select the appropriate driver for the type of data you want to use as a data source (for Access databases, use the Microsoft Access Driver; most database applications install their own drivers on your system when you install them) and click the Finish button. The ODBC Setup dialog box for the data type you selected the driver for appears.

4. Enter a short descriptive name for this data source in the field labeled Data Source Name. This can be the same as the file name if you like.

5. Click the Select button and select your database file from the directory tree that appears.

6. Click the OK button to save your work in the Setup window and OK again to close the ODBC Data Source Administrator window.

To configure Access to import or link to an ODBC data source you've already set up:

1. In the Database window, click the File menu, and then select Get External Data.

2. Choose either Link Tables or Import, depending on how you want the data to be stored.

3. Select ODBC Data Source in the Files of Type text box. The Select data Source dialog box appears.

4. Select the Machine Data Source tab to list all System and User data sources available on your computer.

5. Choose the data source name corresponding to the data source you want to import or link and click OK.

If you've configured the data source properly, Access will be able to use Windows as a mediator between it and the offending application to extract your data. Check your external program's documentation if you have trouble setting it up as a data source. For more information on ODBC, check the online help in Access and Windows, or consider a good book on ODBC.

You might consider the following recommendations as you begin importing and exporting data:

- Access 97 has no trouble reading databases created in earlier versions of Access, but it won't create native database files in any Access format (.mdb) other than Access 97. To allow older version of Access to read Access 97 databases, configure the Access 97 database as an ODBC data source (see the example earlier in this section) and link the Access 97 tables to the Access 2.0 or Access 95 database you're working with.

- If you're not sure what database application another person will be using to read your data, export it as either dBASE III (.dbf) or comma-delimited (.csv). Most database applications will read dBASE files, and almost anything can read comma-delimited files (although some data types will be simplified or excluded if you use .csv).

■ When specifying the data types of fields during import from text files, Access will often recommend Text where Memo is more appropriate. If the data can possibly be longer than 50 characters, change it to Memo before you import.

TIP You may get better results by looking at your data in a text editor, figuring out what the field types should be, and creating an empty table to hold the imported data before you try to import it. Access doesn't always make good guesses as to data types (especially with memo fields) and a little preparation can save you consternation later.

■ Access will sometimes recommend a numeric type for data that is really text, like telephone numbers. Change the type recommended to Text if appropriate.

■ If data is imported into a new table, but some records are not imported, look at the table Paste Errors that Access will create to document the problems. If the problem is due to type mismatches or truncated records, correct the data type(s) in the new table that was created for your import, delete all of the records, and re-import your data into the table you just edited.

■ Exporting data as Text produces different results depending on which file extension you choose. Selecting .txt does not usually produce useful results. Try .csv to place all text fields in double quotes and insert commas between each exported field.

■ You can import or export any Access object, but you can only link to external tables. It wouldn't make much sense to link to an external query, for example.

■ When formatting spreadsheet data to be imported into Access (or any database), try the following:

- Make sure the data is all located in one area of the spreadsheet.
- Use named ranges to mark your data.
- Eliminate all formatting, especially underlines, rows of hyphens, and blank rows and columns.
- Put column titles (soon to be field names) in the cells immediately above each column of data.

Why Duplicating Data Is Bad

In general, when designing a database structure, you should work to keep your tables as small and your keys as complete (composed of as many fields as necessary, but no more) as possible. The rationale behind "good" database design has more to it than just looking for a more efficient way to store data (however you choose to define efficiency—by size, by speed of access, by ease of use, and so on).

It's possible to create database tables that are, well, just plain wrong. Using one of these "wrong" database tables can result in invalid data cropping up in reports, or invalid data being introduced into your tables (which is exactly what you're trying to avoid by using a database instead of a spreadsheet).

The database term normalization refers to the process of ensuring that tables do not duplicate data unnecessarily, and that they include appropriate keys. You should always try to "normalize" your tables to ensure that your database is as efficient as possible and to help you avoid corrupting your data through design errors. For more details on normalization, look up "normalizing tables" in Access Help.

You can use the following guidelines to help make sure that your tables are normalized:

- *Decide what characteristic of the data you're storing is likely to be unique and use that characteristic as a primary key in your tables.*   If there is no characteristic that's guaranteed to be unique, use an AutoNumber field to generate a key for you. For example, you could use a serial number as the key in a computer inventory, or phone numbers (with area codes) as keys in a list of customers.

- *Include the key field in every table relating to the data the key represents.*   In a computer inventory, you would include the computer serial number in every table containing data pertaining to individual computers; in a customer list, the customers' phone numbers could identify every record in every table that concerned customers.

- *Split your data into as many small tables as necessary to group only related information together.*   In the computer inventory, you might group hardware and software information in separate tables.

- *Avoid duplicating data among tables.*   If you use a phone number to uniquely identify customers, the customers' names only need to be in one table. You can use referential integrity to link the table containing the names to the table containing orders, because both tables include the unique phone number field.

Using the Table Analyzer Wizard

A useful tool for novices that experienced database designers might be well advised to try, the *Table Analyzer Wizard*, is provided to save you from yourself. Like all Access wizards, it's really a program written in Visual Basic for Applications (see Chapters 10–12) that takes apart your database structure and makes recommendations on how to fix it.

This wizard isn't a panacea, but it's close. Its strengths are identifying duplicated data in your tables, and finding typos and offering suggestions for fixes. In the previous example, the Table Analyzer Wizard won't notice the duplicated Serial No field in two tables, because it only analyzes one table at a time. It does greatly simplify the removal of the Brand and Model fields from the Administration table and creates a unique ID number to link them back to Administration.

Running this wizard takes a little practice, and it's probably easier to work out your database designs yourself and find problems the hard way than it is to stab wildly at your design and then use the wizard to clean up the mess. The real value of the wizard, though, lies in its examples; run the Table Analyzer Wizard and you'll see some good graphical examples of how not to design tables in the introductory screens.

To start the Table Analyzer Wizard:

1. Click the Tools menu, and then select Analyze.
2. Choose Table from the three options available. The Table Analyzer Wizard starts.

The prompts from there are self-explanatory. You're not likely to use this wizard often; you may not run it more than once. But it's worth trying that one time.

You *are* likely, however, to need to modify your table structure several times in the course of constructing a database as you refine your design and as the requirements of your application become more apparent. Paying close attention to the elements of good design early on can make the modification process considerably easier and prevent problems from which it may be very costly to recover. ●

Part

I

Ch

2

CHAPTER 3

Entering Data in the Database with Forms

Like painting, creating Access forms permits the database designer to put a different "face" on what lies beneath. If you can visualize a form in your mind's eye, you can create it on-screen and use the form to enter (and view) data in your database. Some "faces" are better than others, and some are easier to work with than others, but the art of interface design is well-served by the Access form designer. ■

Explore the uses of forms

It's already established that you can view data in the Datasheet view of the Table designer. Forms take the viewing of data to a new level.

Understand the parts of a form

Forms have three parts, and each has attributes to set and functions to master.

Work with the different types of forms

Different types of forms are available with different behaviors, depending on their intended use.

Learn about controls

Controls are the elements of forms that make them do useful things. There are several available to you to make your forms display data differently.

Create a switchboard

Access can help you quickly create a single form that helps users navigate your database.

Put a pretty face on your data

The Access AutoForm feature turns a table into a form with one mouse click.

Common Uses for Forms

You can think of forms as screens placed on top of tables; these screens permit certain parts of the table to show through when and how the form designer desires (see Figure 3.1).

FIG. 3.1

A form is a screen through which you can view and change the data in an underlying table or query.

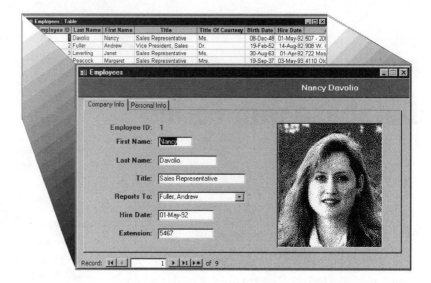

In Northwind, forms are used to create the entire environment through which users see the data in the database:

- ▒ Forms are used for viewing and entering product categories, customer information, and suppliers.
- ▒ Forms control the edits that are permitted on employee records.
- ▒ Forms control the ordering mechanism.
- ▒ A form (called the switchboard) handles the navigation to all of the other forms.

Understanding Form Regions

Access forms can have between one and five regions. These regions are:

- ▒ **Detail**.   This region of the form is where the data appears for each record in the underlying data source. If you have 100 records, the controls you place in the Detail region will be used by each of the 100 records, and they'll either appear "stacked" on top of one another, or you'll use special controls called "navigation buttons" to move among them.
- ▒ **Form Header**.   This region always appears at the top of your form. It's a good place to insert controls containing information that doesn't change with every record, like the name of the company, or instructions on how to use the form. (Optional)

- **Form Footer.** This region appears at the bottom of every form. You usually include information about the date and time the form was created, summaries and totals, or author information in the Form Footer. (Optional)
- **Page Header.** This region appears under the Form Header and before the Detail region. It does not get much use in forms, where page breaks are rarely used, but is useful in reports, which are closely related to forms. Page headers in forms could be used to repeat data that needs to appear at the top of the screen on every page of a long form. (Optional)
- **Page Footer.** These are like Form Footers, but appear above them and after the Detail region. (Optional)

The way these regions appear on-screen depends on how the data and the form work together. In some cases, the only distinction between each section is where it lies on the page; in others, each section acts completely differently.

There may be additional regions as well, depending on how the data displayed in the form is sorted. You can specify that Access should provide a new header and/or footer whenever the value of a certain field changes; this technique is called "placing a sort break." Because sort breaks are much more commonly used in reports than forms, but the method for using them is the same, they're discussed at length in "Using Sort Breaks on Reports" in Chapter 6.

The Detail region is always shown by default. To turn the Form and Page Headers and Footers on or off, click the View menu, and then select Page Header/Footers or Form Headers/ Footers. If the button for either option is depressed, those regions should appear on the form. Figure 3.2 shows the relationship between the regions on a blank form.

FIG. 3.2

A blank form in Design view. Note the Form and Page Header and Footer and the Detail regions.

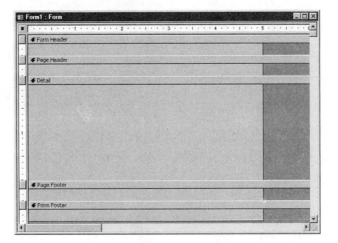

Creating Forms in Access

Access forms are comprised of *form regions*, described previously, and *controls*, which make up the visual objects on the form. Controls can be either *bound* or *unbound*; bound controls are "attached" to a field in the form's underlying data source, and unbound controls are not. Hiding beneath most forms is a *record source*, a table or query, which supplies the data that appears in the form and is affected when users use the form's controls.

To create a new form:

1. Open the Forms pane in the Database window by clicking the Forms tab.

2. Click the New button. A dialog box appears listing several ways to create a new form and a combo box is included for specifying a data source.

3. If you are using any method other than the Form Wizard (described in the list that follows), select a data source (a table or query) for your form in the combo box at the bottom of the dialog box.

4. You can choose any of the following methods to create a new form:

   - **Design view**. A blank form is displayed. Design view is explained in detail later in this chapter; it's where you'll do most of your form design. Use Design view to edit existing forms.

   - **Form Wizard**. A helpful set of dialog boxes that asks where your data is coming from, how you'd like it arranged on the form, and what kind of background picture you'd like (if any). The wizard then creates a form for you.

   - **AutoForm: Columnar, Tabular, and Datasheet**. Creates a simple form with a boring gray background in one click. You must select an underlying record source before using an AutoForm, and you can only include fields from one table or query (unlike the Form Wizard).

   - **Chart Wizard**. If your data lends itself to charting, use this wizard to tell Access how you want the chart to look and it builds the chart for you. Imagine using this wizard at a sales meeting when someone asks a question like "How has order volume changed over the course of a year?" A minute and five dialog boxes later, you can show her the answer.

   - **Pivot Table Wizard**. This completely counterintuitive process takes an Access table and changes it into an Excel spreadsheet, summarizing the data in the table under columns and rows of your choice.

5. Choose one of the methods described here and click OK to start creating your form.

A better understanding of the working of each of these methods will help you decide when each tool is appropriate to use.

Using the Form Wizard

If all you need is to get a form out fast, the Form Wizard is worth considering. Once you start it, it takes you through the steps of creating a basic form: selecting fields, choosing one of four prebuilt layouts, picking a coherent style for the form, and saving it. Using the Form Wizard, you can produce a form in about ten mouse clicks (see Figure 3.3).

FIG. 3.3
A form created with the Form Wizard. It took ten mouse clicks and no typing to create this form. A similar form, created by AutoForm, would take one mouse click.

The biggest disadvantage to using the Form Wizard is the lack of direct control over the layout and choice of the controls on your form. The Form Wizard doesn't create combo boxes, list boxes, or option groups, and it doesn't insert graphics or borders. Unless you're looking for bare-bones results, you can expect to have to modify the design the Form Wizard creates.

▶ **See** "Access Control Descriptions," **p. 263**

You can edit a form created with the Form Wizard as you would any other form: select it in the Database window and click Design to open it in Design view. You can then use the Toolbox and Palette to modify the controls the Form Wizard created for you.

▶ **See** "Using Design View," **p. 23**

TIP In many cases, you can convert one kind of control to another related type. For example, you can change a boring text box to a combo box, a list box, or a static label. Right-click any control and then choose Change to from the pop-up menu that appears. Note that changing a control to another type doesn't start the wizard for that type of control, even if you have the Control Wizard's button on the Toolbox depressed. So if you change a text box to a combo box, for example, you'll have to manually modify its Row Source property to tell Access what to show in the combo box rows.

Using AutoForm and AutoFormat

In one mouse click, AutoForm creates a form based on the object you're currently designing. The resulting form isn't necessarily going to win any design awards, but it's a quick way to get data into a table when you don't want to work in the table's Datasheet view.

The related AutoFormat Wizard, available on the Format menu when working with a form in Design view, manages some preset backgrounds and text styling in much the same way that Microsoft Word manages document styles. The background options include sky-blue clouds and a stylized globe with several choices of text colors and fonts. You can choose to have all or some of an existing style applied to the current form, to add a style to the library based on the current form, or to modify an existing style based on the current form. This tool has potential use in keeping a suite of forms looking similar, which is good design practice.

There are three kinds of AutoForms:

- **Columnar.** Records are arranged vertically along the left margin of the page, in the order they appear in the table definition. All of the fields are labeled. One record is viewed at a time; navigation buttons are provided to handle navigation among records.

- **Tabular.** Records are arranged down and across the visible page in a grid. Fields are labeled. More than one record is shown on the form at a time and navigation buttons and scroll bars are provided as needed.

- **Datasheet.** Records are presented as if you were looking at the Datasheet view of a table. Field names are at the top of each column. All of the records that will fit, one line at a time, are displayed; navigation buttons and scroll bars are also provided.

Because the Form Wizard does everything AutoForm does, and with a lot more flexibility, you probably won't use AutoForm much. However, to create an AutoForm, follow these steps:

1. Click the New button in the Database window, Forms pane.
2. Select one of the three AutoForm options available and specify a data source (a table or query) in the combo box provided.
3. Click OK to create a simple form based on the data source you selected.

Using Design View

The most flexible way to design forms is in Design view. The automated form builders are a nice crutch, but the real work gets done in Design view.

The two most important tools you'll use in Design view are the Toolbox and Palette; there are a myriad of other techniques and methods you'll find handy as well, and those are covered throughout the rest of this chapter.

The Toolbox

The Toolbox is visible when you create or edit a form in Design view and contains buttons that, when clicked, permit you to place various controls in any place on the current form. The Toolbox, which normally floats to the left of the form being worked on, contains 18 buttons that represent controls and two used for special purposes (see Figure 3.4).

FIG. 3.4

The Toolbox contains 18 control buttons. It can float in your work area or you can dock it along any edge of the screen by dragging and dropping it.

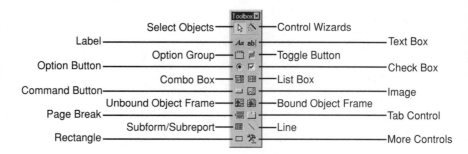

The Select Objects and Control Wizards buttons don't place controls on the form. The Select Object button cancels the selection of a control and changes the cursor back to the default arrow. The Control Wizards button, when depressed (toggled on), activates wizards for those controls that have them (the combo box, list box, command button, image, and subform/subreport). When it's raised (toggled off), the developer of the form must enter all of the underlying properties that these controls require to work correctly.

 The More Controls button brings up a list of all of the ActiveX controls that are registered on your system. You can select rarely used controls from this list.

You'll learn how to use the toolbox to add controls to a form in the section called "Using Controls in Forms," later in this chapter.

The Palette

The Palette (see Figure 3.5) is visible in Design view and acts as a source for adding color (or transparency) to objects. When you select one of the toolbox controls that uses the Palette, the current 40-color palette appears and you can select a color for the currently selected object in your form. There are three controls on the Form Design toolbar that use the same grid-style palette:

■ The Fill/Back color control specifies the color for the form background, rectangles, text boxes, and labels.

■ The Font/Fore color control specifies the foreground color for all controls containing text.

■ The Line/Border color control specifies the border color for all controls with borders and the line control.

Part
I

Ch
3

FIG. 3.5

The Palette gives a selection of colors to use for customizing controls. Recently used colors appear in a row at the bottom (not shown) for quick reference.

To apply color to an object:

1. Select the object by clicking it with the arrow cursor.
2. Choose the appropriate palette control (Fill/Back, Font/Fore, or Line/Border) for the property you want to change.
3. Select a color from the palette that appears.

You're not limited to the 40 colors shown in the grid. You can apply any color that your system supports by using the Properties dialog box of the control you're working with:

1. Select the control you want to modify and display its Property sheet (if it's not already displayed) by clicking the Edit menu, then selecting Properties.

2. Select the appropriate property (Back Color, Border Color, Font Color, and so on) for the control and click the Builder icon that appears to the right of the text box.
3. The Color dialog box appears, giving you the same palette options you had before; click Define Custom Colors to select any color your system can generate (see Figure 3.6).
4. Click anywhere in the rainbow pane to choose a custom color. The custom color is added to your palette. You can have as many as 16 custom colors defined at any time, but you can color any object any color by replacing custom colors as they become unneeded.

FIG. 3.6

The Color dialog box, including the Custom Color selector.

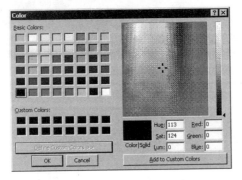

Viewing and Changing Form Properties

 In Access, most objects have attributes that can be used to customize the way they look or work. These attributes, called *properties*, can usually be viewed and changed by right-clicking the object in question and selecting Properties from the shortcut menu. You also can click the View menu, then select Properties, click the Properties button on the Database toolbar, or use macros or Visual Basic for Applications to inspect and modify properties.

▶ **See** "Automating Common Tasks with Macros," **p. 129**

Because forms and form regions are Access objects, they have properties; you'll probably modify form properties more than most objects in Access, because the display and operation of your forms must be precisely controlled to achieve the effect you want. There are more than 20 properties for Access forms, and many are self-explanatory (for example, if you set the Width property to 5 the form becomes 5 inches wide)

To view the properties for a form, as opposed to the objects in a form, you need to select the form. Do this by clicking the Edit menu, then Select Form. Just left-clicking the form (to select it) and then right-clicking won't give you the form's properties—you'll get the properties of the form object you clicked on. After you've selected the form, bring up its Property sheet by clicking the View menu, and selecting Properties.

 You can view the Property sheet for any object in a form by right-clicking the object and choosing Properties from the menu that appears.

 A quick way to select a form is to click in the gray box in the upper-left corner of the form. A black circle appears in the box, indicating that the form is selected. You can then change the form's attributes, view its properties, and so on.

The form's Properties dialog box should look like Figure 3.7.

FIG. 3.7

The Properties dialog box for a form. The tabs break the dozens of properties into different panes.

Part I
Ch 3

You can change any of the properties shown by clicking the box containing the property value and changing that value. Many properties only allow certain values, and a pull-down arrow will appear in the box when you click it if this is the case. You can then select a valid entry from the list that's displayed. Some properties show a button containing an ellipsis when you click in them; this means that you can use the Expression Builder to design complex expressions while avoiding syntax errors and typos.

TIP When there are only certain values available for a given property (as shown by the pull-down arrow appearing in the value box when you click it), you can scroll through all of the possible values by double-clicking the value displayed. Each time you double-click, the next available value in the pull-down list is selected.

Some of the more important properties for forms are shown in Table 3.1.

Table 3.1 Form Property Highlights

Property	Default Value	Use
Record Source	Null	The table or query the data on the form should come from.
Filter	Null	A string describing how to limit the records shown on the form.
Caption	Null	A string that appears as the title of the form when the form is displayed.
Default View	Single Form	Show one record (Single Form), several records (Continuous Forms), or lots of records (Datasheet) in the detail area of one form?
Views Allowed	Both	Allows users to switch between the nicely laid-out form and a Datasheet view of the data specified in the Record Source
Allow Edits	Yes	Permit users to change existing records in the Record Source?
Data Entry	No	Is this form to be used exclusively to enter new data into the Record Source?
Scroll Bars	Both	Show horizontal and/or vertical scroll bars on the form if it's wider than the window in which it's displayed?
Record Selectors	Yes	Show a rectangular region to the left of displayed records that can be used to select an entire displayed record (instead of just a field in the record)?

Property	Default Value	Use
Navigation Buttons	Yes	Show arrows and a count of the records at the bottom of the form to ease moving among records?

The examples in Northwind and the online help are excellent sources of detailed information about how to use each of these properties. By making note of the property settings in the sample forms, you should be able to get a good idea of how they affect the appearance and use of individual forms.

Most of the form-building wizards set the absolutely necessary properties for you, but if you're building a form from scratch using Design view, you'll need to set the properties yourself. Without setting a form's properties, you'll end up with a useless form. For example, if your form is supposed to show data from a table, you'll have to set the Record Source property to the name of that table, or the form won't know where to get its data. Objects inside forms have properties, too. For example, you can achieve some interesting effects by experimenting with the Back Color properties of each of a form's regions and the color and font properties of the objects within the region. In Northwind, the Employees form uses these properties effectively; you also may want to look at the Suppliers form, which uses a bitmapped image (in a file) as the background for all of its regions. To select a region, click its title bar. You then can inspect its properties in the usual way.

The following example demonstrates how to change a property in a form. By default, the background image of the Customers form in Northwind is a stylized globe; we'll change it to a more subdued image suitable for printing.

To change a form property:

1. From the Database window, select the Customers form (in the Forms pane) and click the Design button.

2. If it's not already visible, open the form's Property sheet by clicking the View menu, then select Properties.

3. For ease of use, change to the All pane of the Property sheet by clicking the All tab.

4. Scroll down until you find the property you want to change (for this example, it's the Picture property). Click in the Property box and enter the new value, which may be anything from a simple Yes/No to a long string depending on the property. Some properties, like the one in this example, have a Build button appear when you click in the property box. The Picture property of this form contains the name of the current background. A Build button appears to the right of the property box. Click it.

5. In this example, the Insert Picture dialog box appears (see Figure 3.8), and you can select any appropriate background image. A good choice is \Program Files\Microsoft Office\Clipart\Backgrounds\Leaves on the Side.

6. (Optional) To view any image file on your hard disk, select the image file you want to view and click the Preview button in the file dialog box. A thumbnail of the image appears to the right of the file list (see Figure 3.8) and changes whenever you select a different graphics file.

7. Click OK if any special window (like a file selection window, palette, or builder) was active for this property and close the property sheet by clicking the Close button at upper right to return to your form in Design view to see your changes.

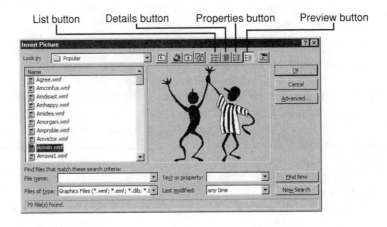

List button Details button Properties button Preview button

FIG. 3.8
The Preview pane is visible in the Insert Picture dialog box when the Preview button is depressed. You also can view file properties by clicking the Properties button.

TIP The image is small because Access repeats it as necessary to fill the form. Using small images minimizes the size of the database on disk.

An Overview of Objects and Controls for Forms

You can create simple forms with only one or two different kinds of controls, but if you are aware of the general uses of form controls it will help you as you design forms. If you're aware that the "tab control" exists, for example, you'll consider using it when the opportunity arises, and it may be the best control for the job.

The Appendix at the end of this book explains most of the major controls, concentrating on how they might be used in a typical application. All of the controls in Access are documented in the online help, which gives examples and caveats as to their use; consider checking help whenever you use an unfamiliar control. In the Appendix, they're presented in order of usefulness, which isn't how they appear on the Toolbox.

N O T E Your Toolbox includes a button at the lower right called More Controls. Click it to display a list of controls (and control-like objects; you can't tell the difference) that varies depending on what applications are installed on your system.

Controls are really programs written in Microsoft's Visual Basic or a related language. Because any system running Windows can run Visual Basic programs (with some caveats beyond the scope of this chapter), other people can create controls for you to perform specialized tasks such as embedding web browsers, maps, and almost anything that another application on your system will manage within an Access form.

Some custom controls require property settings that aren't easily manipulated using the Properties dialog box. Their extra properties are accessed by right-clicking the control in question and looking for a special option on the pop-up menu, usually called XXX Object... (where XXX is the name of the type of control. Left-clicking this menu entry starts a specialized property sheet, which is different for every specialized control. ■

Using Controls in Forms

There are about a dozen "cardinal" controls that you'll use for most of your work, but any Windows application can make other controls available to your Access forms. Because these controls make or break your form, it makes sense to know them.

To view the Toolbox:

1. In Design view, choose Database and then select View, Toolbox. The Toolbox appears to float on your screen, and you can move it around by dragging its title bar. To make it an anchored toolbar, drag it to any edge of the screen and release it.

2. To place a control on your form, click its button in the Toolbox and then click in your form where you want the control to appear.

3. To resize or move the control, select and drag a corner or the center of the control, as appropriate. For most controls, you can click and drag to create the size that you want.

 4. To change a control's properties, right-click the control and select Properties from the shortcut menu. You also can select the Properties button on the Form Design toolbar.

Duplicating and Deleting Controls

After you create a control, create duplicates of it by selecting it and choosing Edit, then Duplicate from the menu. An easier method may be to select it with the mouse, copy it by pressing Ctrl+C, and then paste it by pressing Ctrl+V. To make many copies of the same control, press Ctrl+V as many times as you wish.

Part
I

Ch
3

Delete controls by selecting them and pressing Delete, or by clicking the Edit menu, then selecting Cut or Delete. If you choose Cut, you can paste the control elsewhere in the form by clicking the Edit menu, then selecting Paste (or Ctrl+V). You can only Cut or Copy and then Paste one object at a time, so remember the last object you copied or cut before pasting. Of course, you can always click the Edit menu, then select Undo (or press Ctrl+Z) if you make a mistake.

    You also can use the Cut, Copy, and Paste buttons on the toolbar in Form Design view to move and copy controls.

Aligning Controls

Forms generally look best when the controls on them are lined up. You can use any of the tools in the Format menu to make this easier, including Align and Size. You can align controls by any of their sides, and size a group of controls so they're all the same height and/or width. To select more than one control to align, hold down the Shift key while selecting them or drag a marquee around all of the controls you want to select by clicking somewhere on the background and dragging the rectangle that appears around all of the objects you want to select.

 Be careful aligning controls that are entirely or partially on top of each other. Trying to align an edge of a group of stacked controls will result in them getting terribly out of alignment as Access moves them so they don't overlap. Instead of aligning controls placed like this, use the Horizontal Spacing/Make Equal or Vertical Spacing/Make Equal selections under the Format menu to space them, and then align them.

Access provides an invisible grid to assist in lining up and sizing controls. When Snap to Grid is turned on, controls will align themselves with the nearest grid intersection when they are placed or sized. You can turn this property on or off (it's on by default) by clicking the Format menu, then selecting Snap to Grid. You can change the grid size by changing the GridX and GridY properties of the current form (the default is 24 dots per inch). To see the grid, click the View menu, then Grid.

Moving and Resizing Controls

You move controls around the form by clicking and dragging them around as described previously, but you can make smaller changes (a pixel at a time) by selecting a control and then using combinations of the Shift, Ctrl, and arrow keys. Select the control and press the Shift key while pressing an arrow key to resize the object in the direction of the arrow. To move the control, press and hold the Ctrl key while pressing an arrow key to move the object in the direction of the arrow, a pixel at a time.

Ordering Controls

Controls are typically opaque. If you place one control on top of another, the more recently created control will hide the older one. To change the "order" of stacked controls, select a control you want to change in the stack and click the Format menu, then select either Bring to Front or Send to Back. The object in "front" hides all others behind it.

Converting Controls

Some controls are closely related and Access can change one to another, similar type. Select a control and then click the Format menu, and then select Change To. The related types of controls that can be created using the properties of the currently selected control are displayed in black and can be selected.

 The button at the top-right corner of the Toolbox (when floating) shows whether Control Wizards are enabled. Some controls, most notably, the Combo Box, can use wizards to help you select appropriate properties for them when they are created. Control Wizards are turned on by clicking this button and placing an object that uses a Control Wizard (combo box, list box, command button) on a form.

Inserting Other Objects into Forms

When you're designing and building a form, the Insert menu stays active. Clicking it gives you several objects to insert; these include page numbers and dates, charts, pictures, objects, and hyperlinks. While it's convenient to access these from the menu, they're really no different from any of the controls discussed previously (and in the Appendix). Rather than having to think about the function of the objects you're creating, as you do when using the Toolbox, the Insert menu takes the guesswork out of choosing a control and lets you concentrate on the appearance of your form.

There's no advantage to using either method of inserting controls, although using the menu may be more intuitive for a beginner. For example, it's probably somewhat easier to click the Insert menu, then select Object, and then select the kind of object you want to insert than it is to insert an Unbound OLE Object Frame control and muck with the properties to actually insert the kind of object you want. But once you get the hang of using controls, you'll never use the menu again.

Another way to insert objects is to drag and drop them from Windows Explorer or the Windows desktop into your form. Access automatically creates an Unbound OLE Object Frame for whatever you insert and associates the object with the program that's registered with Windows to handle files of that type. If Windows doesn't know what kind of file you dropped, Access will display it as an icon and complain if you try to double-click it to edit it.

Using Subforms for One-to-Many Relationships

When two tables share a one-to-many relationship, it's sometimes advantageous to be able to work with both tables in the same form. For example, the Customers and Orders tables have a one-to-many relationship established between the field [CustomerID] in both tables. When viewing information about a single customer, it might be nice to see all of that customer's orders.

To see data from both tables in one form, you'll usually want to create a form within a form. Each form will be based on one of the data sources in the relationship, and Access will manage the communication between them. If the Record Source for the outer (parent) form is the Customers table, the Record Source for the inner (child) form would be the Orders table. Access recognizes that a preexisting relationship exists between these two tables, and automatically limits the records displayed in the child form to those with a link to the parent; in this case, you'd only see the order records corresponding to the currently displayed customer record.

Building your forms with linked subforms is a good way to get a lot of data on one form without cluttering the screen unnecessarily, because this kind of form makes efficient use of space by not duplicating data. You can nest subforms up to two-deep (which is about as far as your mind can follow the relationships anyway), and include any number of subforms at the same level in a master form.

One of the nicest new features in Access 97 is the improved Form Wizard. In previous versions of Access, you had to tell the Wizard what kind of form you wanted to build, and then specify where the data was coming from. In Access 97, the Form Wizard asks where the data is, and then suggests an appropriate form.

To display data with a one-to-many relationship using the Form Wizard:

1. In the Database window, click the Forms tab. Then click the New button, and select the Form Wizard from the New Forms dialog box. You don't need to choose a data source at this point. Click OK to continue.

2. In the first screen of the Form Wizard, you'll see a combo box containing the names of all of the tables and queries in your database. Select the data source or sources (tables or queries) for the form. For this example, use the Categories and Products tables; select the Categories table for now.

3. Choose the fields in that table or query (by double-clicking them) that you want in your form from the list that appears below the data source names (see Figure 3.9). For this example, choose the fields CategoryName, Description, and Picture from the Categories table. Then select Products in the Tables/Queries combo box, and the ProductName and UnitPrice in the Available Fields pane. Click Next to continue.

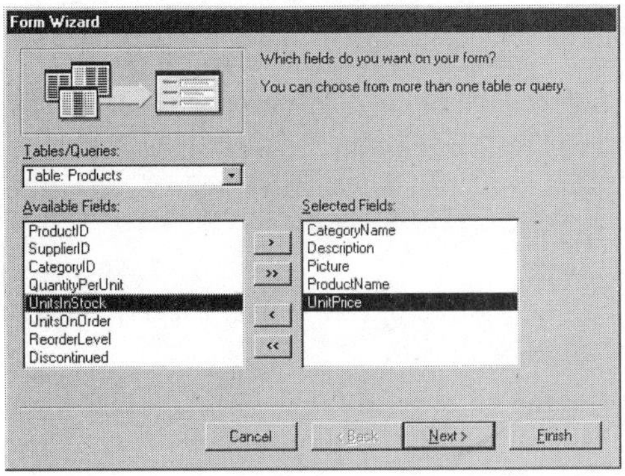

FIG. 3.9
The new Form Wizard enables the selection of data fields from any table or query in the database, or combinations of more than one.

4. Based on the data you just selected, Access realizes that you're designing a form showing data with an existing one-to-many relationship, and it gives you the option of viewing it in three different ways. You can choose any of these formats by selecting a different sort field (in this example, your options are "by Categories" and "by Products") and/or by selecting one of the two option buttons displayed at the bottom of the dialog box (Form with subform(s), Linked Forms, or Single Form). These options work as follows:

- **Single Form**.   Displays the fields from both tables combined into one flat form.

- **Form with subform(s)**.   The fields in the primary sort table are placed on the parent form, and they're linked to the fields in the child table, which reside in a smaller form placed inside the first one. Changing a record on the parent form makes a new set of related records visible on the subform.

- **Linked Forms**.   Access creates two separate forms linked by a command button; the parent form contains the fields in the primary sort table, and clicking the button displays a form containing the related records in the related child table.

You can try various different combinations of sort orders and form styles; Access shows a sample of what the result will look like. After you choose the type of form you like, click Next to continue.

5. All of the remaining screens deal with the appearance of the forms, including details such as colors and backgrounds. These screens are described in detail in the section of this chapter entitled "Using the Form Wizard."

Using the Expression Builder

When you're modifying the properties of a control, it's sometimes necessary to enter long, involved strings that define data sources, that point to other objects in other forms (or even in other parts of the database), or that involve actions or methods that you can't quite remember the name of. For times like this, there's the Expression Builder.

Part
I

Ch
3

The Expression Builder is available when you're editing object properties, writing macros, or building VBA code. You can tell when it's available because the Builder button is visible and not shaded in the toolbar. When you're editing object properties, the Builder button sometimes appears as a button with an ellipsis on it to the right of the property you're currently editing. This is a hint that a complicated expression may be required.

To use the Expression Builder:

1. Click the Builder button when it appears in the Property sheet or choose the Expression Builder from the toolbar.

2. You're presented with the Expression Builder window (see Figure 3.10). It's arranged in four panes:

    *   One horizontal pane across the top, which contains the expression you will create
    *   One vertical pane that contains the types and names of objects in the current database
    *   One vertical pane containing a list of controls in the currently selected object
    *   A vertical pane containing all of the methods relevant to the selected control

    There also are miscellaneous buttons that insert arithmetic and logical operators into your expression and control the workings of the dialog box.

FIG. 3.10

The Expression Builder. Its appearance changes depending on what's selected in it.

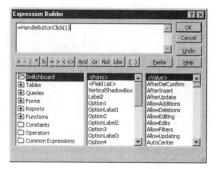

3. To create an expression, select the object you want to reference in the leftmost column. If there are other objects embedded in the object you selected, you will see the folder tree expand in much the same way the Windows Explorer does when traversing directories.

4. Go to the next pane and select a control in that object, if appropriate.

5. Finally, in the last pane, choose the method of that control that you need and click Paste. The expression you built appears in the top pane.

6. Click OK to insert it into your code or Properties box.

This process is easier to perform than to explain. For example, in the Employees form in Northwind, there's a control that displays an employee's name when the record containing her information is selected. But there's no field in the Employees table that contains an employee's full name, so that file has to be constructed. The Expression Builder facilitates this kind of work by keeping track of the names of fields and the syntax for creating the expression. To make it interesting, let's change this property to include a title for each employee, as in "Ms. Nancy Davolio."

To modify the Employees Form to show a courtesy title using the Expression Builder:

1. Open the Employees Form in Design view by selecting it in the Forms pane of the Database Window and clicking Design.

2. Select the EmployeeName control (it's the control nearest the top of the form; you won't see its name until you look at its Property sheet), and open the Properties dialog box for this control (right-click and select Properties). The Control Source property is filled with gibberish; the Expression Builder is a good way to examine it.

3. Click the field containing the Control Source property and the Builder button appears; select it to enter the Expression Builder. The current value for the Control Source,

```
=[FirstName] & " " & [LastName]
```

is carried into the Expression Builder.

T I P If all you want to see the code in this field without starting the Expression Builder, press Ctrl+F2 (Zoom) to make it appear in a simple text window for editing.

Before you re-create this snippet of code from scratch, look at what it's doing. The Control Source for the Employees form is the Employees table, and all of the data on it comes from the Employees table. The entries in square brackets, [FirstName] and [LastName], are fields in the Employees table; Access normally encloses object names in square brackets when they are parts of expressions. The ampersands (&) in the text indicate that the strings should be concatenated, and the blank in quotation marks should be concatenated between the first and last names.

You want to add a title for each employee; the obvious way to do this is to concatenate the title to the beginning of the existing string. You don't happen to know the name of the field in the Employees table containing the title, though; all you know is that you are going to end up with a code string that looks something like this:

```
=[Title] & " " & [FirstName] & " " & [LastName]
```

[Title] may be right or wrong—you'll soon find out. Now that you understand what you're building, do the following:

1. Clear out the part of the code before the [Title] field in the top window pane (select it and press Delete, or backspace over it). You should see the following in the pane:

```
[FirstName] & " " & [LastName]
```

2. To re-create the code string you need, find the Employees table in the leftmost vertical pane. There happens to be an object called "Employees" at the top of the pane currently selected and open, but it's the Employees form you are currently working in. Look farther down the list, to the folder marked "Tables" and double-click it. A list of all of the tables opens, and you can select the Employees table by clicking it once.

 Get comfortable with a naming scheme that works for you to distinguish between objects of different types. One common scheme, proposed in the *Access Developers Guide* series (SAMS), is to prepend each object name with a three-letter identifier like "frm" or "tbl." If that scheme were used here, the Employees table would become tblEmployees and the Employees form would be frmEmployees. It's not pretty, but it's perfectly clear which is which. And casual users never need to see these names.

If that scheme is too foreign looking, you could just use "Employees Form" and "Employees Table." Be aware that including spaces in object names, while perfectly legal in Access, makes coding a little more complicated (because you have to enclose the name in quotes sometimes). It also presents compatibility problems when exporting data.

3. When you select the Employees table, the values in the next column change to reflect all of the objects in the Employees table. Now you can see the field you need to include as part of the EmployeeName. Select the TitleOfCourtesy field by clicking it once.

 Is the field you need in this step "Title," or "TitleOfCourtesy"? Here is an example of poor naming practice; it would be a lot clearer if the field Title was called "JobTitle," which is what it really represents.

CAUTION

Double-clicking the name of an object pastes it into the top pane. If you double-clicked on the field name by accident, select and clear the pasted entry from the top pane before continuing.

4. You want the title to appear before the first and last names, so click to the left of the [FirstName] field in the top window. This places place the blinking cursor just after the equal sign (=) at the beginning of the line of code.

5. Next, click the Paste button. The field [TitleOfCourtesy] is pasted into the expression, along with the word <<Expr>>. Because the Expression Builder maintains syntax, Access is telling you that you need something between these two fields to make it a legal expression.

6. You need to insert two ampersands and a space to create the whole string. Select the <<Expr>> field so anything you type subsequently will replace it.

Click the ampersand key, type " ", and click the ampersand key again. Your line of code should look like this:

```
= [TitleOfCourtesy] & " " & [FirstName] & " " & [LastName]
```

Don't worry about spacing (but don't forget the space between the quotes); Access does the spacing for you.

7. You're done, so click OK to return to the Properties dialog box. Close it to see the form in Design view.

Want to see how you did? Change to Form view (select View, then Form View from the menu). If you got it right, you should see something like Figure 3.11. You can use the navigation buttons at the bottom of the form to see the other employees in the database, all with titles listed.

FIG. 3.11
The Employees form with customary titles added.

Using the Switchboard Manager

Access 97 includes an add-on that creates a form, called a *switchboard*, that helps users navigate to the areas of the database they need to see and use, and prevents users from changing objects and information that could be catastrophic to the integrity of the database application. You can create a switchboard form manually and include all of the navigation and utilities your users might need on it, or you can start with an Access-generated switchboard and modify it as necessary.

To create a Switchboard form click the Tools menu, then select Add-Ins, and then Switchboard Manager from the default menu. Access searches your existing forms for a previously generated switchboard; failing that, you'll see the dialog box in Figure 3.12.

The empty switchboard created is really a form template containing an Option Group control and several Command Buttons. The form is bound to a new table called Switchboard Items, which acts as a lookup between the number of a button a user might press and the action you want the database to take as a result. Each "page" in the Switchboard is bound to a command button Access creates for you.

FIG. 3.12

The Switchboard
Manager dialog box,
ready to add pages
to the application
switchboard.

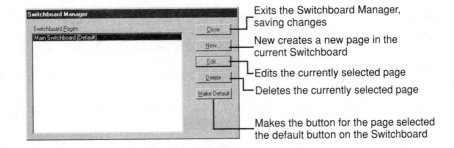

Exits the Switchboard Manager,
saving changes

New creates a new page in the
current Switchboard

Edits the currently selected page

Deletes the currently selected page

Makes the button for the page selected
the default button on the Switchboard

You can have any number of switchboards in your application, but start by editing the default switchboard that was created for you by clicking the Edit button.

The next dialog box reminds you that you're working on the Main Switchboard (this time), and provides plenty of space to add switchboard "pages" under it. Click the New button to add a page, and you'll see the Edit Switchboard Item dialog box.

You'll get the hang of this quickly; you create a new page, decide what the page should do, and enter the parameters to make it do that. If you want to do something not listed, you can edit the Switchboard Items table and Switchboard forms directly to add functionality.

You edit a page in the Switchboard by selecting it in the Switchboard Manager and clicking Edit. This displays the Edit Switchboard Page dialog box, which contains the names of all of the pages (which correspond to buttons) on that page. Several buttons are available to help edit the page:

- **Close** exits the Edit Switchboard Page dialog box
- **New** creates a new page in this switchboard page
- **Edit** brings up another Edit Switchboard Page dialog box to edit the selected page
- **Delete** deletes the currently selected page
- **Move Up** and **Move Down** change the order of the pages (buttons) on the current page

A finished switchboard for the Northwind database might look like Figure 3.13.

FIG. 3.13

A finished switchboard
built for the Northwind
database. Clicking the
button causes the
action listed to execute.

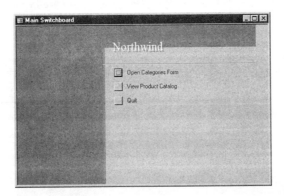

CHAPTER 4

Managing Data with Queries

Access provides several ways to view, change, and extract data from your database. These methods are based on the concept of *queries*, which are short programs that request the data be retrieved, added to, or modified in a table. Queries in Access can stand alone or they can be a part of forms and reports, but they're all constructed in more or less the same way. Once you master Access queries, you can be sure that almost any relational database program works nearly the same way.

Learn the similarities and differences between queries and tables

Queries can create tables, change the data in tables, and delete tables.

Get graphical with the Query By Example (QBE) grid

Access gives you a tool that lets you build queries by grabbing fields from tables and putting them in a new table.

Become familiar with SQL

Structured Query Language (SQL) is an English-like language that Access queries are built around.

Use Select queries to extract data from the database

The most common kind of query retrieves all or some of your data, depending on criteria you specify.

Get comfortable with Delete and Update Queries

These specialized queries are similar to Select queries in syntax.

Learn how to use Append and Make-Table Queries

Two-step queries that select for add records.

Try out a Crosstab Query

This rarely used query extracts data from a table and turns it on its side for analysis.

Writing Queries in Access

When you create a query, it's usually because you know there's a table in the database that contains data you need somewhere else, be it in another table, a form, or a report. The query explains what you need to the database engine, which remembers your request and executes it whenever requested. Because data in the underlying table can change, the results of the same query may be different every time it's run.

Queries that extract data from tables create objects that look and act like tables themselves. Consider the Employees table in the Northwind database. If you extract only the records from that table that contain information about people who live in London, what you are left with still looks like a table (see Figure 4.1).

FIG. 4.1

Records extracted from a table look like tables themselves, no matter how many records or fields are extracted.

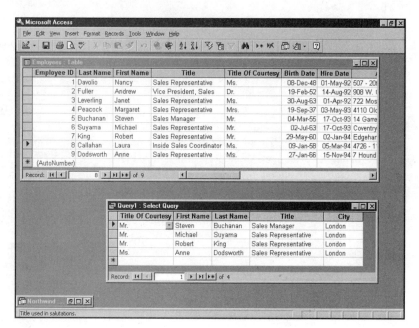

There are several types of queries that you can use in Access:

- **Select Queries.**   You can think of a Select query as a "view" of a table, constructed in such as way as to make the data in the table appear differently depending on how you look at it. Select queries almost always produce subsets of the table (or tables) from which the data is selected.

- **Delete and Update Queries.**   These queries remove or modify records in an existing table.

- **Append and Make Table Queries**. These queries extract data from existing tables (or create new data altogether) and add new records to existing tables, or create entirely new tables by generating new records.

- **Crosstab Queries**. These unusual queries summarize data extracted from tables, counting and merging data from several underlying fields into one or more fields in the output.

It would be ineffective, given the changing nature of data in tables, to permanently store the results of a query and use those same results over and over again. Instead of storing results, we usually store the *request* that the database processed to extract that data. Access stores queries in two ways: the Query By Example (QBE) grid and in Structured Query Language (SQL). These two methods are normally referred to by their initials (pronounced Cue-Bee-Eee and either Ess-Cue-El or See-quel, respectively) and they express the exact same query in very different ways.

N O T E   A few unusual types of queries can only be written in SQL and are not supported by QBE. For more information, look up "SQL Queries" in Access help. ■

Most queries written in one format are convertible to the other, and you may find yourself learning how to achieve certain results in one format and switching back and forth to it when you want to use that feature. Neither method is superior, but you'll probably use QBE most of the time and switch to SQL for fine-tuning or to convert queries to Visual Basic for Applications (VBA) code.

Part

I

Ch

4

Creating Queries with the Query By Example Grid

QBE is the default format, or "view," for creating queries in Access, and you'll use the QBE grid for most of the queries you create.

To create a query in QBE:

1. From the Database Window, select the Queries tab and click New. Several options for creating queries appear in the New Query dialog box.

2. Select Design View and click OK to open the Show Table dialog box and QBE grid (see Figure 4.2).

Because most queries depend on data already in tables to work, Access expects you to select an existing data source. Notice that Access considers both existing tables and queries as valid data sources, because both return tablelike objects from which queries can extract data.

FIG. 4.2
The Query By Example (QBE) grid, as it appears when starting a new query. Access automatically displays the Show Table dialog box to help you select a data source.

Table relationships window——

Query grid——

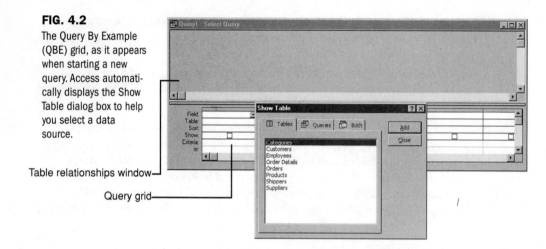

After you've selected an underlying data source, you can close the Show Table dialog box to make the QBE grid easier to see. The QBE grid is made up of two sections: the Table Relationships at the top, and the Query Grid at the bottom. If you selected a data source in the Show Table dialog box, you'll see the table or query you selected in the Relationships pane. Otherwise, it will appear empty. In either case, you can add as many data sources as you need at any point during the development of a query—more on that later in this chapter.

The bottom section is where the real work gets done. By default, there are six lines in this grid. You can directly type in all six; some work like combo boxes (providing a pull-down list of valid values) or use the Expression Builder to fill them in.

▶ **See** "Entering Data in the Database with Forms," **p. 49**

The lines in the Query Grid are used as follows:

■ **Field**.   The entry in each column in this row is the name of a field in an underlying data source. You can enter a field name here for one of two reasons: You want that field's data to appear in the results of the query, or you want to sort or sift the records in the data source according to some value in this field.

■ **Table**.   The data source in which the field listed resides. This is either a table or another query.

■ **Sort**.   How the records the query returns should be sorted, if at all. Valid entries in this cell are ascending (0–9 and A–Z), descending (9–0 and Z–A), and (not sorted) or blank. Sorting takes place on the field listed above the sort order, and any number of fields can be sorted on.

■ **Show**.   This check box is checked automatically, indicating that the data in the field selected should be shown as part of the results of the query. If it's not checked, the listed field is still used for sorting and/or criteria, but is not shown.

- **Criteria**.   A string entered in this cell indicates that the field listed must match the string for the data in its associated record to be included in the results. This string may include any number of criteria for the listed field, separated by the word AND.

- **or**.   A string entered in this cell is part of the Criteria for this field, but this criteria can be matched exclusively of the criteria in the previous cell. If the data in the listed field matches the criteria in either the Criteria cell, the Or cell, or any of the cells below, the associated record will be included in the results.

As an example of how to use the QBE grid, use the Northwind database to write a simple Select query. You'll then write the same query in native SQL for comparison.

In your example, you'll create a query to find a list of current products in the Northwind catalog. All the data needed for this query, the Product Name, ID, and Discontinued field, can be found in the Products table (see Figure 4.3).

FIG. 4.3

The Products table in Datasheet view. Some products have been discontinued, as evidenced by the check marks in the Discontinued column. (Some irrelevant fields have been hidden for clarity.)

Product ID	Product Name	Supplier	Discontinued
1	Chai	Exotic Liquids	☐
2	Chang	Exotic Liquids	☐
3	Aniseed Syrup	Exotic Liquids	☐
4	Chef Anton's Cajun Seasoning	New Orleans Cajun Delights	☐
5	Chef Anton's Gumbo Mix	New Orleans Cajun Delights	☑
6	Grandma's Boysenberry Spread	Grandma Kelly's Homestead	☐
7	Uncle Bob's Organic Dried Pears	Grandma Kelly's Homestead	☐
8	Northwoods Cranberry Sauce	Grandma Kelly's Homestead	☐
9	Mishi Kobe Niku	Tokyo Traders	☑
10	Ikura	Tokyo Traders	☐
11	Queso Cabrales	Cooperativa de Quesos 'Las Cabras'	☐
12	Queso Manchego La Pastora	Cooperativa de Quesos 'Las Cabras'	☐
13	Konbu	Mayumi's	☐
14	Tofu	Mayumi's	☐
15	Genen Shouyu	Mayumi's	☐
16	Pavlova	Pavlova, Ltd.	☐
17	Alice Mutton	Pavlova, Ltd.	☑
18	Carnarvon Tigers	Pavlova, Ltd.	☐
19	Teatime Chocolate Biscuits	Specialty Biscuits, Ltd.	☐
20	Sir Rodney's Marmalade	Specialty Biscuits, Ltd.	☐

Record: 1 of 77

Part

I

Ch

4

N O T E   This book refers to fields, tables, and queries using the syntax that Access (in Visual Basic for Applications) uses to refer to them. In general, fields are surrounded by square brackets, as in [Discontinued]; table and query names appear as plain text unless they include a space, in which case they're surrounded by double quotes, as in "Discontinued Products." ▪

To write a Select query to extract this data using the QBE grid,

1. From the Database window, click the Queries tab, then click the New button.

2. Select Design View from the list of options and click OK to continue. The Show Table dialog box appears.

3. Select the Products table, click the Add button, and then click the Close button. A representation of the Products table appears in the Relationships Window of the QBE grid and the Show Table dialog box goes away.

4. For this example, you'll want the [ProductID], [ProductName], and [Discontinued] fields to appear as returned data when the query is run. To move those fields from the Relationships Window to the QBE grid, just drag them down to an otherwise blank column in the grid or double-click the name of the field in the table.

5. Clear the check mark in the Show row of the [Discontinued] field. That makes the field available for querying but does not show it in the results.

6. To inform Access that you only want those records where the value of [Discontinued] is False (see Figure 4.4), click in the Criteria row in the column containing the field [Discontinued] and enter "**=False**".

 T I P Access tries to help you by not requiring some syntax elements, like the equal sign in the criteria value shown here, if it can figure out what you mean. Similarly, almost nothing (including expressions, constants like "False" and field names) in Access are case-sensitive; if case matters, Access will usually make the changes itself.

FIG. 4.4
The QBE grid, complete with a Select query to show only the active (not discontinued) products in the database.

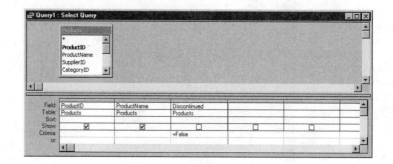

 To run the query, click the Run button (looks like a red exclamation point) on the toolbar. The results of the query are shown in Figure 4.5, which Access calls the Datasheet view of the query.

 To return to Design view, select the View button on the toolbar. You can make several minor changes to this query to see the data in different ways; for example, try entering "**Ascending**" in the Sort row under the field [ProductName] to sort the output differently. Try including different fields from the table in the query.

To see only discontinued products whose names start with A:

1. Enter Like "**A***" in the Criteria row under the field [Product Name].

T I P The asterisk (*) in the expression in Step 1 is called a *wildcard*; it means any character or characters match. So the expression "A*" means "any string beginning with the letter A". The word "Like" tells Access to expect a wildcard in the expression.

FIG. 4.5

The results of the Active Products query. Note the skips in the ProductID field where discontinued products used to be.

2. Enter the following in the same row under the field [Discontinued]:

   =True

3. Your QBE grid should look something like Figure 4.6. Click the Run button on the toolbar to see your results.

 T I P For help on any of the rows in the QBE pane, click anywhere in the row and press the F1 key.

Part

I

Ch

4

FIG. 4.6

The QBE grid before running a query to show only discontinued products with names beginning with the letter A.

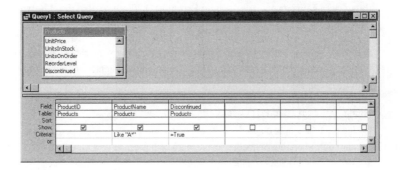

Creating Queries in Structured Query Language (SQL)

In Access, every query can be expressed either in SQL or on the QBE grid, and a query created in one interface is usually translatable to the other when required.

Using SQL is useful to create and understand queries because you can gain a different perspective on any query, and some kinds of modifications to queries are actually a little easier in SQL view.

There is one common activity that makes a SQL query absolutely necessary, and that's when you want to convert a stored query into a VBA module. VBA can run SQL queries directly, and this is especially useful when you expect to print the documentation of the database or want to keep it as portable as possible.

The SQL equivalent of the "discontinued products beginning with A" query can be viewed by clicking the pull-down arrow to the right of the View button on the toolbar and selecting the SQL View from the list that appears (see Figure 4.7).

FIG. 4.7

The same simple Select query in SQL view. Access inserts more parentheses than it needs, but they don't hurt anything.

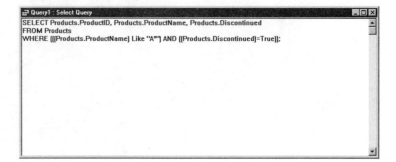

```
Query1 : Select Query
SELECT Products.ProductID, Products.ProductName, Products.Discontinued
FROM Products
WHERE (((Products.ProductName) Like "A*") AND ((Products.Discontinued)=True));
```

The structure of most SQL statements is like this example: SELECT (*fields*) FROM (*table*) WHERE (*criteria*).

The "dot" notation used in this SQL query is common in databases and is used all over Access. Periods are often used between the names of data sources (tables and queries) and fields in those data sources, as in Products.ProductID. They're also used between the names of database objects and methods and properties of those objects.

N O T E   Access' automatic SQL generator makes this query, as simple as it is, even more complicated than it needs to be. Most human programmers would write it as

```
SELECT ProductID, ProductName
FROM Products
WHERE Discontinued=True and ProductName like "A*";
```

leaving the table name out of the field identifiers and eliminating the parentheses. Those elements are required only when they're needed to eliminate confusion, as when the data fields are being extracted from more than one data source.

Also worth noting is that SQL is not case-sensitive and the line breaks shown (which Access inserts) are only for readability. The semicolon at the end is required, however, although Access rarely enforces this and the query runs without it. ▪

Using SQL view, even if you don't become familiar with the language, can sometimes assist in troubleshooting problem queries. If a query designed in QBE doesn't seem to be returning the right data, you should consider viewing it in SQL and just reading it aloud to see if it makes sense.

N O T E   For more information on the ins and outs of SQL syntax, you can use the SQL Command Reference in Access (click the Help menu, then select Contents and Index, then search for "SQL Queries" and select the topic "Work with SQL in queries, forms, reports, and macros") or consider the following Que books:

Special Edition Using Microsoft Access 97, by Roger Jennings, et al.

Access 97 Power Programming, by F. Scott Barker ▪

Extract Data Using Select Queries

The most common kind of query is the Select query. Select queries extract data from a data source and return it in the form of a table. The resulting table can be used as the basis for a form or report, or as a data source for yet another query.

When you open the QBE grid, Access assumes you're about to build a Select query. The Show Table dialog box appears (refer to Figure 4.2) to assist you in selecting a data source (either a table or a query) from the database from which you'll extract data for your query. You can select a data source of your choice and close this dialog box to begin building your query.

N O T E   You can actually use as many data sources as you like to form the underlying data sources for a query. Multiple-source queries are described in Chapter 5, "Advanced Data Retrieval Using Queries." ▪

The use of the QBE grid is explained in the previous section, but there are some additional features and functions that you'll find useful in constructing your Select queries. The most common of these is the use of aggregate functions in the Totals row of your query to compute totals and statistical variances.

Aggregate functions are provided by Access to make calculations based on more than one record. For example, the aggregate function "Count()" counts the number of records in a given data source. When you want to use these functions in a query, you typically use them in the Totals row of the QBE grid.

The Totals Row

 If you click the Totals button on the toolbar (it looks like the Greek letter sigma) while in a query's Design view, a new row appears in the QBE grid entitled "Total:" Click in the Total field and then click the drop-down list. A number of Access functions are available in this row that act on the field entered in the top row of the grid and change the way it looks in the resulting

Part

I

Ch

4

table. Most of these are true aggregate functions, but a few of the entries in this list manage the grouping of data in the results, provide for complex expressions in queries, and filter out some records. The Totals row is used for all of these. These aggregate functions and special operators are:

- **Group By**.   Select Group By for a field when that field will be used to define the sort breaks for another function on another field. For example, if your query computes the sum of the cost of all products in the Products table, it might be nice to break it down by supplier. This is not an aggregate function.
- **Sum**.   Use this to calculate the sum of all of the values of a given field in the query.
- **Avg**.   This function computes the average (arithmetic mean) of all values of the specified field in a query.
- **Min**.   Finds the minimum value of the specified field in all records in the underlying data source.
- **Max**.   Finds the maximum value of the specified field in all records in the underlying data source.
- **Count**.   Counts the number of records in the underlying data source.
- **StDev**.   Determines the standard deviation of the values of the specified field across all of the records in the data source.
- **Var**.   Determines the statistical variance of the values of the specified field across all of the records in the data source.
- **First**.   Returns the value of the specified field in the first record in the data source.
- **Last**.   Returns the value of the specified field in the last record in the data source.
- **Expression**.   Used to denote that the entry in the field row is an expression that uses aggregate functions. For example, to have a Select query on the Personnel table return the full name of an employee, you might enter the following in the Field row:

  ```
  FullName: [FirstName} & " " & [LastName]
  ```

  If you needed to have the Totals row displayed for a calculation on some other field in the query, you would use the Expression function in the column for the calculated [FullName] field. This is not an aggregate function.
- **Where**.   Used to denote that the entry in the field row has some criteria being applied against it. As with the Expression function, this is only displayed when the Totals row is being used for another field. This is not an aggregate function.

All of these will become clearer with a couple of examples. There are a some caveats to using aggregate functions in queries:

- They only work on the rows that survive any criteria you apply. For example, if you write a query on the Personnel table and use a criteria to only return the employees whose names begin with "M", the Count function will only count those whose names begin with "M".

■ The aggregate functions only work on records whose values are not null. When using the aggregate functions, use them on fields that you know will not be empty, such as key fields. Alternatively, you can use Access' NZ function to convert nulls to zeroes for some data; see Access help for more information on this function.

Continuing with this example, write a query that computes the average price of products in the Northwind inventory, and break it down by supplier. The results should be the ID number of the supplier and the average price of the items from that supplier.

To create a query that uses Avg (an aggregate function) follow these steps:

1. Open a new query in Design view; the Show Table dialog box and QBE grid will appear. In the Show Table dialog box, choose the Products table and click OK to make it appear in the Relationships pane. Click Close to make the Show Table dialog box go away.

2. Double-click (or drag) the [SupplierID] and [UnitPrice] fields from the Relationshsips pane into separate columns in your QBE grid.

3. Turn on the Totals row by clicking the Totals button on the toolbar.

4. Select the Avg function for the [UnitPrice] field and the Group By operator for [SupplierID].

5. Finally, sort the list by Supplier ID: in the Sort row of the QBE grid, choose Ascending for the [SupplierID] field.

6. The ready-to-run grid should look like Figure 4.8. Click the Run button and what you should see look like Figure 4.9.

FIG. 4.8
The QBE grid before you run the "Average Price by Supplier" query. Note the SupplierID is included in the grid, not the Supplier Name, which is in a different table.

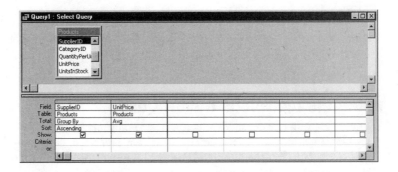

The designer of the Products table has installed a Lookup on the [SupplierID] field that automatically displays the supplier's name instead of their ID number. You sorted by ID number, and this list is sorted correctly, even though it's not alphabetical. There's just no correlation between the suppliers' names and the order of their ID numbers.

Part

I

Ch

4

FIG. 4.9

The averages look OK, but the Supplier Name appears instead of the ID because there's a Lookup established for that field in the Products Table.

N O T E This is a good example of where some of the smoke-and-mirrors capability of Access can be detrimental, as alluded to in Chapter 2. Without modifying the design of the Products table, there's no way to see the supplier IDs in this query or any other. And if you depend on this query returning the supplier names, you lose the portability of your query, because there's no guarantee that any other database will have a Lookup capability. If you go back to the Database window and open the Products table for editing, you can delete the Lookup information for the [SupplierID] field to make this query run correctly. But that may break other queries in the database. This is a flaw in the design of the Northwind database, and it's not recommended for real-world databases. ■

You may want to replace the Avg function with some others (try Sum, Min, Max, Count, First, Last, StdDev, and Var) to see how they work. You may have noticed that Access automatically inserted the GroupBy function in the [SupplierID] column; it's the default, and every column in a function including aggregates needs to have an entry in this row.

Returning the Top Values from a Query

Continuing with this example, what if you were only interested in, viewing the five most expensive suppliers? Access enables you to choose any number or percent of "top values" (that is, the first values to be returned from the query) to return. The default is to return all values, but you can choose to return only the top *n* or the top *n* percent (where *n* is an integer).

T I P The Top Values property can be modified in Design view as shown, or the Top Values property of the query can be modified on the query's property sheet.

In Design view for the query, select the Top Values pull-down list from the toolbar. Access provides six options for the display of top values from a query. These are the:

- Top 5 records (5)
- Top 25 records (25)

- Top 100 records (100)
- Top 5 percent (5%)
- Top 25 percent (25%)
- All records (All), the default.

Changing this value will have the expected effects on your query, with one exception. The query you built earlier is sorted by Supplier ID, and sorting by the top supplier IDs is not useful. Change the sort order to sort instead by the averaged Unit Price for more meaningful results.

"Top" in this context really means the first records displayed in the query results. If you've sorted your values in Ascending order, which is normal, the top values will be the lowest ones because they appear first in the list. If you're interested in the "bottom" values, reverse the sort order of your records before running the query.

You can select any value for the top values or percent; the 5, 25, and 100 values are available from the toolbar for convenience. Type any value in the Top Values box or use the query's property sheet to set the Top Values property to any value you wish.

Expressions and Calculated Fields

It's frequently necessary to perform a calculation on a value in a data source before using it in a query. These calculations can take the form of concatenated strings, as in the example shown previously or may involve intermediate calculations on data that culminate in a final result. These calculations are performed in the Field row of the QBE grid; if Totals are turned on, the Expression function should be entered in the grid for the calculated fields.

To create a calculated field, enter the expression for the calculation in the Field row of the QBE grid. For example, say you wanted to find out the average time between the placing of an order and its shipping, sorted by destination country. It's not hard to write a query that shows the actual dates of ordering and shipping and the destination country (choose the fields [Ship Country], [Order Date], and [Shipped Date] from the Orders table), but it doesn't make any sense to average the actual dates. You really want to average the difference between the two dates, and that can be figured using a calculated field. Calculated fields have the following format:

```
FieldName: Expression
```

As you learned earlier, for noncalculated fields, you usually enter just the field name in the Field: row of the QBE grid. For calculated fields, you enter the calculation, and it's usually a good idea to specify a field name. Access creates field names if you don't, and they have incredibly descriptive names like "Expr1," "Expr2," and so on.

For the date calculation field, the calculation is straightforward: the difference between the Order Date and Shipping Date is expressed as:

```
[Shipped Date] - [Order Date]
```

Part
I
Ch
4

and this is typed in the Field: row, next to the [Ship Country] column. Access isn't sure where the data fields come from when you type them in directly, so make sure you select the Orders table in the Table: row. You can return a descriptive name for the calculated field by writing the expression as:

```
Ship Delay: [Shipped Date] - [Order Date]
```

Running the query at this point will show you the shipping delay for every order in the database; you need to use the aggregate function Avg to obtain an average by country. Turn on the Totals line and enter "Avg" on the Totals line under your calculated field. The "Group By" entry automatically entered under the [Ship Country] column is appropriate in this case. Finally, sort it in descending order by the amount of delay. The resulting QBE grid looks like Figure 4.10.

FIG. 4.10

The QBE grid, including a calculated field with an aggregate function applied.

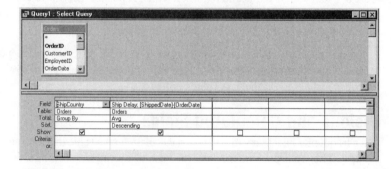

The results, when the query is run, are shown in Figure 4.11.

FIG. 4.11

Note that the date calculation and average is taken to way too many decimal places; this is because dates are stored internally as double-precision floating-point numbers.

This expression was easy to type directly, but you could have used the Expression Builder if you couldn't remember the exact names of the fields, or if you wanted the full array of Access functions available for the calculation. You can use any expression that returns a value in a calculated field; you can even use a constant.

For example, building on the previous example, what if you wanted to flag all countries with shipping delays greater than five days? You could add a third column to show this, and its Field: entry might look like this:

```
Too Long: IIf((Avg([ShippedDate]-[OrderDate])>5),"Too long!","Okay.")
```

The IIf( ) function evaluates its first argument (true if the average delay is more than five days) and returns the second argument ("Too long!") if it's true, and the third argument ("Okay.") if it's false. because this uses an aggregate function in the Field expression, this field must have "Expression" entered in the Total:row. Executing this query returns the same 21 values as in the previous example (refer to Figure 4.11), but each of them has been evaluated for the acceptability of the delay (and all have failed).

You can make queries return constants by including them in the Field: row just as you would an expression. If the delay will always be too long, regardless of the actual delay, you could enter

```
Too Long: "Too Long!"
```

as the third field, and you would always get the words "Too Long!" returned in the query results.

T I P To create any of the query types introduced in the beginning of the chapter, open a new (Select) query in Design view and click in the menu on Query, then either Crosstab Query, Make-Table Query, Update Query, or Append Query, or Delete Query. Alternatively, you can use the Query Type pulldown on the toolbar. You can even switch between query types at will, preserving most of the work you've done in the QBE grid.

Creating and Using Delete Queries

A Delete query removes records from the underlying table. Running an incorrect Delete query can irreparably damage the underlying table. For this reason, it's always a good idea to make a backup of a real data table when writing these types of queries, and to use the Datasheet view of the query to see what it's going to do before it actually does it.

Delete queries are deceptively simple to create. The first column in the QBE grid is always the asterisk, representing all of the fields in the underlying table. If the query contains only that, all of the fields in all of the records in the specified table will be deleted at the press of a button. To create a query that deletes everything in a table, double-click or drag the "*" field from the Relationships pane of the query's Design view to the QBE grid. Note that the entry in the Delete: row changes to "From."

 Click the Run button on the toolbar to delete everything in the table. You'll get a chance to confirm your choice, but once those records are gone, they're gone. There's no "Undo" on a delete.

You can take the more docile approach to Delete queries if you prefer, by deleting some or all records in a table based on criteria. You can have practically any number of criteria that records must meet before they'll be deleted; you enter them in the grid field-by-field. After you move a field to the grid, enter the appropriate criteria in the Criteria row, as described in "Query By Example (QBE)", earlier in this chapter. Remember that this is deletion criteria you're entering; any records meeting the criteria you specify will go away when you execute the query. Listing more than one field and criteria for each has the effect of establishing an "and" relationship: candidate records must meet the criteria for Field 1 and Field 2 and Field 3, and so on before they'll be deleted. Multiple criteria on subsequent rows under one field creates an "or" relationship, requiring records to meet any of the criteria listed to be deleted.

To demonstrate how to use the Delete query use the Northwind Traders database. Assume Northwind has sold all of its overseas business to another company. The sale is final, and it's time to remove all of the customers outside of North America from the Customers table.

CAUTION

Before running this example, back up your Northwind database by selecting it in Windows Explorer and clicking the Edit menu, then Copy, then Edit, then Paste from the menu (or press Ctrl+C, then Ctrl+V). Name it something like "Northwind Backup" for easy restoration later.

Note that you'll have to close the database in Access before you'll be able to copy it.

If you forget to do this, the Northwind database can be copied directly from your Office 97 Professional CD; it's saved as \Office\Samples\Nwind80.mdb. Copy it to C:\Program Files\Microsoft Office\Office\Samples\Northwind.mdb and make sure you remove the read-only attribute from it (in Explorer, right-click the file name, select Properties from the menu, and clear the Read Only check box) before trying to use it.

To create a query that deletes all customers who are not in the United States, Mexico, or Canada, complete the following steps:

1. Open a new query and select the Customers table.

2. Change the default Select query to a Delete query by clicking and holding the Query Type button on the toolbar; select the Delete Query button from the column of buttons that appears.

3. Double-click the asterisk in the Table pane of the Query window to move it to the QBE grid (the Delete: row changes to "From").

4. Double-click the [Country] field as well (the Delete: row changes to "Where").

5. You could set up the criteria in many ways, the most likely of which are listed here:

   - List all of the possible countries to delete on separate lines under the Criteria for the [Country] field (for example, "Germany" [new line] "Austria" [new line] "Poland", etc.)

- List all of the possible countries to delete on one line under the [Country] field, separated by the word OR (for example, "Germany" OR "Austria" OR "Poland", etc.)
- Use the NOT operator to list only the countries you want to exclude in different columns (for example, NOT "USA" in one column, NOT "Mexico" in another, etc.);
- Use the NOT operator to list only the countries you want to exclude in one column (for example, NOT "USA" AND NOT "Mexico" AND NOT "Canada").

6. Only the last of these makes much sense. You could list every country you want to delete as criteria, as shown in the first two examples, but that's a lot of typing. The third approach isn't hard (there's no reason why you can't list one field in as many columns as you like), but it's not as easy as the previous option. In the Criteria row under the column containing the field [Country], enter

```
NOT ("USA" or "Mexico" or "Canada")
```

N O T E The NOT operator is distributive across parentheses. The previous example shows the criteria listed as

```
NOT "USA" AND NOT "Mexico" AND NOT "Canada"
```

for clarity, but it could be written as

```
NOT ("USA" or "Mexico" or "Canada")
```

with a lot less typing. The NOT distributes across the parentheses and changes the intent of the enclosed OR operators to AND NOT. This kind of use takes a little practice, but becomes intuitive over time. ■

After you enter this in your QBE grid, it should look like Figure 4.12.

FIG. 4.12
The QBE grid, ready to do a Delete query. The entries in the Delete: row are made automatically.

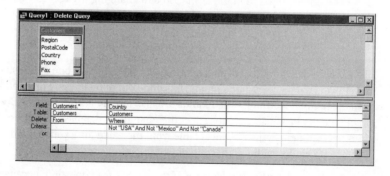

Don't click Run yet! It's always a good idea to see what you're about to delete before you actually do it, and this is where the Datasheet view of queries is most useful. Click the View menu, then Datasheet View (or select it from the View pull-down on the toolbar) to see the records that Access is about to delete. There are normally 91 customers listed in the Customers table; you should see that 70 of them are about to be deleted. If you're satisfied with what you see, switch back to Design view and click the Run button. Access shows a helpful reminder (see Figure 4.13); if you choose Yes, those records will be deleted and you'll need to restore the Customers table from your backup to continue with the examples in this book.

Part
I

Ch
4

FIG. 4.13

The warning Access displays before you delete records.

The warning message shown in figure 4.13 is almost true. Actually, the Customers table is the primary table in a relationship with the Orders table; orders include Customer IDs, and removing the customer record would orphan several records in Orders. For that reason, Access won't let you delete any customers that have related records in Orders and gives you an error message if you try.

If you inspect the relationship between these two tables, you'll see that Referential Integrity is enabled, and that Cascade Update Related Fields is turned on. This forces the Orders table to be updated automatically if you change a Customer ID in Customers. However, Cascade Delete Related Records is not turned on. If you turn it on, Access deletes your customer records whether they have placed orders, and it removes any records of their orders as well. For this example, this is fine, but you may want to carefully consider the implications of this kind of action in a real-world database.

▶ **See** "Understanding Table Relationships," **p. 36**

Creating and Using Update Queries

Update queries work in much the same way as Delete queries, selecting a subset of records based on criteria entered in the QBE grid and changing the records appropriately. As with the Delete query, the records to be updated can be viewed in a datasheet before actually executing the Update query, and like the Delete query, the results of an Update query can't be undone without resting the database. Have you made a backup?

To illustrate the workings of an Update query, let's say that one of the suppliers in the Northwind database, Exotic Liquids, has gone out of business. Fortunately, all of the products you currently buy from Exotic Liquids are also available from Bigfoot Breweries, so you'll need to update the Products table to reflect the change. In database terms, you'll need to change the [SupplierID] field in the Products table from the value for Exotic Liquids to the value for Bigfoot Breweries without affecting any of the other products.

You need to find out the IDs for both of the suppliers in question, because they're not stored by name in Products. This information is easy to find in the Suppliers table; the ID for Exotic Liquids turns out to be 1 and the ID for Bigfoot Breweries is 16.

To create a new Update query that transfers all of Exotic Liquids' products to Bigfoot Breweries:

1. Open a new query and select the Products table.

2. Click the Query type button on the toolbar and choose Update query.

3. Double-click the [SupplierID], [ProductName], and [UnitPrice] fields in the Relationships window to take them to the QBE grid.

4. The QBE row specific to the Update query is the Update To: row; for each field listed in a column, the Update To: row should contain the value to which it should be changed. In this case, you want to change every [SupplierID] of 1 to 16. so Enter 16 (the ID for Bigfoot Breweries) in the Update To: cell under the field [SupplierID].

5. Without some criteria, this query will change every [SupplierID] in the database to 16, which will really mess up your resupply system. You only want to update those records in which the [SupplierID] is currently 1; the expression to enter in the Criteria cell is therefore

   =1

   Enter "=1" (the ID for Exotic Liquids) in the Criteria row under the field [SupplierID].

The resulting QBE grid looks like Figure 4.14, but look at the Datasheet view before running it to make sure the correct records are selected for update. There should be three, and running the query will indeed update their Supplier ID to 16. Note that this query has no effect on the Suppliers table, and Exotic Liquids is still in there. You can remove it from Suppliers, if you like, by running a Delete query (the hard way) or just selecting the record for Exotic Liquids in Datasheet view and deleting it. Either method has referential integrity implications for the Order table.

FIG. 4.14
The QBE grid before running a simple Update query.

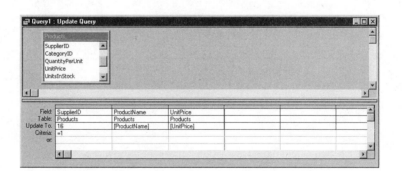

Part

I

Ch

4

Because the only field selected in this query is [SupplierID], it can be hard it tell if you're really updating the right thing in Datasheet view. It's also possible that you'll want to select records based on criteria that aren't related to the field (or fields) you're updating. The solution to both of these problems is to select more fields in the QBE grid, but enter the same field name (in square brackets) in the Update To: row if you don't want them updated. You're really updating them to their current value. You'll see all of the fields you select in Datasheet view, and your criteria apply to entire records, not just individual fields.

Add Records to an Existing Table with Append Queries

You use Append queries when you want to add records to existing tables in the database, instead of just selecting some for later use and/or deleting them.

Append (and Make-Table queries, discussed later) queries add records based on some selection criteria that the programmer supplies. In those cases where one or two records need to be added, or where the data to be added isn't available (or calculable) from an existing data source, these queries aren't appropriate. It is possible to add a record containing constants to a table with these queries, but you're not likely to do that often.

The only difference in the QBE grid between an Append query and a Select query is that the familiar Sort row is replaced with Append To:. Sorting is irrelevant, because the resulting table can be sorted easily enough. In this type of query, the Append To row is used to denote the field in the table to be appended that the data in this column will be appended to.

When you create an Append query (usually by creating a Select query and then changing the type to Append by clicking the Query menu, and then selecting Append), Access asks to which table the data will be appended to, and whether that table is in the current database or another. If you select an external database, you need to supply a file name for it. A file selection dialog box is not provided, so you have to know the name and fully qualified pathname of the external database. If you mistype it, Access will continue until it completes the query and tries to write the records. It's also unfortunate that in this version of Access you can't append to an ODBC data source.

Filling out the QBE grid is straightforward and works exactly as it does for a Select query. As is the case in Delete and Update queries, you can use the Datasheet view to preview the records that will be appended before they actually are written to the destination table.

When writing Append queries, be careful to include any fields that are necessary in the destination table, like keys, before you run the query. Failing to include values for key fields (that aren't of the data type AutoNumber) will result in a "failure to append because of key violations" error message. Similarly, if you are appending records to a table with a primary key defined, make sure that records you append have unique keys and do not duplicate keys already in the table, or they will fail to paste. Access gives you the option of continuing a query like this when some of the records would result in key violations; if some records can be pasted without violating integrity, Access will paste just those if you select OK on the error dialog box warning you of this condition.

It's difficult to show an example of an Append query using the Northwind database, because no data in the database lends itself to be appended. The most common use of Append queries is to merge two tables in two databases, where the structures of the tables are very similar and there is minimal data overlap between the two. For example, if the Northwind Traders organization purchased a competitor's store, it might be appropriate to use an Append query to merge the former competitor's Customers and Suppliers tables into the Northwind database, assuming they contained more or less the same information. This would be accomplished by importing each external table (if the tables were in an Access database, it wouldn't be necessary to import them) and creating Append queries to extract the data out of the foreign tables and paste it into the Northwind tables.

▶ **See** "Importing and Exporting Data," **p. 42**

Add Records to a New Table with Make-Table Queries

Make-Table queries work in exactly the same way as Append queries, except that they paste the selected records into a new table. The QBE grid for a Make-Table query looks exactly the same as it does for an Append query.

Because a Make-Table query selects records from an existing table and pastes them into a new table, it's easier to demonstrate than an Append query. The example used in this case brings forward several of the concepts discussed in earlier sections, including using top values and aggregate functions.

Let's say that you have an internal company Web page that is constantly updated with the names of the company's best customers. The Web page frequently queries the Northwind database, looking for a table called "tblBestCustomers." This table needs to contain the names of the customers with the highest sales during the past two years and the total of the sales.

There are several things you'll need to do in your query to make this happen:

- For a data source, use an existing query instead of a table. The Invoices query contains everything you need (and it extracts the information from six different tables), so you'll use it rather than re-create it.

- You're only interested in sales over the past two years. That will need to be recalculated every time the query is run. You need to look at the Invoice date and compare it to today's date. If the invoice was more than two years ago, it doesn't count.

- You want to add the values of all of the sales to that customer (over the last two years), so you'll use the Sum( ) function to do that.

- The resulting table is called tblBestCustomers.

Part

I

Ch

4

To create a Make-Table query containing the names of Northwind's best customers over the last two years:

1. Create a new query (from the Database window, select the Queries tab, then New), open it in Design view, and select the Invoices query as a record source.

2. Click the Query type button on the toolbar and choose Make-Table query.

3. A wizard asks for the name of the table to be created; enter **tblBestCustomers** and click OK.

4. Select the fields Customers.CompanyName, ExtendedPrice, and OrderDate by double-clicking them in the Relationships window.

5. Click the Totals button to display the Totals row and enter **Sum** in the column under the field [ExtendedPrice] and **Where** in the column under [OrderDate]. The Sum function adds up all of the orders on all dates, and the Where identifier lets Access know that you are not totaling the [OrderDate] field; you are including criteria for it (see Step 8).

6. Select Descending in the Order row under the column under the field [ExtendedPrice] to sort the records in order from highest to lowest price.

7. Turn off the display of the [OrderDate] field by clicking once in the check box in the Show row under that column. The check should clear.

8. In the Criteria row under the column containing [OrderDate], enter

   `>Date()-730`

   This tells Access to select only orders with dates in the last two years (365 days/year times 2 = 730).

9. Select only the top ten suppliers by changing the Top Values control on the toolbar to 10.

After you create the query in the QBE grid, it looks like Figure 4.15.

FIG. 4.15
A Make-Table query that creates a table based on another query and using aggregate functions.

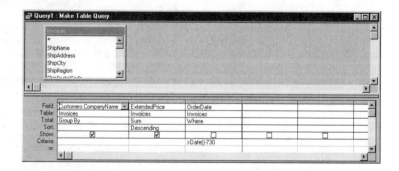

N O T E A Select query would work just as well as the Make query for the purpose of supplying data to ODBC queries, because both queries and tables return data to external clients. In fact, a Select query would be guaranteed to contain up-to-the-minute data, whereas the Make-Table query is only as good as the last time it was run.

There are a couple of interesting things about this query. First, because it's built on another query, you can see the names of some of the tables that the data in the underlying query come from, as in [Customers.CustomerName]. You use the Sum() function, as promised, to add up all of the invoices for a given company. To include only the records pertaining to orders within the last two years, you check the Order Date to see if its date was no more than 730 days (about two years) before today, which is the value returned by the Date() function.

Note that the Total row under the [OrderDate] column contains the option "Where" instead of the default "Group By." If you leave it as "Group By," the criteria will be recognized, but the results also will sort by Order Date. This creates a table that has multiple entries for each order date, giving you the top ten highest individual orders, not best customers. You can give this a try by changing the Make-Table query to a Select query and experimenting with these two settings.

You can preview the results by switching to Datasheet view (which is shown in Figure 4.16), or you can execute the query to create the new table. If you try to run the query more than once, you'll be notified that Access is deleting the table (because you can't create a table that already exists) and is re-creating it. Be careful when running Make-Table queries so that you don't create a table using the name of a table that you don't want to lose. It would be catastrophic to name the results of this Make-Table query "Customers," for example, because a critical table with that name already exists.

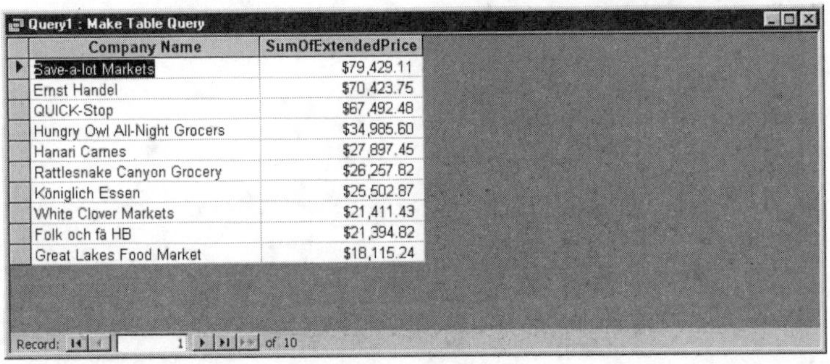

FIG. 4.16

The results of the Make-Table query in Figure 4.15, showing Northwind's top ten customers. This is really the Datasheet view of the query, not the new table.

Company Name	SumOfExtendedPrice
Save-a-lot Markets	$79,429.11
Ernst Handel	$70,423.75
QUICK-Stop	$67,492.48
Hungry Owl All-Night Grocers	$34,985.60
Hanari Carnes	$27,897.45
Rattlesnake Canyon Grocery	$26,257.82
Königlich Essen	$25,502.87
White Clover Markets	$21,411.43
Folk och fä HB	$21,394.82
Great Lakes Food Market	$18,115.24

Part
I

Ch
4

Creating and Using Crosstab Queries

Crosstab queries are infrequently used and rarely understood. Their best and most common use is to summarize financial data in a grid that looks like an Access datasheet, but acts more like an Excel spreadsheet. To use a Crosstab query, the data in the underlying data source must have the following characteristics:

- A data value that is repeated in several records (that is, the same data in the same field in several records)
- A characteristic that lends itself to summarizing (like sales quantity or dollar amounts)
- A field to summarize across (almost always a date or geographical region)

A Crosstab query summarizes the data in an underlying table by sorting it into rows and columns, where

- The row titles contain the names of the things to be summarized (like individual products or salespeople)
- The column titles contain a description of the way the data is summarized (dates or regions)
- The cells at the intersections of the two contain summary data

You can get specific details on how to write a Crosstab query by checking the online help for the topic "Crosstab Queries." ●

CHAPTER 5

Advanced Data Retrieval Using Queries

In Chapter 4, you built queries of various types. All of them had one thing in common: all of their data came from a single data source. In practice, this is relatively uncommon; one of the features that makes queries as useful as they are is their ability to retrieve data from more than one table, from tables and queries, from several queries, and so on. This technique, called *joining*, is one of the most important elements of good database design, and it's one of the hardest database concepts to master. ■

Run queries based on more than one data source

When tables or queries are related through similar key fields, you can write queries that extract data from all of them at once.

Prompt users for information to be used in a query

You can create a query that includes data that a user supplies, like a range of dates or an ID number.

Set global options for your query

Access' query feature includes several options that improve the appearance of returned results, limit the number of records returned, and determine how the system should behave if an error occurs.

Retrieving Data from Multiple Tables

The real value of queries lies in their capability to relate data from different data sources and return it as one cohesive table. You've already seen that you can use tables and queries synonymously in new queries; they work the same as data sources. Now consider building a query that draws data from more than one table and/or query. The Northwind database contains several good examples of multitable queries, including "Employee Sales by Country" and "Quarterly Orders."

For example, if you've set up a relationship between a Customer ID in one table and a Customer Name in another, why couldn't you use that ID to look up the name if you needed it in a query? The Orders table in Northwind contains an Order ID, a Customer ID, and an Employee ID. These raw, numeric fields don't look good on a report, though; it's usually better to use the relationships between the Orders table and the associated lookup tables to fill in the words where the numbers are unclear.

N O T E If you look at the Orders table in Design view, you'll see that the fields [OrderID], [CustomerID], and [EmployeeID] are all there. If you view it in Datasheet view, though, you'll see the Customer Name and Employee Name instead of the ID numbers. This is because those two fields are defined as Lookup fields in the table definition. Access performs a three-way join on the Order, Employees, and Customers tables every time you look at the Orders table in Datasheet view. If you try to create a query or report using those tables, you'll have to define the join. ■

When you specify more than one related table for a query, the tables are considered "joined." *Join* is a database term that means that two tables are merged for the purposes of the current query, usually by a common key or keys. Any number of tables can be joined, assuming they share common primary keys and your computer has unlimited memory. In practical terms, you're unlikely to create a table join that Access 97 can't handle (although this was not necessarily the case with earlier versions of Access).

There are three types of joins in Access (and in most relational databases):

- **Inner Joins.** When you connect two tables in the Relationships window of a query, Access assumes you're trying to create an inner join. An inner join selects all records from both connected tables where the joined key is the same in both tables.

   In the Products and Orders tables of the Northwind database, a query that joins the two tables returns all records where the same Product ID is in both tables. The Products table lists all products and product IDs, but the Orders table only contains the Product IDs of products that have been ordered. You would use an inner join in your Select query to eliminate all products that had never been ordered.

- **Outer Joins.** Like an inner join, an outer join returns all records that appear in both joined tables. However, an outer join also returns records that only appear in one of the two joined tables. Any data fields that the query requests that only appear in one of the joined tables show empty cells where they could not match with the second table.

For example, you can create a Select query that returns the fields Products.ProductID, Products.ProductName, and Orders.OrderDate. Running the select query with an outer join, you see all of the products, but see blanks where the order date should be for any products that have never been ordered.

Outer joins always include all of the records from one of the two tables in a join relationship, but only those fields in the other table where the matched keys are equal. These joins are called left (outer) joins and right (outer) joins. The terms "left" and "right" refer to the position of the two tables in the relationship. Assuming that the relationship between two tables is one-to-many, the "one" table is assumed to be on the "left" side of the relationship. Because left and right joins must be outer, the term "outer" is redundant, but is sometimes included for clarity. There is no such thing as a one-sided outer join, because the results would be the same regardless of which side (or both) was chosen.

In the Northwind database, the query "Quarterly Orders" contains an example of an outer join, which links the Customer ID fields in the Orders and Customers table. This query includes all of the records in the Orders table that fall between certain specified dates, but only those records in the Customers table that correspond to customers that placed orders between those dates.

■ **Self Joins.** When a single item of data can appear in two fields in the same table, you might consider using a self-join to express the relationship. The classic example of this technique is a database table including information for both employees and supervisors, where some employees also can be supervisors (the Northwind Employees table provides such an example). In this case, the field [EmployeeID] could be self-joined with the field [ReportsTo] in a query to return both employees and all their supervisors. A self-join may be either inner or outer.

This example walks you through the process of creating a simple multitable query. This query displays a list of products (from the Products table), the name of each product's supplier (from the Suppliers table), and the name of the category (from the Categories table each product falls under). All of the joins between these tables are default, inner joins, which make up 95 percent of all of the joins you ever create.

To create a query that uses more than one table as a data source:

1. From the Database window, select the Queries tab and click New. In the New Query dialog box that appears, Design view should be selected by default; click OK.

2. The Show Table dialog box appears. The list of tables is shown by default; you can select the Queries tab to show all of the queries in the database, or the All tab to show queries and tables together in one alphabetical list. For this example, you can use the Tables tab.

3. Select each of the data sources you want to use in your query. For this example, double-click each of the three tables Categories, Suppliers, and Products. Alternatively, you can select each table and click Add. Access displays a definition of each table in the Relationships pane of the QBE grid.

T I P It's better to select more tables than you need than to have to go back later and figure out which ones you left out. They're easier to remove than to add.

4. Click Close to close the Show Tables when all of the tables (and/or queries) you need have been selected. If you accidentally added an extra data source or two, close the Show Tables dialog box, right-click anywhere in the definition of the errant table, and select Remove Table from the menu that appears.

5. In the Relationships pane of the QBE grid, all of the tables you selected should be visible. If an existing relationship includes referential integrity constraints, Access shows them by marking the ends of the line between the tables in thicker bars and including a one (1) or an infinity symbol (∞) at either end to denote the relationship type. The infinity symbol denotes the "many" side of a one-to-many relationship.

You can use the vertical scroll bars on each table definition to view its fields, and you can drag the tables around the Relationships pane to make the relationships clearer. You can even create temporary relationships between tables, just for this query, by dragging the primary key field(s) in one table onto the foreign key field(s) in the second table, just like you'd do it in the Relationships window of the Table Designer.

To change the type of join established between the displayed tables or queries, select the link by clicking it once, then double-click it to open the Join Properties dialog box (see Figure 5.1). The three options (1, 2, 3) that appear in the dialog box correspond to inner, left outer, and right outer joins respectively; select the appropriate option for your situation and click OK. This example uses the default (inner) joins, so you don't need to use this dialog box at all.

FIG. 5.1
The three kinds of joins in Access. Option 1 is the default and is the most common.

6. Create your query by double-clicking (or dragging) fields from the Relationships Pane down to the QBE grid, just as you would if there was only one data source. Access "joins" the tables you've selected and considers the group of them as one big data source. For this example, choose the fields Suppliers.CompanyName, Products.ProductName, and Suppliers.SupplierName and sort the results in alphabetical order by Supplier Name and then Product Name. The finished QBE grid looks like Figure 5.2.

FIG. 5.2
The QBE grid for this sample query shows the relationships between the component tables.

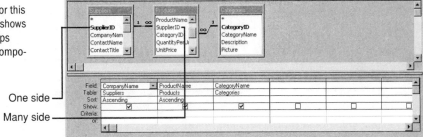

One side
Many side

 7. Click the Run button on the toolbar to execute the query against all of the tables selected. The sample query you are developing looks like Figure 5.3.

Sometimes you'll want to create a relationship between two data sources for a query where no such relationship exists outside of the query. This is common when using queries as data sources, because queries don't participate in relationships except as part of other queries. To join two data sources that don't have an implicit relationship defined, create a relationship by dragging the key from one data source to another as you would in the Relationships Window of the Table Designer.

FIG. 5.3
The results of the sample query combine data from three tables to form a coherent, useful set of records (which is not unlike a table in itself).

Company Name	Product Name	Category Name
Aux joyeux ecclésiastiques	Chartreuse verte	Beverages
Aux joyeux ecclésiastiques	Côte de Blaye	Beverages
Bigfoot Breweries	Laughing Lumberjack Lager	Beverages
Bigfoot Breweries	Sasquatch Ale	Beverages
Bigfoot Breweries	Steeleye Stout	Beverages
Cooperativa de Quesos 'Las Cabras'	Queso Cabrales	Dairy Products
Cooperativa de Quesos 'Las Cabras'	Queso Manchego La Pastora	Dairy Products
Escargots Nouveaux	Escargots de Bourgogne	Seafood
Exotic Liquids	Aniseed Syrup	Condiments
Exotic Liquids	Chai	Beverages
Exotic Liquids	Chang	Beverages
Forêts d'érables	Sirop d'érable	Condiments
Forêts d'érables	Tarte au sucre	Confections

Record: 14 ◄ 1 ► ►I ►* of 77

► **See** "Understanding Table Relationships," **p. 36**

To remove a relationship between data sources (either preexisting or newly created for a query), select the line connecting the data sources in the Relationships pane and press the Delete key on the keyboard. Note that this won't affect relationships between tables outside of this query.

Using Queries Within Queries

Because queries are considered the same as tables for the purpose of subsequent queries, you can "nest" queries inside each other for complex situations or for clarity. There are times when a query might be required to generate a value for use in another query, and these queries can either be constructed as two separate queries or they can be mingled.

Part

I

Ch

5

Consider the query "Products Above Average Price" in Northwind. The query returns only two values, the product name and price, but only those products with a price above the average should be returned. The criteria call for the field [UnitPrice], then, should contain the average price of all of the records in the table; one way to calculate this is to use a Select query that returns all of the records and averages them. This query could be built in the QBE grid, then converted to SQL; the SQL generated query is then inserted into the criteria cell for the unit price field in the final query. Access runs the criteria query first, then runs the query it's contained in.

N O T E The better way to perform this calculation is with the Davg() aggregate function, which averages all of the records in a given domain. Using that function wouldn't illustrate the use of a separate query for criteria, which the database designers apparently intended. ▪

You may have occasion to design a complicated query that requires considerable testing. You can break up the problem by designing several smaller queries, then basing each on the results of an earlier one. The query "Category Sales for 1995" in Northwind works this way, using as its data source the query "Product Sales for 1995." Access runs them all in the correct order.

Using Parameters in Queries

A query's criteria are usually set when the query is defined, by entering them in the Criteria row of the QBE grid. There might be times, however, when you want a user or program to set the criteria for a saved query; entering predefined criteria for the query may not be the best way to accomplish this.

N O T E If you're writing VBA code to run the query, you might create a small form to prompt the user for the criteria, and then pass the criteria to the query in the form of a Filter or by generating a string to use with the RunSQL method. This would have the effect of creating a new query for every execution, but it requires some knowledge of VBA coding. ▪

If your application is small or does not require fancy formatting, you can use the parameter-passing feature of Access to change the criteria row of a stored query at runtime. To prompt the user for a value to use in a criteria string, enter the prompt for the user in square brackets as part of the criteria in the QBE grid.

For example, if you wanted a salesperson to be able to display all of Northwind's customers in a given country, you can create a query and enter the criteria under the [Country] column as

```
=[Which country?]
```

and save the query. When this query is run, users will see the dialog box in Figure 5.4.

FIG. 5.4

Users can be prompted for values to use as criteria in most types of queries.

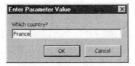

You are limited to about 40 characters in your prompts, so be brief. If your prompt requires more space, consider building a custom form to obtain the parameter and run the query.

You can use any number of parameters in a single query or even in a single criteria. For example, if you wanted to list details about orders between two order numbers (that the user would enter), you could use this string for the criteria in the [OrderID] column:

```
Between [Starting order number:] And [Ending order number:]
```

Be careful that you have considered the results of your parameter query if the user enters invalid or null data. In the double-parameter example shown previously, failure to enter one of the two parameters will be interpreted as zero. If the first parameter is omitted, this isn't much of a problem, but omitting the second parameter will cause no records to be displayed.

 TIP Entering long criteria and parameters in the small box provided can be hard on the eyes. If you need more space, press Shift+F2 while the cursor is in the text entry field and the Zoom box will open, giving you ample room to work. You can use Zoom in most text-entry cells in queries, forms, and reports.

When you use parameters in certain queries, you are required to tell Access the data type of the parameters so it can plan the layout of the results. These special queries include Crosstab queries, queries that use Yes/No fields as criteria, queries that create charts, and queries that depend on criteria gleaned from ODBC data sources. To do this, first create the parameter query as described previously. Next, open the Query Parameters dialog box by selecting Query, then Parameters from the Query Design menu. Enter the names of the fields you're specifying parameters for and their display data types in the grid provided and save the query.

Part

I

Ch

5

Understanding and Setting Query Properties

Queries, like tables and forms, have properties that apply to the query as a whole. These are set either by code or by selecting View, then Properties from the menu.

 TIP Fields in queries have properties, too, just like fields in tables. To set the query's properties, select the query itself by clicking the background of the Relationships window in Design View.

Most queries share the same properties, and these properties are usually reflected in the SQL View of the query as well as in the property sheet. For example, setting the Source Database property appends the SQL keyword IN [database name] to the SQL translation of the query.

▶ **See** "An Overview of Using Access Security," **p. 228**

Commonly used query properties include:

- **Output All Fields (default No).**   Changing this to Yes returns all fields in all source tables and queries. This is a quick way to dump data from several related tables while taking advantage of the referential integrity that queries offer.

- **Unique Values (default No).**   Changing this to Yes guarantees that all fields in all records will contain unique data. For example, if a query selected all customers from the Orders table, any customer with more than one order would be duplicated in the results, unless Unique Values was set to Yes This differs from the Unique Records property in that Unique Records returns records in which at least one value is different.

- **Unique Records (default No).**   Changing this to Yes guarantees that no records which are exact duplicates across all fields will be returned. If a query was written on the Orders table to return the names and dates of all orders, the query would normally return all orders. If Unique Records was set to Yes, duplicate orders on the same day would not be listed twice. If Unique Values was set to Yes, only the first order for each company would appear in the results. Only one of Unique Records and Unique Value can be set to Yes.

- **Source Database/Source Connect Str (default Current).**   These options can be set for queries written on databases that are not linked to the current Access database, such as external databases and ODBC data sources. The Source Database property is usually set to the name or full path of the remote database, and the Source Connect Str is used to specify standard connection information for ODBC databases.

- **Recordset Type (default Dynaset).**   When a query is used as the data source for a form, you might want to prevent users from changing the data values on the form, and you can change the value of this property to control the way the query handles modified data. A better way for most applications to prevent data from being changed on a form is to change the Allow Edits property of the form to No.

- **ODBC Timeout (default 60 seconds, not shown).**   This value specifies how long Access should wait for results to be returned from a remote ODBC data source. An error is generated if this time is exceeded.

- **Filter**.   Filters are used to limit the records returned by the current query depending on the situation. You could enter the name of a filter (which is a text string corresponding to the WHERE clause of a query, such as "OrderDate > #1/1/95#") and change it later using VBA rather than writing separate queries for similar data requirements. You also might consider the use of a Parameter Query for this kind of application. If you intend to enter a string directly in the Filter property to limit the records returned and not to modify it later with code, it might be clearer to include it in the criteria for the query itself.

- **Order By**.   Fields listed here (separated by a comma) will form the default grouping for the results of the query. As with Filters, this property is best used in conjunction with Access macros and VBA programs to make minor modifications to an existing query depending on circumstances. The default order is lowest to highest; to reverse the sort order, insert the keyword DESC after the name of the field(s) that should be listed highest to lowest.

■ **Max Records**.   Queries on ODBC data sources may return hundreds of thousands of records if the remote server is extremely capable. Returning this many records might be desirable for your application, but if the connection is slow, waiting for them may cause Access to time out. You can adjust the Max Records and ODBC Timeout properties to properly retrieve the data you require.

■ **Column Headings**.   In a Crosstab query, the columns for the returned data grid can be specified in the query's property sheet instead of the QBE grid. This permits external programs to slightly modify the query depending on conditions and external user requests without rewriting the query.

■ **Destination Table/DB/Connect Str**.   In a Make-table query, if the destination table is not in the current database, these settings define the path and options necessary to create it in an external database.

■ **Use Transaction (default No)**.   In a multiuser environment, it might be preferable to ensure that all of the results of a long-running query are written to the database at one time. This minimizes the amount of time the database is unavailable to other users. In this case, setting this property to Yes forces Access to store all of the query results in memory or a temporary file until they can all be written at once. Setting this property to Yes might improve database performance as a whole for all users. The local user running the query will probably see decreased performance as Access swaps data to and from the local disk while waiting for an opportunity to commit it to the database.

■ **Fail On Error (default No)**.   If this property is set to Yes, update and delete queries will terminate if all records cannot be updated or deleted due to key violations, sharing problems, and so on. In this case, no records will be changed. The default behavior of this property gives a user an option to continue updating or deleting the records that do not cause errors. This confirmation can be disabled using the SetWarnings method in VBA code.

▶ **See** "Handling Errors and Confirmations," **p. 218**

If you set properties for a specific type of query and then change the query to a type that does not contain that property, the values you entered will be lost. ●

Viewing Your Data with Reports

If the data in your database is destined for paper, Access reports provide a way to make the raw numbers and text look presentable. With a myriad of wizards and automatic formatting options, you can print the data in a simple table in as few as two mouse clicks. ■

Create summaries and calculations for printed data

Because reports can be laid out in just about any way you like, you may want to display the data in several ways on one report. You can show averages, counts, totals—all on the same report.

Create sort breaks and totals

Reports are typically used to summarize data in the form of running totals, subtotals, and intermediate sort levels. You'll see how to lay out data and use breaks for the maximum effect.

Take the easy way out

When you need quick answers, the AutoReport Wizard gets your data on paper as fast as your printer can print.

Creating a New Report

Almost everything you already know about creating forms holds true for writing reports. Some of the controls aren't there (what use is a pull-down combo box on a piece of paper?), but some of them are even more useful, like the page break control. You'll generally find yourself concentrating on the format of data in reports, instead of the color of the background. And you'll learn how difficult it can be to get everything to fit in one page width. But for the most part, the techniques and controls described in Chapter 3 for forms hold true here.

Reports and forms are so similar that small forms can be inserted directly into reports as "subreports," just as they are used for "subforms." Access converts finished forms directly into reports and vice versa (right-click the name of the form or report in the Database window and choose Save As Form (or Report) from the pop-up menu).

When you design a report, the most important thing to do before getting started is to know where to get the correct data. If your report will use a table as the underlying data source, make sure all of the fields you need to reference are in the table. If not, create a Select query to extract the fields you need and make them available to the report.

▶ **See** "Select Queries," **p. 72**

To create a new report, you can either use Access' AutoReport or Report Wizard features, or you can do it from scratch. The Report Wizard is useful when the record source for the report is simple and well-understood by the programmer; it also provides a jumping-off point for more complex reports. AutoReport creates a fast, basic report that's easier to create from a blank canvas than it is to modify. If you create a report using Design view, you get pinpoint accuracy and any type of visual design you like.

Sometimes, it's a good idea to start a new report by creating a "prototype" using the Report Wizard. There's no reason why you can't duplicate a report created automatically by manually creating controls, sort breaks, and summary fields, but it's really easy to modify a report Access has already created for you if it's close to your goal. For the examples in this chapter, you'll see how to create a basic report using AutoReport. You'll re-create the report by using the Report Wizard to obtain a much nicer looking report, and then make some modifications to it by using the manual tools in Design view. Of course, you could use Design view to create the entire report if you prefer; in practice, once you become familiar with all of the controls and features available to you in Design view, you'll probably prefer to create your reports in that environment.

All of the following examples use Northwind's "Sales by Category" query as their record source. It's a simple query that includes the following fields:

Category ID
Category Name
Product Name
Product Sales

Because the Category Name is included in the output fields of the query, you'll have little use for the Category ID in your reports. You should be able to see that there are several ways you can sort this data; you can summarize and total the dollar amounts, and break the data up into groups on the reports that follow.

Using AutoReport

If you've got to have a report in 10 seconds, AutoReport is the way to go, but if you have five minutes, use the Report Wizard. The reports created by the AutoReport feature are basic and not pleasant to look at. They accomplish their major goal, which is to print the data in the underlying data source in an organized fashion, but not much else.

To create a new report by using AutoReport:

1. From the Database window, select the Reports tab and then click New. The New Report dialog box appears.

2. Enter a record source (either an existing table or query) in the pull-down box provided and choose either the Columnar or Tabular AutoReport. The Columnar AutoReport arranges the fields in the underlying data source in a single logical column, broken across the page if it won't all fit along the left margin. Each data element is shown in a text box (or bound object frame, if appropriate) and each has a label created for it. A Tabular AutoReport arranges titles for the data fields across the top of the page and displays the data fields in a grid, not unlike a spreadsheet. In this example, we'll use "Sales by Category" as the record source and create a Tabular AutoReport.

3. Click OK. Your report appears on the screen (see Figure 6.1) in Print Preview view.

FIG. 6.1

A basic AutoReport based on the Sales By Category query. The data is sorted as it was generated by the query, and there are no totals (although there are page numbers, not visible in this screen shot). The column labels leave something to be desired.

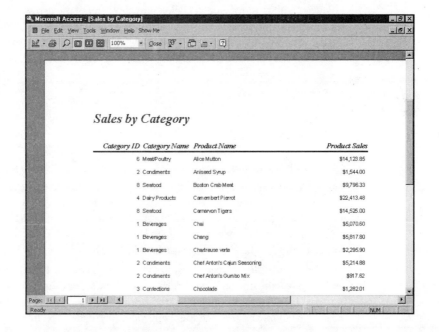

Part

I

Ch

6

A more tailored, better-looking report can be created almost as quickly by using the Report Wizard.

Using the Report Wizard

The Report Wizard steps you through the process of selecting a data source, specifying the fields that will appear on the report, determining sort breaks (groups), grouping options, and sort orders, and applying a polished appearance to the final report. It even gives you the option of including total and summary information and saves the results for you.

Creating the reports in this section by using Report Wizard should take you less than five minutes each. To create them manually, you might spend half an hour to get them right, but their appearance would probably be significantly enhanced. After you create some sample reports by using the Report Wizard, you'll be able to see how to lay out the controls and design elements when you modify them in Design view (later in this chapter).

To create a report using the Report Wizard:

1. From the Database Window, select the Reports tab and click New. The New Report dialog box opens.

2. In the list of design methods at upper right, select Report Wizard. In the pull-down list at lower right, choose a data source. For this example, use "Sales By Category." Click OK to continue.

3. The first dialog box of the Report Wizard appears. In this dialog box, you'll have to select the fields in the data source (from the Available Fields pane on the left) to include on the report. You designate the fields to include by moving them into the Selected Fields pane at lower right; to move a field, click it and click one of the arrow buttons between the panes. The single arrows (left and right) move only the selected field between panes; the double arrow buttons move all of the fields in the pane. For this example, choose all of the fields except for the Category ID, which isn't really useful on a report. Click Next to continue.

 TIP If, at any point in this process, you feel that you don't need to modify the default options on the other dialog boxes, you can click Finish to complete the process instantly. To exit this process without finishing the report, click Cancel.

4. The next dialog box asks whether you want to add any grouping levels. You can select any of the fields in your report and click the right arrow to designate it as a sort break; a helpful diagram of the sorted report format appears on the right. Clicking the left arrow moves a previously designated sort break back into the Available Fields list at left. In this case, you'll want to group on Category Name. Under each Category Name, the products in that category and their prices are listed on individual lines.

   To modify the order of group headers in your report, select any of your headings on the right and use the up and down Priority arrows to order them correctly. If you have only one sort break, as in this example, the Priority arrows will be unavailable. Once you've created headers and ordered them appropriately, click Next to continue.

5. The previous dialog box specified the fields you want to use a group headers; it didn't designate any order in which to sort them. This dialog box contains four combo boxes numbered 1 through 4, corresponding to each of the fields that aren't in group headers (called detail fields). If you want to sort the records, select each of the fields you want to sort in a different combo box. The default sort order is alphabetical; to reverse the order, click the sort order button to the right of the combo box. In this example, sort the records alphabetically by Product Name.

 Any fields you designated as group headings are automatically sorted alphabetically. You can change this sort order after the report is complete by opening it in Design view and using the Sorting and Grouping dialog box (described later in this chapter) to set the sort order for the header fields.

You also use this dialog box to specify whether you want totals to appear on your report. When you click the Summary Option button, a new dialog box appears showing all of the detail fields. For each field, you can specify that a Sum, Average, Minimum, or Maximum should be calculated and displayed for that field by selecting one or many of the check boxes next to each field name. Another option group asks you to specify whether your report should contain only summaries (Summary Only) or the detail records along with the summaries; this is the default. Finally, you can choose to show the sums (if selected) as raw numbers or as numbers and percentages of the total by selecting the Calculate percent of total for sums check box. For this example, select all of the summary options for the Product Name field and also mark the Calculate percent button. Click OK to return to the previous dialog box and then click Next to continue.

6. The next dialog box shows several layout options in the left window pane and two option groups on the right that you'll use to select a layout and page orientation for the finished report. This example uses the default Stepped report layout in Portrait orientation. You also can select the box marked Adjust the field width so all fields fit on a page to compress the field width appropriately for the paper orientation you selected. This option is selected by default. Click Next to continue.

7. The next dialog box enables you to select one of six predefined styles with various typeface and font colors. This example uses the default Corporate. Click Next to continue.

8. The final dialog box in the Report Wizard asks for a name under which to save the report, whether you want to view it in Design view or Print Preview, and asks whether you want online help to appear in conjunction with the displayed report. You can choose a convenient title; the defaults (Print Preview and no help) will suffice for most applications. Click Finish to create the report and to display it in Print Preview (see Figure 6.2).

9. Save the generated report (you'll need it for an example later in this chapter) by clicking the File menu, then selecting Save. You can close the report if you like by clicking the Close button in the upper-right corner.

Part

I

Ch

6

FIG. 6.2
The Sales by Category report, as generated by the Report Wizard. It looks a lot like the report generated by AutoReport; the addition of a Category sort break adds considerably to its readability.

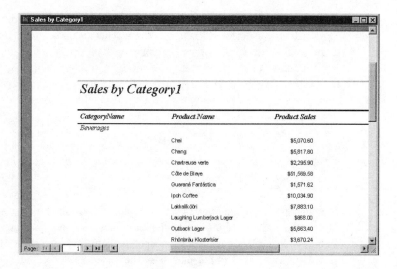

The summaries created by the Report Wizard are a great help; these formulas are difficult to generate from scratch. At the bottom of each sort group, text boxes have been created with aggregate functions entered to calculate sums, averages, and so on. The functions used to generate these totals (shown in Figure 6.3) are described in "Using Aggregate Functions on Reports," later in this chapter.

FIG. 6.3
The same report, showing the generated totals a little farther down. The formatting is poor, but the numbers are correct.

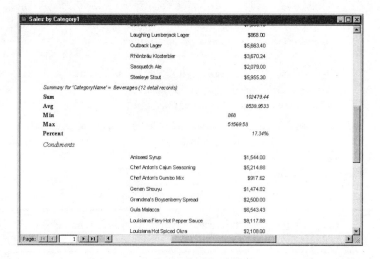

The way to correct the problems in this report is to use Design view, where you can see the individual controls that make up this report and modify their properties. You'll almost always end up using Design view when you create reports, either to adjust automatically generated reports or to create custom layouts from scratch.

Before you edit this report, you should become familiar with Design view by working with a new report's blank canvas. Then you can open the automatically generated report in the same environment to make changes.

Creating a Report Manually

To create a new report in Design view:

1. From the Database window, select the Reports tab.

2. Click the New button, and select Design view from the options that appear. From the pull-down box at the bottom of the dialog box, select any table or query and click OK.

3. The Report design window opens, and you'll see what looks like a blank screen with a grid (see Figure 6.4).

FIG. 6.4
A report being born. The dots represent a grid to help align controls, and can be adjusted or removed.

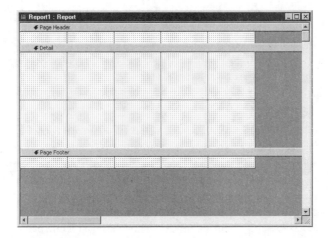

If your new report doesn't show the grid, the View Grid option is turned off. To turn the grid on, click the View menu, and select Grid. The grid acts as a bumper along which you can precisely line up controls as you work.

 After the new report is open in Design view, turn on the Toolbox (if it's not already open) by clicking the View menu, then Toolbox. The most commonly used controls are visible here; you can place any of them in your trial report by selecting a button in the Toolbox and then clicking anywhere on the design canvas to place the control. You can move controls around by clicking and dragging them with the mouse. You can resize controls by selecting them and dragging any corner or side (except the upper left) in or out with the mouse.

 You may find it convenient to use the Field List from the toolbar to show a list of fields in the underlying data source. You can quickly create text box controls for those fields by dragging them off of the field list and into the report.

The controls you place may not align with the grids automatically. To align the controls, click the Format menu and select Snap to Grid.

To adjust the grid spacing:

1. Right-click anywhere on the background of your report.
2. Choose Properties from the menu that appears.
3. Change the GridX and GridY properties; the number represents the number of dots per inch.

The default spacing is 24 dots per inch; below about 10 dots/inch, Access will not display the dots (but will continue to snap to them).

Another layout tool you may find useful is the Ruler, which shows the actual dimensions of the current report in the default units. To toggle the ruler on or off, from the Report Design menu select View, Ruler.

If you're creating a new report from scratch, after the controls are in place on the report, you can use the AutoFormat wizard (from the Format menu) to apply consistent look to the entire report. The AutoFormat wizard "remembers" several sets of settings for fonts, colors, and backgrounds, and applies them to your report on command. The real value of the AutoFormat wizard lies in its ability to be customized; you can customize the settings and save them so all of your reports reflect your own personal style.

A Review of Regions

As is the case with forms, there are three default regions to a report: a Page Header, Detail, and a Page Footer. The Detail region is where the data controls belong; you can put standard titles and page numbers in the Page Header and Footer. These regions appear on every physical page, so you probably don't want to put a lot of extraneous material in them, as this material will detract from the amount of data you can fit on the page. A Page Footer is an excellent place to put a page number and date, and it's helpful to include a descriptive title for the report in the Page Header. These steps help identify a multipage report if one page becomes separated from the rest.

Two optional regions, the Report Header and Report Footer, can be activated by clicking the View menu and then Report Header/Footer. These regions only appear at the beginning and ending of a report, before the first page of data and after the last. This is a useful feature for creating cover pages and summaries; see the Northwind Catalog report for an excellent example.

You can create any number of intermediate headers and footers by defining sort breaks for your data. For example, if you have a report based on the Customers table and you create a sort break on the field [Country], Access gives you the option to add a new header and footer every time the value of [Country] changes. This is especially useful for intermediate titles and subtotals.

Choosing Data Sources and Controls for Your Report

Access gives you the option to select a data source when you create a new report, and you can select one at any time by modifying the report's Record Source property (click the View menu, then Properties). Access provides a pull-down menu of all of the tables and queries in the current database for use as potential data sources.

Any field that is visible in the Datasheet view of the selected query or table is available to you in the Report Designer. Query fields with the Show property set to off in the QBE grid are not visible in the Datasheet view of the query and are therefore unavailable for reporting. If an underlying query has user-supplied parameters, a user previewing or printing a report based on that query will be asked to supply those same parameters.

▶ **See** "Using Parameters in Queries," **p. 100**

Once you select a data source, you can use the Report controls to put data on your report. You may notice that the control toolbox for reports is exactly the same as the toolbox used in designing forms.

▶ **See** "The Toolbox," **p. 54**

Viewing and Changing Report Properties

There's more to writing a good report than placing controls on a canvas. The properties of the report have a good deal to do with the way the data is presented, and appropriate selections of properties can make the difference between an adequate report and a great one.

To use a report's property sheet, you have to select the report (and not a control inside it). To select a report, do any one of the following:

- Click the background area of the report and click the Edit menu, and then Select Report.
- Press Ctrl+R when any control in the report is selected.
- Click the small square that sits in the upper-left corner of the report, where the two rulers meet. A small black square appears in this box when the report, and not an object in the report, is selected. Then choose any of the methods described previously to open the properties sheet for the report. To view a report's property sheet, do any one of the following:
  - Select the report. Click the View menu, then Properties.
  - Right-click the background of the report and select Properties from the menu that appears.
  - Click the report background and click the Properties button on the toolbar.

You'll see a dialog box that looks like Figure 6.5.

FIG. 6.5

The Properties dialog box for a typical report. There are several more properties not visible in this figure; you can scroll to see them. The tabs at the top help organize the properties into useful categories.

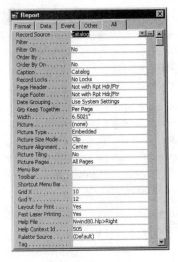

The primary properties you'll need to work with on reports (there are many) include the following. To view them in the order described, click the All tab in the Properties dialog box.

■ **Record Source**.   The table or query containing the data on which this report is based. This field can even contain a SQL statement instead of the name of an existing query.

■ **Filter**.   The name of a query (or a SQL statement) that limits the number of records in the underlying table that are displayed in the report.

■ **Filter On**.   A toggle that determines whether the filter in the previous cell is applied. This is most useful when debugging or when manipulated using VBA code in response to a user action.

■ **Order By**.   The name of a field (or fields, if separated by a comma) in the underlying data source which determines the sort order of the records displayed.

■ **Order By On**.   A toggle that determines whether the ordering fields in the previous cell are used. Like the Filter On property, this is most useful when debugging or when manipulated using VBA code in response to a user action.

■ **Caption**.   In the Print Preview, the string entered here appears as the name of the report in the title bar. The Caption property has no effect on the printed report.

■ **Record Locks (default No Locks)**.   If set to All Records, other users can't change values in the table underlying the report while the report is being viewed or printed.

■ **Page Header/Page Footer (default All Pages)**.   Page headers and footers normally appear on all of the pages in a report. However, if you want to suppress the display and printing of the Page Header or Footer when various combinations of the Report Header and/or Footer are visible, you can do so by changing this property to Not With Rpt Hdr, Not With Rpt Ftr, or Not With Rpt Hdr/Ftr. The Page Header and Footer are controlled separately (these are two properties).

■ **Picture**. If you want a picture to appear over the entire background of the report, you can enter the path and file name to any bitmap (.bmp or .dib) or Windows metafile (.wmf or .emf) here. This seemingly useless feature can actually be used as an understated effect if you don't mind the data obliterating the image (see Figure 6.6).

FIG. 6.6

An image used as a background for a report. This technique can destroy a report or add considerable visual interest, depending on how it's used.

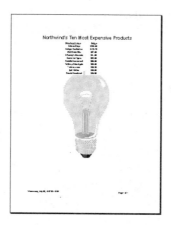

■ **Picture Type/Size Mode/Alignment/Tiling/Pages**. These options determine how the picture specified in the previous property appears on the page:

- The Type property determines whether the picture is stored in the database or in a separate file.
- The Size Mode determines how a picture that is too big for the page is cropped or shrunk.
- Alignment centers or left- or right-justifies the picture on the page.
- Tiling copies the picture all over the page if it's smaller than the page itself.
- Pages determines whether the picture should appear on all of the report pages, just the first page, or nowhere (which you might use if there's a memory problem, or if the user selects a low-res printing option).

■ **Layout for Print (default Yes)**. If this is set to Yes, the fonts available for report design are limited to fonts your default printer has installed natively (designated by a little printer icon in the font list on the toolbar) or TrueType fonts available to Windows. If you change it to No, the fonts available change to TrueType and screen fonts particular to your system. If you design a form by using a particular font and try to print it on another system or by using a different printer, Access may warn you that the fonts required are not available; Access will then choose what it considers appropriate substitutes.

■ **Fast Laser Printing**. If you're printing this report on a printer that understands Hewlett-Packard's PCL print language, Access will tell the printer to generate straight lines instead of sending it the locations of tiny dots to arrange on the page whenever there's a line in the report being printed. This generally saves a few milliseconds per report printed.

Several other properties in the property sheet pertain to Windows help or report events and are discussed later in this book.

▶ **See** "Distributing Applications (ODE)," **p. 256**

The best way to discover how properties work is to play with them and see what effect they have on your final result. Keeping property modifications to a minimum ensures that your report will be easy to modify and maintain, but here's an opportunity to show some flair if you like.

Using Sort Breaks on Reports

In the absence of other guidance, Access displays the data on a report in the order in which it is stored in the underlying query or table. This may or may not be meaningful to those who will use the report, and it can be changed by using sort breaks appropriately.

Sort breaks are an element that distinguishes reports from forms. Whereas forms always display data in one monolithic list, reports allow you to break up the data in as many pieces as you like, based on the data itself. Even better, the report designer gives you the option of adding sections (regions) to your report whenever the value of any field in the data source changes.

 To specify sort breaks, use the Sorting and Grouping dialog box, which is activated by clicking the Sorting and Grouping button on the toolbar while in Design view. A blank grid appears, into which you'll enter the names of fields you want to use as breaks in your report (see Figure 6.7).

FIG. 6.7
The Sorting and Grouping dialog box. Field names go on the left and sort options are selected on the right.

The fields listed here are sorted as you specify, but the real value of this dialog box is in using the five Group Properties in the lower half of the dialog box that can be set for each field listed in the Field/Expression area. Fields specified here can generate headers and footers whenever their value changes, and Access tries to keep data in a given sort break together on one page if you so desire. These properties are:

■ **Group Header (default No).** If set to Yes, Access creates a new header region below the Page Header for this field. Whenever the value of this field changes, Access writes a new header, including any controls you place in it. This is an excellent place for summary information that pertains to all records that fall within this group. Setting this to

Yes for the field [CategoryName] in your example creates a header, which is reprinted every time a new category starts. It might include information about the definition of this category (if that were stored in the database), or a count of the number of products in this category.

- **Group Footer (default No).**   Setting this to Yes creates a new footer every time the value of this field changes. A group footer is normally used for subtotals of all of the values in a group.

- **Group On (default Each Value).**   Access creates a new header or footer (or recognizes that data is related if those options are turned off) every time the value of the specified field changes if this property is set to Each Value. The other options available here are different depending on the data type of the field referenced. If the field is of type "text," the option Prefix Characters causes a break only if the first number of characters specified in the GroupInterval property in the string don't match. For example, with a GroupInterval set to 3, "Beverages" and "Beer" are considered to be in different groups (because "Bev" and "Bee" don't match); if the GroupInterval were set to 2, they would be grouped together (because "Be" and "Be" do). For dates, the options here include "Year," "Quarter," "Month," and so on.

- **Group Interval (default 1).**   For numeric data types, the number of different values to group together at a time. For text, the Group Interval represents the number of characters to match to cause a break. To use any value other than 1 here, you must have either Group Headers or Footers turned on (because it would make no sense to break if there were nothing to show the break).

- **Keep Together (default "No").**   Determines whether Access will make an effort to keep group headers, footers, and detail on the same page. If set to No, Access creates page breaks whenever the page is full. If set to Whole Group, the group header, footer, and detail are all printed on one page if it will fit (a break is generated before printing the header if necessary). If set to With First Detail, Access starts a new page before a Group Header if it can't fit both the header and at least one record in the group on the current page. You'll want to experiment with this one for best effect with your data.

Using Aggregate Functions on Reports

When someone looks at a report generated by a database, they usually expect the information to be totaled or summarized. The Report Wizard makes this pretty easy, as described earlier, but you can create your own controls based on expressions and functions as well. The report shown in Figure 6.9 looks good, but it might be nice to know how many products are in each category, what the total sales by category were, and to see some grand totals for the entire set of records. These are easy to generate by using aggregate functions such as Count() and DSum() in the footers.

▶ **See** "Extract Data Using Select Queries," **p. 79**

Using aggregate functions in footers (or headers) is almost as easy as inserting a field from the record source in the report.

To create an aggregate data control on any report, follow these steps:

1. Insert a text box into the report at the point where you want the total or summary to appear. A group footer is generally a good place to put totals.

2. Select the control you just created and open its Property sheet (click the View menu, then Properties). Make sure you selected the correct control and you're viewing the properties for this control, not the report.

3. Enter as the RecordSource property of that control any expression (or aggregate function) that calculates the value you want.

4. Close the property sheet if you're done modifying properties for this control by clicking the Close button.

The beauty of doing this in a report is that Access limits the records considered by the expression to those in the current group. If you include an aggregate function in a group header (or footer), only the records in the group are included. If you put the function in a Page Header or Footer, only the records on that page are considered, and an aggregate function used in a Report Header or Footer totals everything in the report. This allows you to create as many subtotals as you have groups.

For example, to calculate the number of products in the Sales by Category query, you would use the expression

```
=Count([ProductName])
```

as the record source for a control. Placing that control in the Group Footer for the field [CategoryName] (the CategoryName Footer in the Design view, which you'll have to enable using the Sorting and Grouping dialog box) starts a new count of records every time the category name changes. Copying the same control to the Report Footer counts all of the records in the report.

For counting records, you can use any field that appears once per record (like a key field) as an argument to the Count function. Most other aggregate functions only work on numeric fields, including Currency (but not including Date/Time).

Other common aggregate functions you'll find useful include

Totals:	Sum([*numeric field*])
Average:	Avg([*numeric field*])
Min:	Min([*numeric field*])
Max:	Max([*numeric field*])

You can even use functions to refer to other fields containing functions. For example, if you want to compute the percent of the grand total that a subtotal comprises, you could give the control containing the grand total a descriptive name, such as [GrandTotal]. Then, you could create an expression for your subtotals such as

```
=Sum([ProductSales])/[GrandTotal] & "%"
```

The value of [GrandTotal] is computed before the result of this expression is displayed, even though the control [GrandTotal] doesn't appear until the bottom of the report.

The aggregate functions and expressions used in the Sales By Category example report include:

Category Footer	="Summary for " & "'CategoryName' = " & " " & [CategoryName] & " (" & Count(*) & " " & IIf(Count(*)=1,"detail record","detail records") & ")"
Sum of Sales	=Sum([ProductSales])
Average of Sales	=Avg([ProductSales])
Maximum Sale	=Max([ProductSales])
Minimum Sale	=Min([ProductSales])
Percent of Total Sales	=Sum([ProductSales])/([ProductSales Grand Total Sum])

Access shows the value of the RecordSource property in the control in Design view.

Editing Existing Reports

Earlier in this chapter, you created a report based on the query "Sales By Category" by using the AutoReport and Report Wizard features. Both were lacking in style, and several modifications needed to be made to either version to make it ready for the corporate boardroom. These modifications are easily made in Design view, taking advantage of the work Access did earlier by opening the saved Report Wizard report in Design view.

Several minor changes could be made to this report in Design view to improve its appearance:

- Some highlighting could be applied to make the summaries stand out.
- The column titles should be changed (Access uses the field names, which rarely make decent column titles).
- The format of the totals and averages should be specified in the control properties to make them look like currency.

Use Design view and the techniques described earlier to make these changes. To modify an existing report (specifically, the example report based on the Sales By Category query begun earlier):

1. Open the report you want to work on by selecting it in the Report pane of the Database window and selecting Design. If you followed the example earlier and didn't rename the report, it's probably called "Sales By Category1." The report appears in Design view (see Figure 6.8).

Part

I

Ch

6

FIG. 6.8

The example report in Design view (grid turned off). You can see the report regions and the text boxes that calculate the aggregate functions.

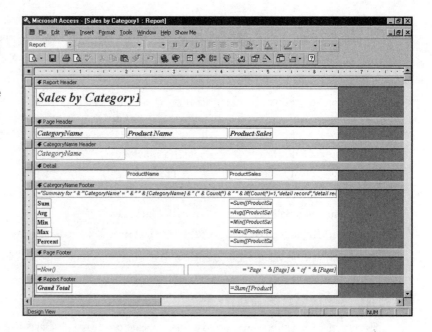

2. Addressing the desired modifications listed in order, you'll first highlight the summary information and make it easier to read. First, move the label controls containing the summary headers ("Sum," "Avg," etc. closer to the values they describe by selecting the entire group of them and moving them right a few inches. To select all of them, select each one in turn while holding down the Shift key. The pointer changes to an open hand; left-click any of the selected controls and drag them to the right until they're closer to the aggregate values on the right margin.

You can also move them one at a time; the grid helps keep them aligned. To align a group of controls with or without Snap To Grid turned on, select all of them, then choose Format/Align from the menu. You'll have the option of aligning their left sides, right sides, tops, or bottoms. You can also align them with the grid if Snap to Grid is disabled.

Finally, make all of the values in the text boxes bold like their labels. Select the text boxes containing the aggregate functions (to the right of the labels) either by using one of the techniques described for the labels or by using a "marquee": Left-click somewhere the report background near the bottommost control you want to select and drag upward until all of the controls you want to select are enclosed in the box that's drawn as you drag. When you have them all, release the mouse button; all of the controls should be selected. Make them bold by clicking the Bold button on the toolbar; all of the selected controls become boldfaced.

TIP You don't have to completely enclose the controls to select them with the marquee; the default behavior selects any controls enclosed or touched by the marquee box (you can change this in Options if you like).

If you accidentally move a control while trying to select it or while working with a marquee, the easiest way to replace it is to stop what you're doing and press Ctrl+Z (Undo).

3. To change the column titles, first select one of them with the mouse. There are two ways to modify the boxes' Caption property: You can right-click to display the property sheet and modify the Caption property directly, or you can left-click in the text box after you've already selected it to edit the displayed caption. Either method works; change the column headers and the report title by adding spaces where necessary to separate words and removing any numbers from the report header.

4. Lastly, to correct the format of the totals, select all of them again except the Percent field, and display their property sheet by right-clicking any of the selected controls. Select the Format tab of the property sheet that appears. This property sheet represents all of the selected controls. Where the controls have property values in common, the value is displayed (for example, they're all set to Auto decimal places). Making a change in this property sheet affects all of the controls. Click in the Format property box and click the pull-down arrow that appears at the right side of the box. Scroll down and select the Currency format for these fields. Now select the Percent text box (you may have to move the property sheet out of the way) and change its Format property to Percent. Close the property sheet by clicking the Close button at upper right. You'll be returned to Design view.

5. Display the report in Print Preview by clicking the View button on the toolbar. Your formatted report should appear, including a summary section that looks something like Figure 6.9.

You can continue to make modifications by returning to Design view as much as you need to get the report looking just right. A considerable amount of the effort involved in the creation of reports is spent in this kind of tweaking and testing.

Included with the Northwind database is a report called "Sales By Category" (which is why the Report Wizard version you created was called "Sales By Category1"). If you open that report in Print Preview (from the Database window, select it and click Preview), you'll see that it's not unlike the one you just created, except that it includes a useful chart. Charts like this can be generated in an external program (such as Excel), or by using the Access Chart Wizard.

Part

I

Ch

6

FIG. 6.9
The summary area of the modified report. All of the number formats are appropriate, and the labels and values are easy to associate with one another.

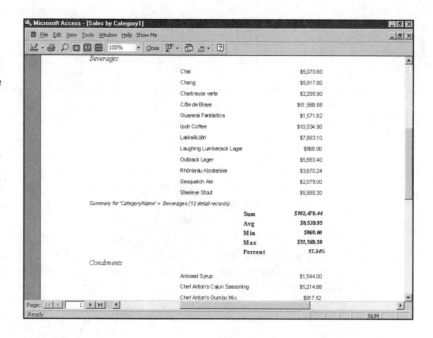

Using the Chart Wizard

The Chart Wizard, given a data source, collects the values in a field you specify and plots them on one of several dozen types of graphs. If you can picture your data in a chart, this Wizard can produce it. The colors, fonts, and styles of text are configurable; if you've created charts in Excel or PowerPoint, you'll feel right at home in the Chart Wizard (because it's really the same application, called Microsoft Graph, doing the work).

Unfortunately, the Chart Wizard as it's implemented for reports is badly flawed. Because charts are OLE Objects, and reports can't update OLE Objects in Print Preview, there's no way to see the chart design you create with the Chart Wizard except to print it on paper. There is a workaround, however; it involves creating the chart in a blank form, changing some properties of the chart, and copying it back into a report. The Insert/Chart menu options from with the Design view of a form are nearly the same as the Chart Wizard from within a report, so the notes below (which are tailored to creating charts in forms) are largely the same if you use the Chart Wizard from within a report.

N O T E You can read more about this issue on Microsoft's Web site at: **http:// www.microsoft.com/kb/articles/q154/4/54.htm**. ▪

To create a chart using the Chart Wizard (via the Form Designer), again following the example started previously using the Sales By Category query as a data source:

1. From the Database window, select the Forms tab and then click New. The New Form dialog box appears; Design view is selected by default and you can click OK to continue.

2. A blank form appears. From the menu, click Insert, then Chart. The cursor changes to an icon of a chart; drag a large rectangle anywhere on the blank form. Make it as large as you can while constraining it to one screen. When you release the mouse button, a dialog box appears asking you to specify a record source for the report. Click the Queries option button at the bottom of the dialog box to display all of the queries in the database. Select one and click Next; for this example, select the query "Sales By Category."

3. The first dialog box of the Chart Wizard appears.

   In the left pane of the two-paned dialog box that appears, select each field that you want to appear on the chart from your data source, and click the greater-than arrow (>) to move that field to the right pane. To select all of the fields, click the double greater-than arrow (>>); to move one or all fields from the right pane to the left, select the field and the less-than arrow (<) or double less-than arrow (<<). For this example, select the fields ProductName and ProductSales. Select Next to continue.

4. Twenty different chart types are displayed; select one (the horizontal Bar Chart on the second row works well with this data) and click Next to continue.

5. The Chart Wizard displays a sample of your chart, listing the data fields you selected on the right. Access makes a guess as to which of the fields should be shown on each axis; in this example, ProductName is displayed on the vertical axis and Access computes an aggregate SumofProductSales as the data for the bars. This is exactly what you want for this example; if it's not right, drag and drop the data fields into the appropriate places on the sample chart, placing them in the predefined Data, Series, and Axis areas. This screen takes some getting used to and you will want to try several options for best results. Click the Preview Chart button to see what your chart will look like with real data (the preview will probably be too small to see much; click Close in the preview window to continue), and click Next to continue.

6. Finally, enter a title and select the appropriate actions to display a legend if you like, and click Finish to create your chart.

7. The chart that you'll see displays sample data—the title and format may be correct, but the data series says "North," "East," and so on. You need to change some of the chart's properties to work with it and update it properly. Right-click the report, select Properties from the menu that appears, click the Data tab, and change the following two properties:

   Enabled   Yes

   Locked   No

8. Save the form by clicking the File menu, then Save. Accept the default title or create a new one. After it's saved, open the form you just created in Form view by selecting it in the Database window and clicking Open (not Design).

Part
I
Ch
6

9. Your chart should appear correctly, but probably needs editing. Select the chart and click the Edit menu, then Chart Object, then Open.

10. Microsoft Graph opens with your chart in it. You can make almost any change you like to the chart while in this environment; a tutorial on Microsoft Graph is available by searching for the topic "Changing the Display or View of a Chart" from Microsoft Graph help. After you're done editing your chart, click the File menu, then Exit and Return to *form*. Graph closes and your chart is updated in the form.

11. The chart should still be selected. Click the Edit menu, then Copy. Close the form, saving your changes. Now open any report that you want to put the chart in (or create a new one) in Design view.

12. Paste the chart into your report by selecting Edit, then Paste. It's best to place a chart in a header or footer region instead of Detail, because any control in the Detail region will be repeated with every record.

Your finished report looks like Figure 6.10.

FIG. 6.10
A chart, created in a form, pasted into a report. You can use the Chart Wizard from within the Report environment, but you can't edit the charts you create that way.

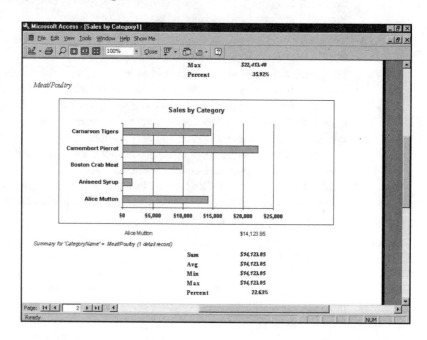

Using the Label Wizard

The Label Wizard takes the data you specify from a table or query and arranges it to fit on standard Avery labels, or on a custom label you can specify. You decide which fields appear on the label, how they're sorted, and you can modify the layout of this specialized report (which is really just the detail region of a simple report, sized and arranged on the grid to fit the labels you specify) to include pictures or whatever else you like. This is a really nice feature, akin to the Mail Merge Helper in Microsoft Word, but much easier to use because there's no question about how the data is organized. If you're considering using an Access database as a mail merge data source for address labels in Word, think again and consider printing the labels directly from Access.

To use the Label Wizard:

1. From the Database window, select the Reports tab and then click New.

2. Enter a record source (either an existing table or query) in the pull-down box provided and choose the Label Wizard.

3. Select the Avery label type (by number or size) from the list that appears. If you don't know the number, measure your label and see if it matches a standard Avery size. To create custom-sized labels, click the Customize... button, which will allow you to create your own label type of almost any size. Click Next to continue.

4. Choose the font, color, and style for the text on your labels and click Next.

5. Select the fields you want to appear on your label and click the greater-than arrow (>) to move them to the sample label shown. You can type spaces, additional text, and carriage returns directly in the sample label, around your data fields if you like. Click Next to continue.

6. Select the fields, if any, that you want to sort the printed labels by, and click Next to continue.

7. Assign a name to this new report if you like and click Finish to display either the label design report or a Print Preview of the labels you designed.

Part
I

Ch
6

Creating Database Applications

Automating Common Tasks with Macros

Macros, the poor person's method of programming in most Microsoft Office applications, provide a way to perform simple tasks in a database application with a minimum of sweat for the developer. There's no syntax to remember, no error handling to worry about, and plenty of room to comment your code. On the other hand, there's only so much you can do with macros; their biggest limitation is their lack of flow control, but that's why you have modules. ■

The Macro Builder window

The canvas on which you create macros has a couple of sections and properties worth understanding.

Macro actions

There's a slew of individual actions that a macro can perform; this chapter talks about the most useful ones and explain how to use them.

Work with macro groups and conditions

Macros have the capability to include function-like groups of commands in one macro and the capability to perform actions based on criteria you set.

Discuss running and debugging macros

The various ways to start a macro are discussed, and the simple debugging you can perform on them is covered.

Why Use Macros?

Developing applications in Access is often a circular process: You have a feature or design goal in mind, you try something, you tinker with it until it works, and then you save your work in a logical and maintainable form. Sometimes, a problem just screams out "use a macro!" and you'll recognize those cases when you come across them if you know how to use macros when you need them.

In the context of Access, the meaning of the term "macro" is somewhat different than its meaning in Word or Excel. In those applications, macros are keystroke (and sometimes mouse-click) recordings that can be played back when needed to perform a repetitive process. In Access, you don't record keystrokes per se; you specify a process and save that process in a macro. The actions that make up a macro may or may not correspond to keyboard or mouse sequences.

Macros are excellent prototyping tools—you can usually create a macro for a simple action, like opening or closing forms, running reports, or setting options in a few minutes. Macros can run VBA code or execute menu commands; they can import and export tables and other database objects; they can resize windows and quit Access. If you can do it by clicking a toolbar or menu option, you can do it with a macro.

Access provides another programming feature, called *modules*, that contain programs in a language called Visual Basic for Applications (VBA). Modules are well-suited to complex, involved operations that involve many steps or require the code to make some sophisticated decisions. Macros, in contrast, are typically short bursts of high-level code (called actions) that require little or no looping or decision-making (flow control). For example, to make the terminal beep, you can write a one-line macro using the Beep action; it takes about 15 seconds. To do the same thing in a module you'd need at least three lines of code and maybe as many as eight, and it would take a couple of minutes.

Many beginning Access programmers start with macros and move to modules when it becomes clear that macros won't always do what they want. Access even converts your macros to VBA code on demand, making the action your macro was performing more flexible and usually faster.

Macros, in general, are slower than an equivalent module. The reason for this is that macros are *interpreted*, meaning that they are read and converted to executable code (parsed) one line at a time when they are run. That process takes a few milliseconds for each line of macro code. Modules, on the other hand, are (usually) *compiled*, meaning that the parsing and conversion to machine instructions takes place before the database is saved, and they're ready and waiting when the code is run. Furthermore, compiled modules can sometimes be *optimized*, or reorganized by Access so they run more efficiently. With macros, the order of execution that the programmer specifies, no matter how inefficient, is how they're run.

Macros come in handy when you can't remember how to do something in VBA. Want to change the cursor to an hourglass while a query runs? You have two options: a module or a macro. Without getting into the details of how to write a module, the processes can be compared as in Table 7.1.

Table 7.1 Changing the Cursor to an Hourglass with a Macro versus with a VBA Module

Module Actions	Macro Actions
Kick off Access Help	Create a new macro
Search the title index for "hourglass"	Choose the Hourglass action
Decide which topic includes the syntax	Save the macro
Read the topic	
Copy the code example	
Create a new module	

Even if you remember the syntax in VBA (it's DoCmd.Hourglass True, by the way), you still have to write at least three lines of code. And the best part is that once the macro's written, Access will convert it to VBA for you on command.

There are some things that only macros can do. They are as follows:

- **The assignment of actions to keyboard keys**.   If you want F3 to open up a report menu, no matter where in the application a user is, the only way to do it is with an AutoKeys macro (described later in this chapter).

- **Run startup actions**.   Access 97 includes a dialog box that allows you to force the execution of a macro when the database is opened (in earlier versions of Access, this was called the "Autoexec" macro). You can have that startup macro call VBA code if you like, but your startup options only enable you to call a macro directly, not code.

- **Control what menu and toolbar buttons do**.   Access 97 includes a complicated mechanism for managing toolbars and menus (which used to be accomplished in earlier versions of Access with—you guessed it—macros), and the actions those buttons and menu entries perform have to be listed in macros.

Creating a Macro Using the Macro Builder

You can create a simple macro in about 30 seconds once you understand the Macro Builder, the environment in which macros are written. This example takes you through the steps involved in creating a macro that pops up a message box with a friendly greeting. To create a macro:

1. In the Database window, click the Macros tab.

2. Click New. The Macro Builder window is displayed (see Figure 7.1). The empty Macro Builder window looks a little bit like a sheet of lined paper. The lines are, by default, separated into Actions and Comments. There are more columns available that initially are hidden. Each row in the lined section of the Macro Builder represents an opportunity for an action to take place. One row contains no more than one action, although rows may be left blank to separate groups or provide comment space.

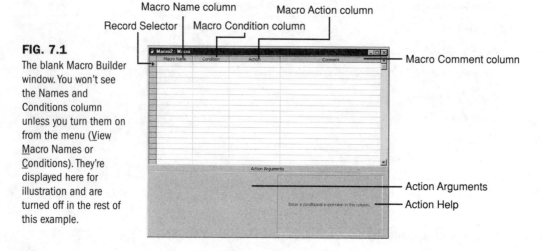

FIG. 7.1

The blank Macro Builder window. You won't see the Names and Conditions column unless you turn them on from the menu (View Macro Names or Conditions). They're displayed here for illustration and are turned off in the rest of this example.

3. The first line in the Action pane has a pull-down arrow in it; click the arrow to display a list of all of the actions available to you. You can select any action in the list; for this example, select the action MsgBox.

4. When you selected an action, the valid arguments for that action appears in the Arguments pane at lower left, and a description of how to use the arguments appears in the Action Help pane at lower right. Fill in appropriate values for the action's arguments. For this example, you should enter "Hello, World!" (without the quotes) in the box labeled Message; leave the default Yes in the Beep argument. Click in the Type box and click the pull-down arrow to see a list of valid Message Box types (select Information), and enter a title ("Greeting") in the box labeled Title. As you select different arguments, the help at the lower right changes appropriately.

5. Save your new macro by clicking the File menu, then Save. A dialog box appears asking for a name for your macro; the name you enter will appear in the Macros tab of the Database Window. For this example, use "Greeting." Click OK to save the macro. You must save a macro to run it.

6. To run your macro from the Macro Builder, click the Run button (or click the Run menu, then Run). You should see your Message Box appear as in Figure 7.2.

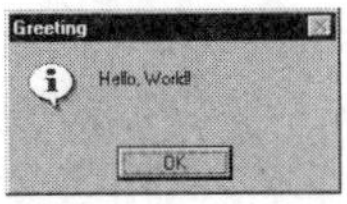

FIG. 7.2

The balloon icon in the Message Box is determined by what type of Message Box you choose.

N O T E Most macros have certain predefined arguments that take some of the work out of writing useful programs for your database.

Actions and Comments

The functions that a macro performs are called *actions*. Actions are predefined by Access and run the gamut from such mundane activities as causing the PC speaker to beep (the Beep action) to complex activities such as sending an Access object (a form, a table, and so on) to an e-mail recipient. The Achilles' heel of the Macro Builder is its inability to provide flow control mechanisms. After an action has been performed in a macro, the only place for the program to go is to the next line. You can't jump to subroutines or perform loops. You can, however, skip lines if certain conditions hold (see the section "Setting Conditions," later in this chapter).

Maintaining a general knowledge of the kinds of things macros can do is more important than remembering exactly what macro action does what; you always can find the action in the short, alphabetical list of actions (there are 49 in Access 97). Knowing what actions are available to macros is like knowing what controls you can use on a form or report. You can find a particular element if you need to, but it helps to have a good feel for what's available.

Access provides a short description of each macro action at the bottom of the Macro Builder window whenever you choose one, making a helpful syntax reference available when you need it. The more useful macro actions include the following:

■ **Close.** This action closes the currently active window, or whatever object you specify in the arguments (see "Action Arguments," later in this chapter).

■ **DeleteObject.** Deletes the currently active database object, or any object specified. Very dangerous, very useful.

■ **Echo.** If your macro manipulates screen objects, setting the "Off" argument to the Echo action doesn't update the screen while the macro is running. This saves a lot of time during long or screen-intensive macros.

■ **GoToControl/GoToPage.** If your form is particularly long, you may want to provide a button or menu option to jump to specific sections of it. Binding these actions to keys (like the Page Up and Page Down keys) makes your form that much easier to navigate.

■ **MsgBox.** Access provides five different prebuilt pop-up forms in which you can provide text. These can inform the user of a potential problem, provide information, and so on. Creating a macro to display a particularly common warning or condition is easy with this action.

Part
II

Ch
7

- **OpenForm/OpenReoprt.** You can get a form or report onto the screen (or onto the printer) easily by using this action, and you can even make some choices about how it will appear (blank for new data entry, with a filter applied, as a dialog box, and so on) by using the arguments.

- **PrintOut.** Want to give your users instant validation of what they entered in a form? Bind a key or menu option to this action and the current database object (usually a form in an Access application) will be printed.

- **Quit.** Closes Access and returns to Windows.

- **Requery.** Causes the current or specified object to be reevaluated, depending on its data source. If it's a control with an underlying query, the query is rerun; if it's a function, the function is rerun.

- **RunApp.** Runs another Windows program. Great for toolbars.

- **RunCode.** Runs an Access module. Sometimes the only way to get a module to run, as in the case of startup options or menu actions. Note that RunApp can only run VBA functions, not subroutines (see Chapter 11, "Beginning Programming for Your Database Using VBA").

- **SetWarnings.** Annoyed by all of those confirmation messages? Running the SetWarnings action can turn them off or on, as desired. This only affects dialog boxes that don't require user input such as "You are about to append 132 rows."

The last column in the upper half of the Macro Builder window is entitled Comment, and it's intended for just that. It's good programming practice to enter a short description of what each line in your macro is doing in the Comment column. One of the beautiful things about macro comments is that they're maintained by default if you later convert the macro to VBA, making your VBA code even more readable.

Action Arguments

Most actions have arguments, which provide parameters for running that action. The arguments for any given action are invisible until you select that action in the Macro Builder window; when available, the arguments are shown at the bottom-left corner of the window (see Figure 7.3). It would be unusual to edit macro properties in VBA code (although it's certainly possible), so you will normally do any customization of the actions in your macro here.

Different actions have different arguments; you can look up any action in Access help for a list and description of its arguments, or you can rely on the short syntax help provided in the Macro Builder.

FIG. 7.3

The Arguments pane of the Macro Builder window. This only appears when an action is selected, and changes depending on the action in question.

Selected action ⟶

Arguments for the ⟶ selected action

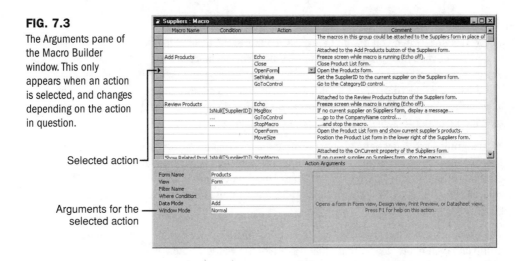

Some typical actions and their commonly used (and largely self-explanatory) arguments include:

Action	Commonly Used Arguments
Close	Object Type, Object Name
FindRecord	Find What
GoToPage	Page Number
Minimize	(no arguments)
OpenTable	Table Name, View
Quit	Options
Save	Object Type, Object Name
SetWarnings	Warnings On
StopMacro	(no arguments)

For details on how different values for these arguments affect these (or any other) actions, see Access help.

Action arguments provide the supplemental information that's necessary to complete the specified action correctly. Some actions have no arguments at all (like the StopMacro action, which stops the currently running macro), but some have as many as seven (like FindRecord, which searches the current datasheet for a specified record).

The arguments available for each action correspond to the *properties* and *methods* for each action, which are extensively used in Access modules. A good way to get accustomed to the properties and methods of any Access object is to start Access help and search for the name of that object in the Index. Relevant properties and methods are usually referenced in the online help, complete with examples.

Part

II

Ch

7

Using Macro Groups

There are times when you'll want to include several small macros in one object. This feature exists for convenience; you may want to include all of the macros used by a certain form in one object so the number of saved macros visible in the Macro window is minimized. Additionally, if you have one macro that calls another as the result of a condition (see "Setting Conditions," later in this chapter), it's especially convenient to include both macros in the same object to make them easier to debug. This feature is rarely used in practice.

Macro groups are collections of short, simple macros that are all saved separately under one macro name. They are separated by a single blank line in the Macro Builder window, and each macro in a macro group needs a name. Those names are entered in the Macro Name column, which you can display by clicking the View menu, then selecting Macro Names from the Macro Design menu.

The Customers macro (shown in Figure 7.1) provides a good example of the use of a macro group and comments. The comment at the top of the window notes that all of the macros in this group are attached to the Customers form, and other comments precede each macro explaining how it's used. Each macro in the group starts with a macro name in the leftmost column and the actions begin on the same row in the Action column. When these macros are run, each action is executed in order until a blank line in the Action column is encountered, which stops execution.

N O T E   To run a macro within a macro group from a VBA module, specify the group name, followed by a period and the name of the macro in your code. For example, to run the ValidateID macro in the Customers macro group, you'd write

```
Customers.ValidateID
```

in the appropriate method of the code calling it. If you want to run a macro in a macro group from the Database Window, make sure that the first action appears on the first line of the Macro Builder window, or execution will stop when Access encounters a blank action line. ▪

Setting Conditions

Access provides rudimentary, one-way control flow for macros in the form of macro conditions, which can be entered in the Condition column of the Macro Builder window. To show the Condition column, click the View menu, then select Conditions.

Macro conditions act like "if" commands to control the flow of actions in a macro. An expression entered in the Condition column tells Access to execute the action on the same line only if the condition is true. If the condition is false, Access skips the action listed on the condition line and skips to the next row and executes the action listed there.

For example, consider the macro "Hide Footer" in the macro group "Sales Totals by Amount" (from the Database window, click the Macros tab, then Sales Totals by Amount, then click

Design). It includes only one action, "Cancel Event," which stops the execution of the code that called this macro. It also includes a condition:

```
[Counter]=10
```

which means that this action is executed only if the value of the variable Counter (which presumably exists in the code that calls this macro) is equal to 10. Since the next line of this macro is blank, the macro stops executing after this condition is evaluated and executed if necessary.

A condition applies only to the action on the same line with the condition; if the condition is evaluated as false, execution continues with the next line after the condition (if it's not blank). There is one exception to this rule: If you include an ellipsis (…) in the condition column immediately below a condition, Access will consider that line part of the condition and will execute it only if the condition is true. In the Customers macro, the ValidateID macro group specifies the condition:

```
DLookUp("[CustomerID]","[Customers]","[CustomerID] = Form.[CustomerID] ") Is Not
➥Null
```

This complicated-looking snippet of code checks to see if the Customer ID entered on the Customers form is in the Customers table. If the ID is found, then you are about to duplicate a Customer ID (which is bad in this context). The action specified is to use the MsgBox action to display a message to the user trying to enter a duplicate ID. The important thing to recognize here is that if the condition evaluates to be true, the action is executed.

The line after this condition has an ellipsis in the Condition column, so you know it's also part of the code that Access should execute if the preceding condition is true. The CancelEvent action clears out the erroneous ID that caused the macro to be run in the first place.

Because the next line is blank, there's nothing else to do and the macro is finished. If there were an action listed on this first blank line after the condition and ellipsis, Access would execute it whenever the condition above evaluated false. For good form, you should be careful to include blank lines between macros in macro groups to make it clear that the macro ends there. Access 97 recognizes that a new name starts a new macro, but earlier versions of Access weren't that intelligent (this was a "feature," not a bug), so it's a good idea to make it clear that you intend execution to stop at the blank line.

Using the AutoKeys Macro

A useful application for Access macros is the AutoKeys macro, which Access recognizes for special treatment if you create it. When you create a custom application, it may be useful to create key combinations that make your application do certain things. For example, maybe you want to print the current form whenever a user presses Ctrl+P, or you want to open a certain form when he presses F7. You can assign almost any key combination on the keyboard to any action (or group of actions) you can specify in a macro, and there's no way to do this with VBA code.

You can assign macros to most key sequences. If you assign a macro to a sequence that Access is already using (like Ctrl+V, which is usually Paste), Access will run your macro instead of the usual action for that sequence. This can be confusing for users, so try to stick to unassigned or uncommon sequences. You can't assign macros to single alphanumeric keys or keys normally used in combination with others (like Ctrl and Alt), although you can assign macros to the function keys and the Insert and Delete keys.

To specify combinations of keys, use the special syntax described in Table 7.2. To specify the key in the first column of Table 7.2, use the character(s) in the second column:

Table 7.2   Key Sequences for AutoKeys Assignments

Keyboard Key	Macro Character	Example
Control	^	^Z
Function key	{}	{F7}
Shift	+	+{F2}
Insert	{INS} or {INSERT}	{INS}
Delete	{DEL} or {DELETE}	{DEL}
Combinations	Use the macro characters above	+^{F5}

To assign an action to a key sequence:

1. Create a new macro (click the Macros tab in the Database window and click New).

2. Turn on the Name column (select View, then Macro Names from the menu) and use the special syntax described in Table 7.2 to enter the key sequence you want to assign in that column.

3. Enter the action you want that sequence to perform in the Action column. If there are several actions you want to perform in sequence, enter them on successive lines with no blank rows between them.

4. Close the macro and save it as "AutoKeys." The name is important; Access only recognizes a macro with this name for key assignments.

5. Close your database (click the File menu, then Close) and reopen it (click the File menu, then Open Database) to activate the AutoKeys macro.

When you close and reopen your database, Access executes the macro actions you specified whenever the specified keys are pressed. To end a sequence of actions, leave a blank line between the last action in a sequence and the next macro. This isn't strictly necessary, but the additional white space makes your macro code easier for humans to read.

Macro Execution and Debugging

You can run a macro in one of several ways:

- **From the Database window.** Click the Macros tab, then double-click the name of the macro. Note that the macro must begin on the first line of the Macro Builder for this method to work.

- **From VBA code in a module.** Use the RunMacro method, as in

  ```
  DoCmd.RunMacro macroname
  ```

- **From another macro or from a custom menubar/toolbar.** Use the RunMacro action, specifying the name of the macro you want to run as an argument.

- **When a database opens.** Enter the name of the macro in the Startup option under the Options dialog box (click the Tools menu, then select Options), or save the macro with the name "AutoExec."

You can run a macro one line at a time to inspect its actions and decide whether to continue running the rest of the lines. To debug a macro:

1. Open the Macro Builder window, displaying the macro you want to test.

2. Click the Single Step button on the toolbar.

3. If your macro starts on the first line of the Macro Builder, you can click the Run button to start your code at the first line. If you're debugging a macro group (as are all of the macros in Northwind), you'll need to run the code that calls the macro; once you select the Single Step button, any macro the code runs will stop at each line. When the macro starts running, the Macro Single Step dialog box appears (see Figure 7.4).

4. Click the Step button to step through successive lines, the Continue button to cancel stepping and run the rest of the macro, or the Halt button to stop execution.

FIG. 7.4
The Macro Single Step dialog box, which appears only when you step through a macro, or one terminates abnormally.

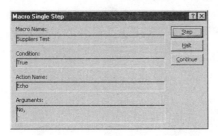

You also can stop execution of a macro and start single-stepping by pressing Ctrl+Break while it's executing; that causes the Macro Single Step dialog box to appear, and you can then start stepping.

Part
II

Ch
7

TIP There's no way to set a breakpoint in a macro, but you can insert an action that stops execution (like a MsgBox) and press Ctrl+Break when it appears to allow you to start stepping from that point. Remove the debugging MsgBox when you're done debugging.

Creating Menus and Toolbars

Earlier versions of Access used macros to create custom menubars that could be distributed with applications. These menu bars typically replaced the standard Access menu bar and were useful for limiting the kinds of action typical users could execute, or to make common actions (via macros) easily accessible at application runtime.

These earlier versions of Access included an add-on tool called the Menu Builder that made it easy to write macros that created menus. The Menu Builder add-on is no longer supplied with Access, however; while macro-based menus still work, the new model of menus and toolbars treats new-style menus as separate entities that have their own properties and a special editor.

Menus created in earlier versions of Access still work fine, however, and you can still create these menus with macros. You can create new menus using the old, macro-based method, or by using the new Customize Toolbar command. Because menus in Access have traditionally been created using macros (and still can be), this discussion is included here instead of in another chapter.

To create or edit a new-style menu bar or toolbar (they're essentially the same in Access 97; it was very hard to create a toolbar in earlier versions of Access): In the Database window, click the View menu, select Toolbars, and then Customize. The Customize dialog box appears as in Figure 7.5.

FIG. 7.5

The Customize dialog box for toolbars and menus. Any currently visible menus and toolbars have checks next to their names; they must be visible to edit them.

You can delete a toolbar or menu bar you've already created by selecting the toolbar and clicking the Delete button. You can't delete built-in Access toolbars. ●

CHAPTER 8

Building Web Pages

As the popularity of the Internet increases, so does the number of people wanting to leverage the effort they've already put into organizing their data into a database. And why not? There's no reason why you shouldn't be able to build a Web page based on the data in your forms and tables, and Microsoft markets Office 97 as "Internet-enabled." Access, in particular, includes some features that make it easier to get your data on the Web.

This chapter assumes you know something about the Web and the language of the Web—hypertext markup language (HTML). To be comfortable using Access to build Web pages, you're going to have to understand how to use a Web browser, what kinds of things a Web server can do, and how to get connected to the Internet. ■

See how to design forms for use on the Web

Some form elements just don't work on the Web due to the limitations of HTML. There are workarounds covered in this chapter.

Look at the "Save As HTML" Wizard

Access translates your form to basic, static HTML. This is convenient for those situations where you have data in the database that you want to clean up manually before publishing.

Work with the Web Publishing Wizard

Access organizes a whole database (or parts of it) into a coherent Web site and push it to your Web server, if you dare.

Talk about the differences between static HTML, Internet Data Connector pages, and Active Server Pages

Depending on your audience and your data, you've got to make some tough design decisions before your pages get stored on your Web server.

Database Design for Web Presentation

Designing an Access application for use on the Web is different from designing for local use, primarily because the capability of Web browsers is so limited in comparison with native Access. Even in the best case, where your Access forms translate directly to Web forms, you still lose half of the functionality of Access because you can't use modules or macros on the Web. The only Access objects that are of any use on the Web are forms and tables, and even their functionality is severely limited. However, the Web is an inexpensive, effective way to get your data out to as many as six million United States users (O'Reilly & Associates 1996 est., **http:// www.ora.com**), and many more elsewhere in the world. No other technical solution is as fast and as cheap and if you can work around the limitations, you can obtain quite impressive results.

N O T E Access converts queries and reports to HTML, but they come out looking and acting like tables and forms, respectively. So why bother, when you have so many more design options with tables and forms?

An exception is when you have created a report for printing that you want to convert to HTML. Reports are essentially the same as forms, but it may be convenient to have similar online and printed documentation. Furthermore, page breaks in reports are interpreted as instructions to create new pages in HTML; Access creates different Web pages for each different page of a report converted to HTML. ■

Some things you should consider before even starting work on a Web database include the following:

- Are your table relationships in place and correct?
- Do your tables include all of the fields you need, and are the fields the appropriate type?
- Are your forms laid out simply and effectively, and have you tried them out on users?
- Do your forms include any extraneous items, like graphics you can live without or integrated buttons that call macros or modules?
- Do you have several megabytes of free space on your Web server to store and experiment with your pages?

When you publish an Access database to the Web, you need to consider how the data will be used. The type of access you require to your data, and the types of operations you'll allow remote users to perform have a significant impact on the kinds of pages you'll create.

Access can create three kinds of Web pages:

- **Static HTML pages** are set in stone when you create them. Access extracts the data you specify from the database (via a form, table, or query) and writes it directly into a Web page for you to put on your server. For environments where the database being accessed via the Web doesn't change frequently and the generation of the pages can be made more or less automatic, a static HTML solution may be your best bet.

If you're comfortable with VBA coding, you could use a code module to generate new Web pages every time the data in your database changes.

■ **Dynamic HTML pages** work with the Web server software to update the data in them at the time the page is requested by a remote user. Because these styles require some custom software to be run by the Web server, they're only useful if your Web server runs on a PC. There are two types of dynamic pages supported by Access:

- **Internet Data Connector (HTC/IDX) pages** contain data that's up-to-the-second when generated. These pages don't allow data to be written back to the database, so they're only good for viewing data. These pages can be generated by almost any PC HTTP server, and can be viewed by any remote user using any browser.

- **Active Server pages (ASP)** contain data that's up-to-the-second when they're generated, they allow any number of custom (ActiveX) controls and they permit data to be written back to the database. However, the Web server must be running Microsoft's Internet Information Server, and the remote user must be using Microsoft's Internet Explorer browser to see the custom controls. Otherwise, remote users will get an error (if the HTTP server is misconfigured) or the pages will look like gibberish (if the remote user is running the wrong browser).

If you want to create Web pages that anybody, anywhere can use to query and update your database in real time (a flexible arrangement), you must use Microsoft's server and your user must use Microsoft's browser (an inflexible solution). Conversely, if you want to use any server you like and allow users to do the same (flexible), you are limited to static, difficult-to-maintain Web pages that may be out of date as soon as they're created (not very functional). Finding a happy medium is where the hard work begins.

Which Server Will You Use?

You may not have any choice as to what kind of server on which you're going to be publishing your pages. If you control your site, you might consider running Internet Information Server (IIS) on Windows NT Server; it's free (if you don't consider the cost of the operating system), it's quite capable, and it's easy to configure. Best of all, it enables you to create both kinds of dynamic pages. If you can't run IIS, but your Web server is still PC-based, you can install the Microsoft Access Desktop Driver, which comes with Access, to permit your server to use ODBC to read Access databases.

 You can get detailed instructions on installing the Access Desktop Driver by searching Access help for "Install the Microsoft Access Desktop driver."

N O T E   The real issue for Web servers to be able to handle ActiveX and Active Server Pages is their capability to use the Access Desktop driver. Theoretically, any ISAPI-compliant server should be able to do this, but the only commercial ISAPI server available at this writing is IIS. ▪

If you can't run a PC HTTP server, or you can't get permission to configure it (as is probably the case if you use a commercial Internet Service Provider), you're stuck with static HTML.

What Browsers Will You Support?

If you're creating content for an office intranet, where you can specify the browser that everybody reading your pages will use, you can consider creating any kind of pages. Unfortunately, Microsoft's ActiveX controls are only understood by Microsoft browsers, so you'll need to make sure that your clients are using Internet Explorer to surf the Web if you're going to create pages using these controls.

If you can't guarantee that your viewers will be using any particular browser, there's no sense in creating Active Server Pages, because they won't work any better than Internet Data Connector (HTX/IDC) pages in any other browser. The bottom line here is that only users running Internet Explorer can add data to your database unless you use third-party Web/database gateway software, which is outside of the scope of this book.

N O T E   Netscape says that they'll include support for ActiveX controls (which should enable you to see Active Server Pages in a Netscape browser) in the Mercury enhancement to Netscape Navigator. Mercury is due in early 1998 and will include support for Java Beans, which in turn supports ActiveX.

It will be interesting to see how Netscape and Microsoft play each other when this happens. If Netscape adds support for ActiveX, will Microsoft change the specification so it doesn't work anymore? We'll see.

Details on Mercury are available at **http://home.netscape.com/comprod/at_work/white_paper/vision/print.html**. ▪

Web/Database Gateways

You're not limited to the meager options Access gives you to publish your data on the Web. If you've got a programming staff and some time, there are several third-party products (called database gateways) that you can use in conjunction with Access on your server to provide a programming interface to your database. All work in about the same way:

1. Configure your Access database as an ODBC data source.
2. Write HTML that uses special codes to tell your Web server to get data from (or put data in) your database.

3. The gateway software manages the communication between your Web server and Access.

Some of the more popular products for this kind of work include Allaire's Cold Fusion (**http://www.allaire.com**) and Bluestone's Sapphire/Web (**http://www.bluestone.com**). Neither is difficult to use and each has advantages and disadvantages to its use. Microsoft's similar dbWeb product, which used to work with any PC HTTP server, has been modified since Microsoft purchased it from Aspect and is now only compatible with Internet Information Server.

Templates and Limitations of Forms on the Web

As you create Web pages from your Access database, you would do well to keep two things in mind:

- **Use a template to keep your site consistent**. In Access more than in most applications, the use of templates is absolutely necessary to introduce any custom formatting into your pages. If you don't create and carefully design a template, your automatically generated Web pages will look flat and boring.

- **Only use controls that your style of Web page supports**. Static HTML pages always look like datasheets; there's no sense in creating elaborate forms for them if this is the style you've settled on. For HTX/IDC pages, you can use labels and text boxes, period. For Active Server Pages, you can use almost any controls you like, but unusual controls may not convert and increase the complexity of the page, which may cause the conversion to fail.

Consider your server and browser limitations and the ways your remote clients will use your data when settling on a style. After you decide on a style, create an appropriate template and include in it the controls that will be supported by your server.

When you convert your Access forms and tables to HTML, you will be prompted to enter the name of a template file. This file, which you should have created beforehand using an editor of your choice, contains all of the formatting, graphics, and nondata objects that you want to appear on your page. Depending on the output format you choose, Access inserts the data and maybe some navigation buttons in your pages for you, but Access doesn't know anything about images and logos.

This discussion assumes you know how to create simple HTML pages. Microsoft Word works reasonably well as a basic editor for Web pages, or you can use any editor of your choice. You can even use complex HTML constructions such as tables, frames, and forms; Access preserves any tags it doesn't recognize.

To create a template:

1. Start Microsoft Word 97.
2. Click the File menu and select New.

3. Select the Web Pages tab from the dialog box that appears, then the Web Page Wizard, then click OK.

4. In the Web Page Wizard dialog box, select the Simple Layout (it should already be selected as the default), then click Next. Choose any page style you like from the next dialog box, then click Finish. The style may take a few seconds to update.

5. Replace the heading and introductory paragraph with some text that's appropriate for the kind of pages you'll be creating. Delete the two lines that say Type some text here and the list bullets between them. Also delete the hyperlinks at the bottom of the page (Related Page 1, etc.), unless you're comfortable customizing them.

6. Enter the special tags (described in the next paragraph) into your document at the appropriate places and change them to HTML tags in Word by selecting them after you've typed them and changed their style to HTML Markup. They'll disappear in Word, because Word doesn't know how to interpret them, but they are there.

7. Save your document by clicking the File menu, then Save. Word recommends the extension .htm, denoting an HTML document.

You'll need to insert several special tags that act as markers for Access to use when it creates your pages. These tags masquerade as HTML comments, ensuring that browsers that don't understand how to use them will ignore them. Ideally, if you accidentally publish an Access template to the Web without including any data in it, it will just look blank.

The tags you'll use include:

■ **<!--AccessTemplate_Body-->** (required)

This tag is replaced with the raw data itself when the page is created. Exported tables and forms are inserted in the template at the point where this tag appears, pushing everything after this tag farther down the page.

■ **<!--AccessTemplate_Title-->** (optional)

All Web browsers show a title for the currently displayed page at the top of the browser. Access replaces this tag with the name of the exported table or form, producing a different page title for each exported object. If you don't like this, you can always provide your own title tag.

■ **<!--AccessTemplate_PageNumber-->** (optional)

If your exported report, form, or table spans more then one page, Access will place them on different Web pages and number the pages for you. This tag displays the current page in the user's browser. Note that this is not the same as exporting several tables, forms, or reports; these are all considered separate objects and are not numbered.

The following tags all assist with navigation within multiple-page objects (as opposed to multiple pages in an exported site):

■ **<!--AccessTemplate_FirstPage-->**

Provides a hyperlink to the first page of the set.

■ **<!--AccessTemplate_PreviousPage-->**

Provides a hyperlink to the previous page in the set.

■ **<!--AccessTemplate_NextPage-->**

Provides a hyperlink to the next page in the set.

■ **<!--AccessTemplate_LastPage-->**

Provides a hyperlink to the last page in the set.

If you're using a WYSIWYG HTML editor (like Microsoft Word), you should use the "Custom Tag" (or equivalent) function to insert these tags in appropriate places in your document. If you're creating your template page in a simple text editor, you can type them in directly. Spelling must be correct, but these tags are not case-sensitive.

For examples of how to use Access' HTML export capabilities, refer to the Customers form and table in the Northwind database. Using Netscape Composer as an HTML editor, you can create a new HTML template from scratch (see Figure 8.1).

FIG. 8.1

The template used as a background for the exported tables and forms. You can't see the Access fields, because they look like comments to the browser.

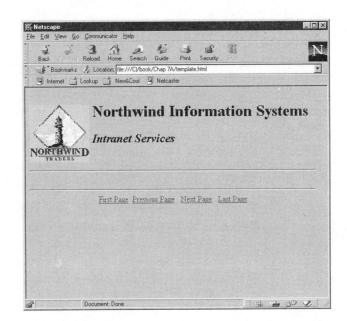

The code that creates this template (with the irrelevant tags removed for clarity) is shown here:

```
<HTML>
<BODY TEXT="#000000" BGCOLOR="#C0C0C0" LINK="#0000FF" VLINK="#800080">
<CENTER><HR></CENTER>
<!--AccessTemplate_Title--><BR>
```

```
<!--AccessTemplate_Body-->
<CENTER><HR></CENTER>
<CENTER>
<A HREF="<!--AccessTemplate_FirstPage-->">First Page</A>
 <A HREF="<!--AccessTemplate_PreviousPage-->">Previous Page</A>
  <A HREF="<!--AccessTemplate_NextPage-->">Next Page</A>
  <A HREF="<!--AccessTemplate_LastPage-->">Last Page</A></CENTER>
<DIV ALIGN=right>
        <!--AccessTemplate_PageNumber-->
</DIV>
</BODY>
</HTML>
```

None of this (except for the horizontal rules) is visible in the browser window, but it will be when it's replaced with Access data after conversion.

After your template meets your requirements, save it to disk. Access, by default, expects to find templates in \Program Files\Microsoft Office\Templates\Access, but you can save it anywhere you want to.

Using the Publish to the Web Wizard

It's unlikely that you'll want to publish your entire database to the Web. Certain forms and maybe some tables and reports are your likely targets; it will be helpful if you decide which you'll be working with ahead of time and write them down somewhere for reference. After you start running the Publish to the Web Wizard, it's hard to go back and browse through your database objects.

CAUTION

Not all database objects can be saved in every page type. This table summarizes your options:

	Static HTML	Dynamic (HTX/IDC)	Dynamic (ASP)
Forms	X (datasheets)	X (datasheets)	X
Tables	X	X	X
Queries	X	X	X
Reports	X		

You can't save modules or macros as HTML.

As an extended example, this sample Web site includes the following objects from Northwind, chosen to show how certain controls and formats export:

- The Customers and Categories forms
- The Orders table
- The Catalog and Summary of Sales by Year reports

Running the Publish to the Web Wizard can be a long, drawn-out process. Give yourself plenty of time to do this and be prepared to make several attempts. This example, turns all of the above objects into static HTML, which is be visible in any browser and runs on any Web server.

Netscape Navigator is used as the browser for all but one of the examples in this chapter. Seventy percent of the browsers used on the Web as of this writing are made by Netscape, so your pages are likely to appear as shown for most Web users. For the Active Server Pages (ASP) examples, you have to use Microsoft Internet Explorer because that is the only browser that supports ASP.

In most of the dialog boxes displayed during this process, you have the following options:

- **Next** carries you forward to the next set of options to be configured
- **Back** returns you to the previous screen to modify the entries you've already made
- **Finish** skips all of the intervening screens, selecting the defaults (or the values previously saved in a Web Publication Profile), and takes you to the last screen before creating the pages
- **Cancel** stops the process and returns you to the Database window

To use the Publish to the Web Wizard:

1. Click the File menu, and then select Save as HTML. The Publish to the Web Wizard starts and you're presented with an overview of the process.

   There is one selectable option on this page: you can choose to use an existing Web Publication Profile, if you've created one earlier, to save you from having to go through all of the publication steps again. Saving a Web Publication Profile is covered in Step 7 of this section. Click on Next to continue, or Cancel to exit the wizard.

2. The wizard lists all of the objects in your database. Select the ones you want to publish individually by clicking in the check boxes to the left of their names, and clicking on the appropriate tab to change the display to a different type of object (tables, forms, and so on).

   The All Objects tab shows all of the publishable objects in the database in an alphabetical list. You may select every publishable object in the database by clicking Select All, or clear all of your selections by clicking Deselect All.

   After you've marked the objects you want to publish, click Next to continue.

3. The next screen asks for the name of the template file, if any, you want to use to create your pages. Click the Browse button to locate your template file if you're using one template for all of your pages.

   You can create (and use) as many templates as there are objects to be published. This is useful when you want the pages to have different appearances, or if you intend to use different publishing methods for some pages. If this is the case, click the check box labeled I want to select different templates for some of the selected objects and click Next to select different templates for every object you've marked.

   After you've chosen a template file or files, click Next to continue.

If you enter a default template in this screen and note that you want to select different templates for some objects, you only have to specify templates for the objects that will not use the default.

4. It's time to specify the type of page(s) you want to create: Static HTML, Dynamic (HTX/ IDC), or Dynamic (ASP). Before you get to this step choose which formats you want to use on which pages. Select the option button appropriate for one of these formats and click Next to continue.

   If you want to specify different formats for some of the pages, check the box labeled I want to select different format types for some of the selected objects and click Next. Like the template selection page, you can select any one of the three options for each page. Click Next to continue.

 The same thing applies here as for templates: You only need to select a different format type for pages that will not use the default. It's possible not to have a default template, but you'll always have a default format type.

5. The next dialog box asks you to specify the directory into which you want Access to save your new Web pages. If you're running Access on the Web server machine (or on a machine attached via a local network to the Web server), you may want to create the pages directly in the directory that they will be served from. This is especially useful if the pages will be generated automatically.

   Note that you select a directory in this step, not a file. The File Selection dialog box does not show any file names; don't worry, your files are still there.

   If you've installed the Web Publishing Wizard, which comes on the Office 97 Professional CD, you'll see three additional options. These are discussed in "Using the Web Publishing Wizard," later in this chapter. If not, your only option is to publish objects locally, which is automatically selected.

   Click Next to continue.

6. Access gives you the option of creating a rudimentary home page, which contains links to all of the pages it is about to generate. This is a nice feature for debugging your pages, but you'll probably want to stop using it after your page format and options are set in stone. The home page Access creates is functional, but not much else.

   If you decide to create a home page, you can specify what to call it. Access suggests "Default," which creates a home page called Default.html. Most Web servers will return a page called "default.html" if a remote user selects the directory containing Web pages, but does not specify a particular page, making this a good option to leave alone.

   For this example, turn on the Home Page option and click Next to continue.

7. Finally, you have the option of saving all of the settings you've just entered in a Web Publication Profile, which is saved on disk for the next time you want to generate pages with the same options. If you select this option, you can name the Profile anything you like, and it will be available to you the next time you run the Publish to the Web Wizard.

It's almost always a good idea to save a Profile every time you change options. If you make a mistake or the pages don't come out quite right, having a saved Profile makes it easy to rerun the process. If you have several similar batches of pages to run, saving a Profile makes it easy to make slight modifications and save more Profiles for the other runs.

After saving (or not saving) your Web Publication Profile, click Finish to create your Web page(s). It will take a few seconds to create your pages, but when it's done, you'll be returned to the Database window.

Using Access to Create Static HTML Pages

In Step 4 of the general example in the previous section, you could choose Static HTML as the output type for your pages. you If you did, you created static HTML pages of five objects in the Northwind database, including forms, reports, and a table. The figures below compare their appearance in Access to their appearance in a browser. The home page, default.html appears as in Figure 8.2.

FIG. 8.2

The automatically generated home page for this batch. The pages linked change every time you run the Wizard, wiping out any previous links. The graphic and title in this page (and the subsequent ones) were created as part of the template (see Templates and Limitations of Forms on the Web earlier in this chapter) and are not included in the code sample in the previous section.

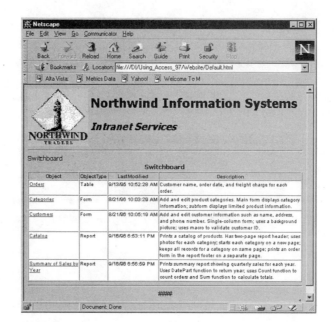

This effort includes links to each of the pages for the other objects created at the same time, the type and last modification date of each object, and a description of each object.

TIP The Description field on the home page is generated using the Description property of each object saved as HTML. You access this property for any of these objects by right-clicking the name of the form, table, report, or query in the Database window and selecting Properties from the menu that appears.

Let's begin with the Orders table. In Access, it looks like Figure 8.3. In Netscape, it looks like Figure 8.4.

FIG. 8.3

The Orders table (Datasheet view) in Access.

FIG. 8.4

The Orders table in HTML.

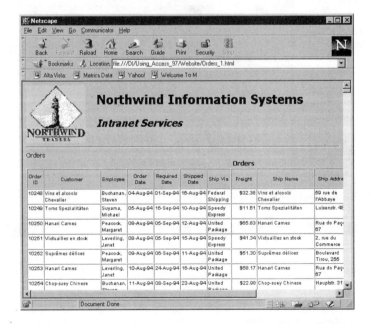

This is a big page—more than a megabyte—and it would take more than two minutes to download over a 28.8 MBps modem. Depending on the memory resources available in your machine, you may not be able to view it at all. But all of the data is preserved.

Next, consider the Customers and Categories forms. Figure 8.5 shows how they look in Access; after conversion to static HTML, the forms look like Figure 8.6.

FIG. 8.5

The Customers and Categories forms in Access (Form view).

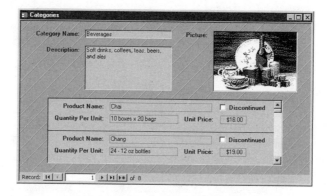

Comparing Figures 8.5 and 8.6, you'll notice that the Customers form looks fine after conversion—even the special ASCII characters used in some of the names are preserved. The Categories form didn't fare as well, however; the field [Picture] was not converted to HTML, because the Publish to the Web Wizard doesn't convert fields of type OLE Object.

The two reports converted come out particularly well, as shown in Figures 8.7 and 8.8.

FIG. 8.6

The Customers and Categories forms in HTML.

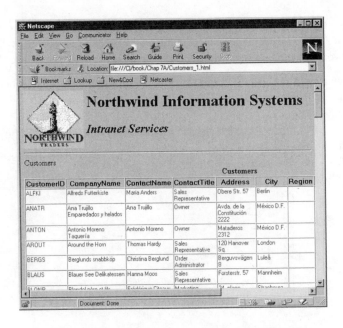

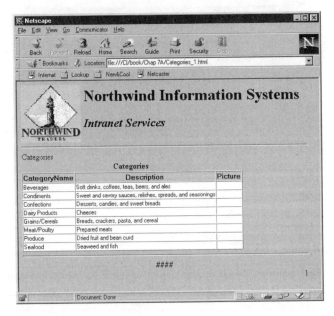

FIG. 8.7

The Catalog and Summary of Sales by Year reports in Access.

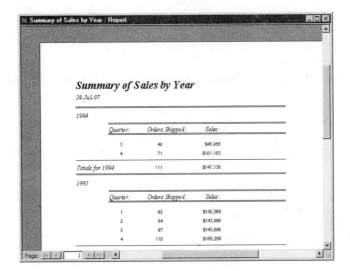

As with the forms, the OLE Objects (pictures) in the reports don't convert, but everything else is true to form.

The page number at the bottom of every page created from a form or table is 1. That's because Access doesn't maintain any relationship between the different pages of the entire site, except in the home page; every individual Web page is therefore the first. In multipage reports, every page is numbered sequentially, so page numbers may make more sense in that case.

FIG. 8.8

The Catalog and Summary of Sales by Year reports in HTML.

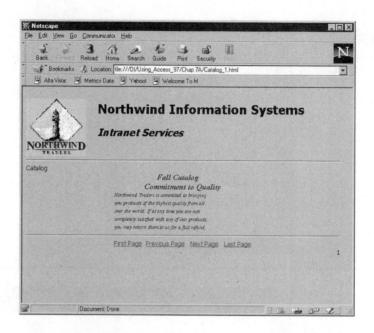

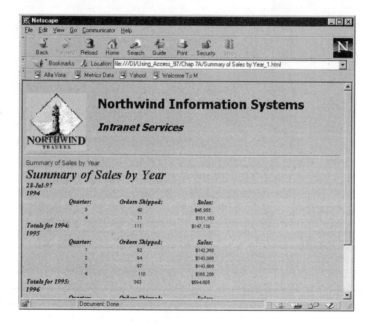

The navigation hyperlinks you created in the template ("First Page," "Next Page," etc.) also are useless except in the case of the reports, because there's no relationship between the separate pages in the forms and tables. In the reports, these hyperlinks are useful.

In general, you'll want to use the <!--AccessTemplate SomePage> and <!--AccessTemplate PageNumber> tags in your templates for reports, and not other kinds of pages. These tags won't hurt, but they aren't useful either.

Creating Internet Data Connector (HTX/IDC) Pages

If your data changes frequently, or you want to make sure that remote users are seeing the latest data, you might consider using Internet Data Connector (HTX/IDC) pages. They can be viewed on any browser, but you only can create them on a system running Microsoft Internet Information Server (IIS). Also note that you only can store forms, tables, and queries as HTX/IDC; reports are saved as static HTML, even if you specify HTX/IDC. There's no difference in the way you create HTX/IDC pages from static pages using the Publish to the Web Wizard, except that you choose the page type HTX/IDC when prompted (step 4 of the example used earlier in this chapter). Choosing this page type causes Access to display an extra dialog box (see Figure 8.9), which asks for the name of the ODBC data source you've set up (and any username and password, if required by ODBC). The options at the bottom of this dialog box pertain only to Active Server Pages, which are discussed later. After you've entered a data source, you can continue with the instructions given previously.

FIG. 8.9
The dialog box in which you enter information about the data source for HTX/IDC and ASP pages. You won't see this if all of your pages are static HTML.

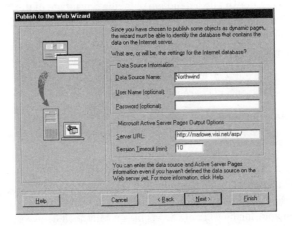

Instead of creating individual HTML files (with the extension .HTM), Access creates pairs of files that, together, are used to generate a Web page on demand. Most of the HTML is stored in the HTX files, along with special tags that IIS recognizes when a user tries to view a page. When IIS receives a request for an IDC page, it parses the page, looking for information about how to connect with the database and what data to extract. It then reads the associated HTX file and replaces those special tags with the data it retrieved. IIS then generates a new, standard HTML page, using the format specified in the HTX file, and returns the generated HTML to the user's Web browser.

Remember that you must have created a "system" ODBC data source referencing your database file to use Internet Data Connector pages. During a Web session, when a remote user requests an HTX/IDC page, IIS communicates with Windows to obtain the data for the page via ODBC. If you don't have an ODBC data source set up correctly (as detailed in Access help), your users will see error messages when trying to view your pages. All of the HTX/IDC pages generated look exactly the same as the static HTML pages in Figures 8.6, and 8.8. The only difference is that external users request IDC files and not HTML files, and the data is regenerated as of the moment when it's requested.

Active Server Pages (ASP)

The creation and use of Active Server Pages (ASP) is a mixed blessing. Yes, you can create Web pages that look like the forms you see on the screen in Access. The layout is essentially preserved, most of the controls you'd normally use in a form survive the conversion, and you can actually change the data in the database (which you can't do with either of the other types of pages).

Unfortunately, there's a lot that can go wrong in the process of creating ASP pages, and they really don't look good as they come out of Access. The script language that creates ASP pages is flexible, but Access doesn't do a good job of taking advantage of the language. If you're comfortable manually designing ASP pages, you can create incredibly flashy, extremely dynamic pages with ASP; however, you'll probably be disappointed with the results you get creating them directly from Access.

You may not be able to get ASP to work correctly at all, especially if you're setting up ASP for the first time on a Web server. There are several common problems you may encounter:

- **Not using a Microsoft Web server.** Your Web server must be running Internet Information Server (IIS) on Windows NT or Personal Web Server (PWS) on Windows 95.

- **Not using a Microsoft browser.** At this writing, the only generally available Web browser that supports ActiveX controls is Microsoft Internet Explorer (IE). Other browsers can read ASP pages, but the buttons and custom controls you may have included in your forms will only be visible on Microsoft browsers.

- **The server must have ASP installed correctly.** ASP and the Microsoft Access Desktop Driver must be installed on the server; neither is installed by default with IIS. ASP can be downloaded as part of the IIS 3.0 update from Microsoft (**http://www. microsoft.com/iis**), and the Access Desktop Driver is installed as part of the default Access (not IIS) installation process. Additionally, the server must have a directory (or directories) designated for ASP pages, and the permissions on those directories must be set to Read and Execute in the IIS configuration.

- **A data source must be set up.**   The server must have a system data source config-ured for the database your pages access. This is done with the ODBC applet (32 Bit ODBC on Windows 95) in Control Panel.

- **Your pages can't be too complex.**   Pages using custom controls (including the Tab control) or that depend on code won't work, because ASP doesn't support them. Additionally, you may have problems if your tables or forms include too much data (the server will time out) or special characters (like % and \), because the server interprets those as ASP commands.

Figure 8.9 shows the additional dialog box in the Save as HTML process that is used to specify data source information for HTX/IDC and ASP pages. For ASP, you need to specify the name of the ODBC data source (and user name and password, if required by ODBC), as well as the server uniform resource locator (URL) and timeout.

Getting the Server URL correct is particularly critical, and Access help is sparse on this topic. The value you enter in this block should be the fully qualified URL for the final destination of your pages. In Figure 8.9, the pages live on the machine marlowe.visi.net in the virtual direc-tory asp. This is not necessarily the physical location of the files on the machine; this is where they appear to be to remote users. Enter a forward slash after the end of your URL and don't use quotes or special characters. This value is hard-coded into your ASP pages; if it's wrong (or if your pages are moved), they won't work anymore.

N O T E   Two files make up every ASP page. The one we are usually referring to is called *object*.asp, where *object* is the name of the database object saved as HTML. It contains layout information for the page that is returned to the remote browser.

The other half of this pair is called *object*alx.asp. This file, called the ALX file contains the code that includes the location of the data file and the URL of the server. The values you enter for the data source name and server URL are stored in this file, which must accompany its associated ASP file wherever it goes.

If you move your pages from one server to another (or just to a different location on the same server), you can manually edit the ALX file to correct the reference instead of regenerating the pages, if you like. Similarly, if you change the data source name, you can make the modifications in the ALX file if you don't want to regenerate the pages and aren't afraid of the code. ▪

The value you enter for the timeout applies only to your remote clients. The default value, 1, means that remote browsers should wait no more than one minute for the data to be sent from the server before giving up. This value may well be too small if you work over a slow data line or if your network is slow. Furthermore, this value doesn't affect the server's timeout at all. That value, set to 90 seconds by default, is often too slow for large pages (like the Orders page below). It must be changed by manually editing the ASP pages or changing a Windows regis-try setting on the server.

ASP is only useful for dynamic database objects like forms, queries, and tables. Reports are static and are saved as static HTML even if you tell Access to save them as ASP. In this ongoing example, the two reports saved as ASP really were stored as static HTML, and look like Figure 8.8. Tables do pretty well, too; refer to Figure 8.4 for a reminder of how the Orders table looked in Access, and see how it looks as an Active Server Page in Figure 8.10.

FIG. 8.10

The Orders table as an Active Server Page. This page will almost always time-out both server and client.

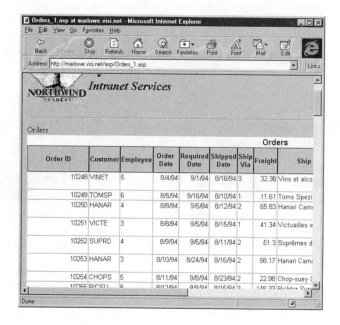

All of the data is here, and it looks good. You can even change it and the changes are saved in the database (if the database permits changes).

Forms don't fare so well. Consider the Categories form in Figures 8.6 and 8.7. Created as an Active Server Page, it looks like Figure 8.11.

There are a few of things to note here:

- The organization of the page is based on the maximum sizes of the data fields, not the actual size of the data in them. This makes the control for the Description field appear too large for the data displayed in it.

- The Products subform looks good, largely because it uses the datasheet layout, which converts well. The relationship between the master and child forms is preserved.

- The buttons at the bottom of the screen are provided by Access and are automatically inserted on any form converted to ASP. The arrow buttons traverse the records in the database, and the three buttons commit changes to the database, delete records, or refresh the values on the display, respective to their positions on the screen.

While this form shows the data in the data source correctly, it leaves a lot to be desired in the way of layout. Similar results are obtained by converting the Customers form, which translates correctly, but not very pretty (see Figure 8.12):

FIG. 8.11
The Categories form in ASP. The logo at the top of the page has been cropped out for clarity.

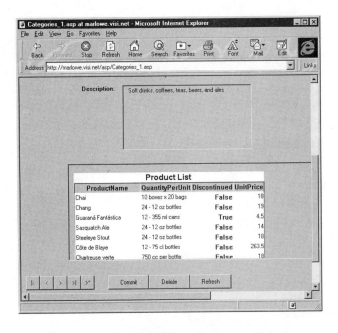

FIG. 8.12
The Customers form as ASP. Note that the colors and placement of the controls are maintained, but their sizes are not.

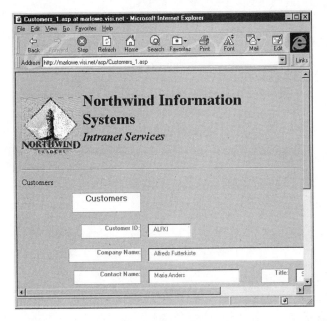

Using the Web Publishing Wizard

An additional Wizard is provided on the Office 97 CD that can make the task of publishing your Web pages a little easier. The Web Publishing Wizard is not installed by default, but if you'll be using Access to update pages on a Web server frequently, you may want to install and use it.

The manual way to publish Web pages involves creating the pages, saving them on the local machine, and copying them to the server machine in the appropriate directory. If the remote machine is a locally connected PC, you can use NetBEUI (via the Network Neighborhood) to copy the files across, which is pretty easy. But if the remote machine is on another network or across the Internet, you'd usually have to use File Transfer Protocol (FTP) to copy your files, and FTP isn't very easy to use without special software and a little experience. Instead of FTP, you can try the Web Publishing Wizard.

To install the Web Publishing Wizard:

1. Insert the Office 97 CD into your CD drive. If a directory of the files doesn't appear automatically, open it in Windows Explorer.
2. Change to the directory Valupack\Webpost.
3. Double-click Webpost.exe to install the Web Publishing Wizard. You'll have to restart your computer after installing it.

The Web Publishing Wizard can be used in two ways: independently, or as part of the Save as HTML process in Access (and other Office 97 applications). In general, it's easiest to run it independently to set it up the first time, and then use it from the application creating the Web pages from then on.

To configure the Web Publishing Wizard for your Internet provider:

1. Start the Wizard by clicking the Start button, then Programs, then Accessories, then Internet Tools, and finally Web Publishing Wizard. A Welcome dialog box appears; click Next.
2. You'll be asked to specify the local location of the files you want to publish to the Web. If you've already created them, use the Browse button to specify their directory on the disk. If the directory you specify includes files in subfolders, be sure to select the Include subfolders check box. If you haven't created the files yet, don't worry—you can still proceed to set up the server information. Just select any file on your disk to proceed. Click Next to continue.

N O T E You can either select a directory (with or without its subdirectories), or a file. You can't select multiple files in different directories, or a subset of the files in a given directory. ▪

3. The third dialog box asks for the name of your Web server. If your ISP is either CompuServe or SPRY, you're in luck—they're already configured. Most of you will need to click the New button to set up our individual servers.
4. After you click on New, you can specify a name for the connection you're setting up. The Wizard suggests "My Web Site"; you may want to be a little more descriptive by typing another name in the box. The name you enter here is the name by which this connection is referenced from now on; Access calls it the "friendly name" of your server during the Save as HTML process.

5. In the same dialog box, choose the name of your Internet Service Provider (ISP). If you use America Online, CompuServe, GNN, or SPRY to connect to the Internet, there are entries already made for you. If you are using Microsoft FrontPage to manage your Web site, FrontPage knows how to connect to your ISP and you should choose FrontPage here. Otherwise, select <Other Internet Provider> and click Next to continue.

6. The next dialog box asks you to enter the URL for your pages on your ISP's Web server. Many ISPs host Web services on computers running the UNIX operating system; these servers usually store your pages in a directory identified by your username proceeded by a tilde (~), as in ~jones. If you're not sure of the URL for your pages on your ISP's server, ask the ISP. After you've entered it, click Next.

7. The next dialog box asks how you're connected to your Web server. If you have a full-time connection to the Internet or your server is located on the same local network as your development PC, select Local Area Network. Otherwise, choose the name of the Dial-Up Networking connection you use to contact your ISP. You can even create a new dial-up connection from here by clicking New Dial-Up Connection.

8. When you click Next, the Wizard attempts to connect to the server you specified. If it succeeds, you're done and you can use this Wizard directly from Access from now on. If not, you have a few more questions to answer. The next questions asks whether to use FTP or Windows networking to transfer your files; if your server is running IIS and is on a local network drive, you can choose Windows networking and click Next (follow Step 9a). Otherwise, choose FTP and click Next (follow Step 9b).

9a. If you chose Windows file transfer in the previous step, enter the name and directory of your Web server in the standard Uniform Naming Convention (UNC) format. This is usually two backslashes (\\), the name of the server, a backslash, the name of the folder or shared directory on the server, and the directory path to the destination. Also enter the URL for your home directory on the Web server again (this is probably the same as in Step 6). Finally, click Next to start the process of sending your pages to the server via Windows networking.

9b. If you chose FTP in the previous step, enter your username and password for the server; these are required for FTP. Click Next and enter the name of your FTP server (which may be the same as the name of your Web server; they are probably the same physical machine in any case). Click Next to continue, and enter the name of the folder (directory) on the FTP server where your files should be placed. You also need to enter the URL for your home directory on the Web server again (this is probably the same as in Step 6). Finally, click Next to start the process of sending your pages to the server via FTP.

Ideally, your pages should be pushed to your Web server and you're ready to go. Next time, choose the name of the connection you just set up and you won't have to go through all of the configuration screens again. ●

Improving Database Performance

After you have a database in place, you may want to consider taking a look at your design and making some modifications to improve the reliability and performance of your system. This process can start at any point in the development process; in fact, modifying the database often helps ensure good design and trouble-free use. Access provides several tools that can help you get the most out of your database and out of the Access environment. ∎

Use the Performance Analyzer

The Performance Analyzer inspects the design of each object in your database and makes recommendations as to how it can be improved.

Decrease disk space requirements

As you create and delete database objects, the space that Access has allocated for them becomes free, but Access saves room until you tell it to stop.

Use the Repair tool to resolve corruption

In rare cases, objects in your database may become corrupted and cause errors in the operation of your system. The Repair tool fixes some of the more likely problems.

Set Overall Options for the database

Instead of writing special code to open a form on startup, prevent users from changing forms, and so on, Access includes a dialog box that sets options for the entire database at the outset.

Consider other performance-related issues

There are several things you can do to improve the performance of your application without the help of automated tools.

Using the Performance Analyzer

The Performance Analyzer tool, new in Access 97, inspects the objects in your database that you specify and recommends changes to improve the operation of your database. Its changes may not necessarily improve the appearance or maintainability of your database, however. For example, one of the Performance Analyzer's favorite suggestions is that you convert SQL statements in code modules to saved queries. While this may improve performance marginally, it certainly increases the clutter in the Database window when you're trying to find a particular query to edit. You have to take the Analyzer's recommendations at face value and apply the power of your developer's intuition to its suggestions to decide whether the recommendations are worth taking.

To run the Performance Analyzer on an existing database:

1. Open the database. From the Database window, click the Tools menu, then select Analyze, and then Performance.

2. You can select any specific object in the database by choosing a tab (Form, Table, Query, Report, Macro, Module) and clicking the check box next to the names of the objects you want analyzed. There are two special tabs:

    *   The All tab lists all of the objects in the database in one pane (making it easy to select all of the objects at once).

    *   The Current Database tab lists the Relationships and VBA Project objects, which are maintained separately from the user objects but can still be analyzed.

    You also can use the Select, Select All, and Deselect All buttons at the right side of the Performance Analyzer window if you prefer. Choose OK to continue after you've selected the objects to be analyzed.

3. The Performance Analyzer runs and you'll see the Analysis Results window on the right side of the window; in addition to buttons for selecting specific problems is an Optimize button; if you select a problem that Access can fix all by itself (like converting a SQL command to a stored query), clicking Optimize will make it happen.

The Analysis Results window (see Figure 9.1) includes a top pane (the Analysis Results) that contains a list of identified problems and a bottom pane (Analysis Notes) that gives details on each problem as you select it.

Each problem is marked by one of four icons representing the severity or status of the problem:

 Recommendations are solutions for major problems that will adversely impact the operation of the database if not corrected. Access can automatically implement Recommendations.

 Suggestions point out less severe problems that should be fixed for optimum performance, but they may have significant side effects to consider. Access can automatically implement Suggestions.

FIG. 9.1

The results of an analysis of the Northwind database. Naturally, there are no Recommendations or Suggestions to fix.

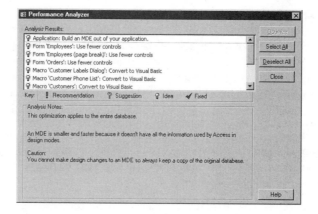

Ideas are general comments about database design that may improve performance, but are not simple to implement. Access cannot automatically implement Ideas.

Fixed items used to be Recommendations or Suggestions, but were corrected by clicking the Optimize button after selecting them. If you run the Performance Analyzer again, they won't appear.

While the recommendations of the Performance Analyzer may seem esoteric or to have minimal impact when taken individually, you may see quantifiable results from implementing a group of recommendations. Certainly, there's rarely any reason why you shouldn't take action on a Suggestion as identified by the Analyzer, and you should almost always follow recommendations given as Recommendations. Of course, with experience you'll begin to recognize that certain suggestions the Performance Analyzer makes may have a detrimental effect on your ability to maintain the database, but you can really only learn to recognize those after you've already implemented them once.

Compacting and Repairing

Databases, like any disk-based program, can sometimes get damaged by the forces of nature and the vagaries of PC architecture. Lost clusters, power surges, network confusion, and small gremlins that live in Windows 95 and NT that feed on programmer anxiety are all to blame; fortunately, Access provides a method for fixing databases that are corrupted by one or more of these things.

The Database Repair tool provided by Access isn't a panacea, however. Its biggest limitation is that it only repairs damaged tables and queries; if a corrupt element in a form or report is making your database act flaky, Repair can't help. For those times when a database application just doesn't seem to be working right, though, Repair may be able to help.

A less serious, though related problem, is the issue of database bloat. Whenever you create objects in your database, Access allocates space for them in memory. When your database is saved to disk (as happens frequently in Access), space also is allocated on the disk. When you delete an object, Access reports to Windows that it's done with the memory that object was using, and Windows reclaims available memory from Access. However, the size of your database on disk won't necessarily decrease without some user intervention, because Windows keeps putting the (now smaller) database file back in the same place on the disk, and that place may be too big for the database after a few deletions. When you compact your database, you ask Access to make a copy of it in a new place on the disk, using only the space it really needs instead of the maximum space it's needed in the past.

A new feature in Access 97 enables you to compact and repair databases that you haven't yet opened. The procedures for repairing or compacting a closed database are almost identical to the procedures for fixing an open one.

To compact or repair a database that's already open in Access:

1. Click the Tools menu, then select Database Utilities, then either Compact Database or Repair Database.

2. Access closes the open database and performs the action you selected, replacing the current database in memory and on disk with the fixed one. If you select Repair Database, you'll see a confirmation message telling you that the database was successfully repaired, even if no errors were found.

To compact or repair a database that's not open:

1. Close any database you have open.

2. Click the Tools menu, then select Database Utilities, then either Compact Database or Repair Database.

3. Access opens a file selection dialog box, enabling you to select a database file and click OK. If you select Compact, Access opens a second file selection dialog box and recommends db1.mdb as the destination for the compacted database; generally, you should select Save and then Yes when asked for confirmation to replace the file.

4. Access performs the action you selected, replacing the database you selected with the fixed one. If you chose Repair Database, you'll see a confirmation message telling you that the database was successfully repaired, even if no errors were found.

If you're sure your database is corrupted and you can't fix it by using these tools, make a copy of your database and try to figure out which database object is causing the problem, working from the copy. If you have problems consistently while working with a particular object, try to delete that object and re-create it from scratch. If you're using any custom controls (including the problematic Tab control), try deleting those. If all else fails, create a new database and import the objects from the problem database one by one (click the File menu, then Get External Data, then Import from the menu; choose the database to import from and select each object to import). After importing each object, test the new database and make sure it's working correctly until you find the offending object.

Setting Database Options

While the Options dialog box doesn't strictly impact the performance of your database (as measured by its speed or size), it has a great effect on the behavior of the database as you develop your application. It's relevant as a performance issue because setting these options appropriately can significantly ease your development effort, making development faster and more efficient and the operation of your application more streamlined. Because the amount of time it takes to develop an application may affect the bottom line as much as the actual running of the delivered product, why not optimize the development process?

To view and change Access' options, click the Tools menu, then select Options. The Options dialog box appears with ten tabs pertaining to different parts of the database. Many are self-explanatory (and pressing F1 while the cursor is in a particular pane gives application-specific help), but some highlights of each tab's options are discussed here:

- **View**.   The visibility of certain database objects can be changed with options on this sheet. For example, if you frequently create macro groups, you may want the Macro Names column of the Macro Builder visible by default.

- **General**.   The default location where databases are stored is saved in a text box on this sheet; if you don't normally save your databases in C:\My Documents, you can change this option to make it easier to load database files into Access. Other options available on this sheet include the default page margins for reports and a toggle to turn sound effects on or off.

- **Hyperlinks/HTML**.   The appearance of hyperlinks in tables and forms is set here, as well as the options for database objects saved as HTML. These options are also set as part of the Save as HTML process.

- **Edit/Find**.   Several options for searches and filters are set here, but the most useful options to change on this sheet are the Confirm Record Changes, Document Deletions, and Action Queries options. All are on by default, but you can turn one or all of them off here if the confirmation dialog boxes annoy you.

 T I P It's not a good idea to change these options if you're developing a database you intend to distribute, because the options may not be set the same in the users' copies of Access. These confirmations also can be modified in VBA code, which you know will get distributed with your application by using the SetWarnings action.

▶ **See** "Handling Errors and Confirmations," **p. 217**

- **Keyboard**.   When users enter a text box on a form, the arrow and Enter keys have certain default behaviors. This sheet enables changing those defaults, which may be confusing to some and beneficial to others.

- **Datasheet**.   The default Access datasheet looks like an Excel spreadsheet—black Arial text on a white background, with gridlines separating rows across 1-inch columns. If you prefer gaudy colors or fonts and textured cells, you can set those options on this sheet.

Part
II

Ch
9

■ **Tables/Queries.** When you create a table, Access assumes that each field you create is of type Text, length 50. If you change a field to the data type Number, Access assumes it's a Long Integer. If you're creating a table and you know from the start that all (or most) of the fields will be numeric, you can change the default field type on this sheet and save a lot of clicking during table design. It's always a good idea to use the smallest data type you can; doing so can have a positive impact on the performance of your application as the memory and disk overhead of your database decreases.

 ■ **Forms/Reports.** If you're creating a form or report, create a control, and edit the control's properties, sometimes a small ellipsis button appears in the Property sheet. This means that a Builder is available for this property. Usually, you're prompted to run the Macro Builder, the Query Builder, or the Code Builder when you click that button. Most of the time, you want to create an Event Procedure, so you almost always choose the Code Builder. Selecting "Always Use Event Procedures" on this sheet bypasses that selection process and always starts the Code Builder during form or report design. Other options on this sheet include the behavior of marquees drawn around multiple objects and the default templates for forms and reports.

■ **Module.** The appearance of the code development environment (colors, fonts, and so on) is defined on this sheet. You also can turn off the hints and syntax checking that Access performs by default while you enter code (see Figure 9.2). A useful option, turned on by default, is Require Variable Declaration. This option forces programmers to declare variables instead of letting Access guess as to their data types, preventing potential problems during program execution.

▶ **See** "Select Queries," **p. 72**

▶ **See** "Using the Publish to the Web Wizard," **p. 148**

▶ **See** "The Code Builder Window," **p. 175**

FIG. 9.2

The Options dialog box, opened to the Module sheet. You can customize most aspects of the Access environment with the options available in this dialog box.

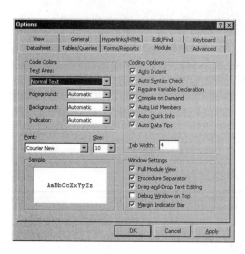

■ **Advanced**.   These options concern the way Access handles requests from external applications (using ODBC and DDE) and users connected via a network. You'll rarely be concerned with any of these.

It's important to realize that changes made in the Options dialog box affect only the local installation of Access. If you're developing applications for distribution, or setting up a system for training, you'll probably want to stick with the defaults to prevent the problems that will arise when your database (or customers) use different machines.

Other Performance Considerations

The Performance Analyzer and Repair and Compact tools work well, but they only affect the performance of a specific database. In Access, there are several things you can do to improve the performance of your applications. Many of these recommendations are common sense to experienced developers, but all of them can have a real impact on the performance of your application:

■ **Don't skimp on system memory**.   Surprisingly, a dearth of available memory will slow your system down more severely than an underpowered CPU will. Access 97 runs quite capably on an older 486 CPU with 32M of memory, but it's a dog on a Pentium Pro with 12M. At this writing, memory is cheap (about $5 per megabyte), and adding memory increases development speed and decreases programmer frustration considerably. Also try to limit the number of applications you run while you're running Access. Access is a resource hog, both for system memory and disk activity. You don't want to try to download an enormous file from the Internet while you're timing an Access application.

■ **Cut down on the glitz**.   Background images and bitmaps look nice on forms and reports, but they take time to load and they eat memory like candy. If you use a 1M bitmap as a form background, you increase the size of your database by slightly more than 1M both on disk and in memory. On a 16M machine, a couple of bitmaps can bring the system to a crawl.

■ **Use MDE files**.   If your application is essentially finished and you're running it more than changing it, consider saving it as an MDE file. MDE files are the same as normal database files, but Access removes all editing capabilities from them. This "lightening" of the application usually improves performance noticeably, but at a cost—you can't edit an MDE file. Save the original MDB file for modifications and development, and give users the MDE version instead.

■ **Pretend you're a server**.   If you're running Windows 95, your machine is probably not configured for maximal use of its CPU and RAM resources. You can make a simple change to help this:

1. Open Control Panel and select the System applet.

2. Click the Performance tab and click the File System button at the bottom of the window.

Part

II

Ch

9

3. If the Typical role of this machine is set to Desktop Computer, change it to Network Server even if it isn't really a network server.

4. Click OK twice and close Control Panel.

You can check Access help for many more ideas that may help improve database performance. From the menu, click Help, then select Contents and Index, then type **Performance** in the search box. ●

CHAPTER 10

Programming Using Modules and Visual Basic for Applications

If tables, queries, forms, and reports comprise the major pieces of an Access database, modules are the glue that keeps the pieces together. These groups of functions and subroutines, written in the standard Visual Basic for Applications (VBA) language, provide all of the underlying functionality of a database; in most database applications, there's a lot that isn't immediately obvious from what you see on-screen. Calculation, data validation, graphic effects, and communication between database objects are all normally handled by customized code residing in modules. The inclusion of code modules in a database converts the database from a storage warehouse for data into an application—an environment in which users perform work with the data.

The topic of modules and the workings of VBA are sufficiently intricate that this topic will take three chapters, and parts of a few more, to cover. Chapter 11, uses the code modules included in the Northwind database as examples as you explore the ins and outs of writing programs in Access. In Chapter 12, you will use code to manipulate Access' built-in error handlers and internal structures, and learn how to write programs that interact directly with Windows.

What is a module, and how do you write one?

The Code Builder environment gives you a blank sheet of paper to write on, and it even tries to help you.

Changing properties with VBA

You can use code to change the properties of objects, the same properties you manipulated in the objects' Design view in earlier chapters.

Dealing with events

Access is constantly watching your database for notable occurrences, like the changing of records and the opening of forms. You can write code that jumps in and takes charge whenever one of these events is detected.

Using subroutines and functions

It's good practice to write code in small, reusable blocks called *subroutines* or *functions*. This chapter discusses the similarities and differences.

Using Access' built-in functions

Access includes dozens of functions that perform calculations, extract data, and manipulate the appearance of objects. Knowing what functions are already available keeps you from having to write new ones.

This chapter starts with the ins and outs of the coding environment. If you're not particularly interested in writing full-blown applications using Access and just want to increase the functionality of your existing databases, this chapter may be all you need. ■

The Visual Basic for Applications Environment

The language in which you program Access, called Visual Basic for Applications (VBA), represents an attempt by Microsoft to standardize the programming language used across all of the Office applications. Before Office 95, each application had its own programming language and environment for coding; these were called "Access Basic," "Word Basic," and so on. Starting with Office 95, all of the Office applications use the language called VBA, with appropriate customizations for each application to match its capabilities. In VBA under Word, for example, you typically write code that affects a selected block of text; the concept of selected text is all but irrelevant in Access, so those constructs are specific to Word. Access has plenty of its own customizations that aren't useful when programming other Office applications, and you'll become familiar with several of these as you read on.

While the general feel and flow of VBA is now the same across all of the Office applications, the programming environment isn't quite standard. Every VBA-compliant application, except for Access, uses a standard programming environment, called the Visual Basic Editor, for writing code modules. Access has such a large installed base of programmers and applications that would be seriously inconvenienced by a major change in the environment that Microsoft decided to preserve most of the major elements of the old Access 2.0 programming environment even through Access 97. For the most part, the skills you develop writing Access code will serve you well if you decide later to learn "standard" VBA, or even Microsoft's full-featured Visual Basic programming language. But it's worth remembering that the development environment in Access is a different than the environment in the other applications, even though the programming language is more or less the same.

NOTE Curious about how the Visual Basic Editor differs from Access' Code Builder? After you're familiar with Code Builder, start the VB Editor by starting Word 97, clicking the Tools menu, then Macro, then Visual Basic Editor. ■

The Two Types of Modules

In Access's Database window, the six tabs across the top represent the most commonly used objects: tables, queries, forms, reports, macros, and modules. Access modules come in two flavors, however, only one of which is accessible via the Modules tab in the Database window:

■ Standard modules are stand-alone programs that have names and can exist independently of any other object in the database. It's possible to design a database that includes nothing but standard modules; these modules can create any other type of object on demand. In fact, the Access wizards that create new databases (click the File menu, then New) are really just groups of standard modules saved in separate files. As you select the options you want to include in your database, those standard modules create the tables and forms your database will need. You manage and edit standard modules via the Database window, where all standard modules appear under the Modules tab.

- Class modules are modules that are associated with other database objects, like controls, forms, and reports. A module that performs some action after a user clicks a button on a form is usually implemented as a class module associated with the button on the form. Class modules don't show up in the Database window.

To view a class module associated with a form, report, table, or query:

1. Open the object in Design view.
2. Click the <u>V</u>iew menu, then select <u>C</u>ode from the menu.

If the object is a control on a form or report:

1. Open the form or report containing the control in Design view and select the control.
2. Click the <u>V</u>iew menu, then select <u>P</u>roperties to view the control's properties
3. Select the Event tab in the Property sheet. You can tell that there are class modules associated with events for this control when the expression [Event Procedure] is listed next to an event name in the Property sheet.

4. To view the code associated with a given event procedure (which is really a class module), select the event procedure you're interested in and click the Builder button that appears next to it when you select it.

▶ **See** "Events," **p. 200**

You can create a new class module in the same way that you view an existing one. If there is no module currently associated with a given event or object, Access will open up a blank Code Builder window, assuming you intend to write code.

N O T E In rare cases, Access 97 allows you to write class modules that appear in the Database window. This special kind of class module is associated with a custom object that's not one of the standard Access types, such as an Excel spreadsheet or PowerPoint presentation. This kind of module is used in "Controlling Other Applications" in Chapter 12. For the most part, only standard modules are visible in the Database window. ■

To create a new standard module from the Database window:

1. Select the Modules tab.
2. Click <u>N</u>ew.

Unlike the other object types, there's no wizard to help you here. You'll end up in a blank Code Builder window.

The Code Builder Window

To edit existing code or start to write a new module, you use the Code Builder. Figure 10.1 shows what the Code Builder looks like when you open the standard module "Utility Functions" in the Northwind database in Design view.

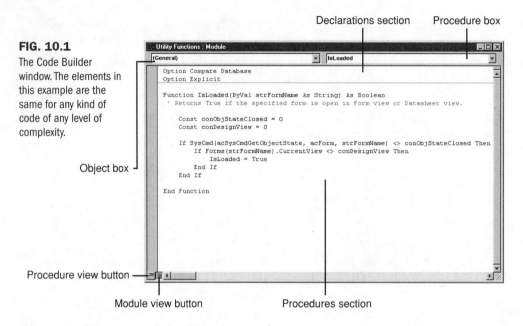

FIG. 10.1

The Code Builder window. The elements in this example are the same for any kind of code of any level of complexity.

Declarations section

Procedure box

Object box

Procedure view button

Module view button

Procedures section

Ignoring the code in the window for now, let's look at the regions of the window:

The Declarations section contains statements that set global options for this module and tell Access the data type of any variables used in the code. Variable dimension (Dim) statements (which declare the types of any variables you care to use) located in this section are available to any procedure in this module; if the Dim statement is placed within a procedure, that variable is only available within that procedure. Option statements must not be in the module procedure itself (because they're needed to determine how the module will run), so they're declared in this region. To add new options, you place the cursor in this region (delimited by the horizontal bar at the bottom) and start typing. Access won't let you put any procedural code (that is, code that actually does something, rather than set up variable storage or set options) in this region.

▶ **See** "Variables and Variable Scope," **p. 205**

The Procedures section is where the meat of the code belongs. To enter or edit statements in the Procedures section, place the cursor in this region and start typing. Access won't let you put Option statements in this region; they belong in the Declarations section.

The Object box is a pull-down combo box containing the names of objects in a form or report that may have code associated with them. This feature allows you to view class modules associated with various controls on a form or report without returning to Design view to select them. Clicking the down arrow in this box lists all controls in the form or report, allowing you to write new code or edit existing code for any control in the form or report. In standard modules, this box only contains one entry, "General."

The Procedure box lists by name all subroutine and function defined so far in the current standard or class module. The Declarations section is also listed here. Selecting a procedure in this box quickly takes you to the beginning of that subroutine or procedure to view or edit it. This box only lists subroutines and procedures in the current class or standard module.

▶ **See** "What's the Difference Between a Subroutine and a Function?" **p. 181**

The Procedure view and Module view buttons change the way code is displayed in the Code Builder. The default is Procedure view, which displays all procedures (declarations, subroutines, and functions) in the current module in one list. This view makes it easy to navigate among several related procedures (by scrolling up and down), but can be overwhelming. Switching to Module view (by clicking the Module view button) lists each procedure in a separate section, navigable by selecting individual procedures in the Procedure box.

Part
II

Ch
10

In the standard module shown in Figure 10.1, you can discern the following things about this procedure:

- The title bar on the window tells you that it's a standard module called "Utility Functions."
- The Procedure view button is depressed, so you're probably seeing all there is to the module. If there were any other procedures in it, they would be visible and separated by a horizontal line.

N O T E   Blank lines don't affect the running of code and can help readability. It's possible in this case that there's another procedure off the screen, separated from the one that's visible by many blank lines. But it's unusual to include more than one blank line in a module, so that's unlikely. Also, the vertical scroll bar at the right side of the window is full, implying that there's no scrolling to be done. In any case, you can confirm that there are no other procedures in this module by pulling down the list in the Procedures box. ▪

- The procedure IsLoaded is active, and that procedure's name appears in the Procedure box. If the cursor was in the Declarations section, (Declarations) would be visible in the Procedure box.

Access automatically color-codes VBA code as follows:

- Blue text represents reserved words in Access, such as Function, True, If, and so on. Most lines in a procedure start with a reserved word or Access-recognized function name.
- Black text makes up most of the body of the code.
- Green text denotes comments, included by the programmer to document what the code is doing. You create a comment in VBA by starting any text with a single quotation mark ('); Access will ignore anything from the quotation mark to the end of the line. You can start whole lines with quotation marks, or enter one at any place in a line of text.

■ Red text contains errors that won't get by the Access compiler, such as misspelled commands or incomplete statements. By default, Access watches for this kind of error as you type and lets you know when you make a syntax error of this type. The offending text remains red until the error is corrected.

TIP If Access' constant error-checking is annoying, you can turn it off by clicking the Tools menu, then selecting Options. Select the Modules tab and turn off the Auto Syntax Check option. Access still flags these errors later when you save or compile the module.

You can have as many code windows open at a time as you like; just follow the instructions given previously to open a new window. The standard Window commands (Cascade, Tile, and so on) are available to you to manage your desktop; this makes it especially easy to compare and copy code between modules.

A note about terminology is important here: Visual Basic for Applications is an *interpreted* language. This means that, when the code is run, a special program called an *interpreter* (Access in this case) reads every line of code one by one, *parses* each line (converts it to machine instructions the CPU can understand, called *object code*), and *executes* (runs) the object code. VBA programs are saved just as they appear on -screen. In *compiled* languages, like C and C++, a special program called a *compiler* does the interpreting and parsing ahead of time. The results of the compilation (called *object code*) are saved and that object code is what's actually executed. When talking about Access, we sometimes use the word "compile" to mean "examine all of the code for obvious errors." VBA code is usually compiled before saving it, but in this context it's important to understand that it's not really saved as object code as in traditional compilers.

Procedures

All VBA code is written in *procedures*, which are blocks of code with a definite beginning and end. Procedures stand-alone in modules; you can't nest procedures within procedures. In most cases, though, procedures can call other procedures, and well-written code generally consists of a lot of short, easy-to-understand procedures that call each other. This type of programming is called *modular*, and it's easy to understand and easy to maintain.

In Access, most of the things that you want a program to do are simple and straightforward. You might want to write code to set the properties of a form, or to save the results of a query in a table. If possible, you should limit the length of your procedures so they fill no more than about one screen in the Code Builder window at a time. Sometimes, this is impossible, but most of the time you'll be able to break your code down into separate procedures that are all less than one screen in length.

Organizing Your Thoughts in Pseudocode

You may find it useful to plan your code before writing it by using a style called *pseudocode* to organize your processes. You write pseudocode by outlining the processes that your code will follow in much the same way that you might write a paper. Instead of outlining in sentences, though, you write short names for the actions you want your program to take. Once you have the pseudocode outline written, all you have to do is fill in the blanks to make your program work.

Consider this example: You want to write a program that will instruct a robot to do your grocery shopping. To program the robot, you first organize the process in your mind, then you write an outline of what the robot should do, and then you write the actual instructions the robot can understand. Your first pseudocode outline might look like this:

```
go_to_store
get_groceries
come_home
```

N O T E Use lowercase letters to start the names of procedures and variables because that's a convention that many programmers follow. You can do it any way you like, but the use of uppercase letters to start words usually implies to most programmers that the word means something specific to the compiler, like "If" or "True." ■

When coding, you generally use the underscore character (_) instead of spaces in the names of objects and procedures. Access usually doesn't mind spaces, but they can complicate the coding process later when it's not clear where a word or phrase ends. Under each of the major tasks above ("go to store," etc.), there are a lot of subtasks. You can fill in some of the blanks as you break the process down in your mind, and a second try might look like this:

```
go_to_store
        make_shopping_list
        get_in_car
        drive_to_store
get_groceries
        go_in_store
        retrieve_items
        check_out
come_home
        get_in_car
        drive_home
        put_away_groceries
```

Obviously, you can break each of these down even more, until you're finally at the level where you can write instructions in the robot's programming language (probably not VBA) that actually makes it do these things.

Programming in almost any *procedural* language works the same way. After the pseudocode is written, each of the lines in the outline becomes a procedure. You can even call the procedure the same name as the line in your pseudocode. The more you can break the process down before you start coding, the better-organized the final code will be.

N O T E Some programming languages are not procedural. These are languages with special uses, and most often languages that emulate thought processes (like expert systems and artificial intelligence systems). Non-procedural languages don't follow a specific sequence of events; you're not guaranteed that lines of code will be processed in order. Needless to say, this kind of code is difficult to write and is very unusual, but it's worth noting that this style of pseudocoding is most useful for procedural languages. ▦

Converting Pseudocode to VBA Procedures

There are two types of procedures in VBA:

- ▦ *Subroutines* are procedures that don't return a value. They have a definite beginning (a Sub statement), and a definite end (an End Sub statement). Subroutines can take parameters by including the name and type of the parameter on the first line of the subroutine, as in the following:

```
Sub drive (destination as String)
```

- ▦ *Functions* are procedures that return a value to the procedure that called them. They have a definite beginning (a Function statement), and a definite end (an End Function statement). The first line of a function usually defines the data type of the value it will return. Functions can take parameters by including the name and type of the parameter on the first line of the function, as in the following:

```
Function drive (destination as String) as Boolean
```

In VBA, each of the lines in the pseudocode outline might represent a procedure, because each line implies that it uses code that completes a specific action.

VBA syntax can be quite involved, but the online help is quite detailed and helpful. For information on any VBA keyword or method, you can type the keyword in the Code Builder window and press F1 for context-sensitive help.

To create a new subroutine:

1. In the Procedures section of the Code Builder, type **Sub *subname***, where *subname* is the name of your subroutine. Access automatically inserts a horizontal line above the subroutine declaration and writes the End Sub statement in a new line for you.

2. Enter variable declarations and options in the Declaration section.

3. Enter statements between the Sub and End Sub statements.

To create a new function:

1. In the Procedures section of the Code Builder, type **Function *functname***, where *functname* is the name of your function. Access automatically inserts a horizontal line above the subroutine declaration and writes the End Function statement in a new line for you.

2. Enter variable declarations and options in the Declaration section.

3. Enter statements between the Function and End Function statements.

To save a standard module, click the File menu, then Save. Access prompts you for a name, which then appears in the Database window. To save a class module, save the object the class module is attached to. In either case, you could also use the Save button on the toolbar.

 TIP To save your code to a text file (for printing or pasting into another application), click the File menu, then Save As Text. You'll be prompted for a file name.

What's the Difference Between a Subroutine and a Function?   Some of the procedures in the example outline don't need to provide any feedback. For example, we might assume that the procedure `make_shopping_list` will always complete successfully, and it's therefore a good candidate for a subroutine. But what if the car doesn't start? In that case, you can't finish the shopping trip. You might implement this in code with a function, a procedure that returns a value. The function `drive_to_store` might return the value `True` if you actually get to the store, or `False` if something breaks and you don't. If `drive_to_store` is false, you can stop right there—the trip is over.

Passing Parameters to Procedures   There are a couple of lines in the outline that are only a little different: `drive_to_store` and `drive_home`. You can see that these are really the same activity, with different destinations. In most programming languages, you'd implement this kind of action with a parameter to a subroutine or function. Parameters are specified when the procedure is started, telling the procedure some piece of information that it needs to know to run. You usually denote parameters by enclosing them in parentheses after the name of the procedure, so these lines might become

```
drive (store)
```

and

```
drive (home)
```

You would write a procedure called "drive" that would expect to be told where to go when it is called. The "drive" procedure would include a variable corresponding to the destination, and it would always refer to the destination by the name of that variable instead of the literal destination. This way, the "drive" procedure needs only to be written once and a program could presumably use it to drive anywhere.

It is very common to have functions that use parameters, because functions are often used to perform calculations. A reference to a function that calculates the tax on a cartful of groceries might be written as

```
tax = calculate_tax(110.95)
```

where the function is called `calculate_tax` and the floating-point parameter `110.95`, representing the value of the groceries in the robot's shopping cart, is passed to it. The calculate_tax function multiplies the value of all of the groceries by the tax rate and returns it to the calling procedure, which assigns that value to the variable called `tax`.

The Anatomy of a Typical VBA Procedure   What if you don't know the total value of the groceries ahead of time? What you really need to do is take each item out of your cart, add up the

Part

II

Ch

10

prices, and calculate the tax on that sum. This corresponds to the procedure check_out in the outline. In VBA, this procedure might look like this:

```
1   Option Explicit
2   Dim item_id, items_in_cart As Integer
3   Dim total_cost, tax, total As Currency
4   Sub check_out()
5   While (items_in_cart > 0)
6       item_id = pick_up_item
7       total_cost = total_cost + cost(item_id)
8       bag_item
9       items_in_cart = items_in_cart - 1
10  Wend
11  tax = calculate_tax(total_cost)
12  total = total_cost + tax
13  End Sub
14  Function pick_up_item() As Integer
15  End Function
16  Function cost(ByVal id As Integer) As Currency
17  End Function
18  Sub bag_item()
19  End Sub
20  Function calculate_tax(ByVal basis As Currency) As Currency
21  End Function
```

(The line numbers are added in the figure for reference; you don't use line numbers in VBA.) This block of code, which compiles nicely in VBA, breaks down line-by-line as follows. Don't worry so much about the syntax of the statements as in their flow; each statement leads logically to the next one, completing a sequence of steps to check out the groceries in the shopping cart.

(**Line 1**) There are several options you can set to change the way Access interprets your code. Option Explicit, which Access includes by default, requires you to declare the type of all variables you use, which is good practice anyway.

(**Lines 2 and 3**) The Dim (dimension) statement tells the interpreter what variables you intend to use so it can reserve storage space in the computer's memory for them. You're declaring two variables to be integers and three to be Currency, which is a floating-point number with two decimal places.

(**Line 4**) The Sub statement begins a subroutine. The empty parentheses are created by Access to make it clear that there are no parameters to this subroutine.

(**Lines 5–10**) While is a VBA keyword that starts a loop. This loop, beginning on line 5 and ending with the Wend statement on line 10, will be executed as long as the condition specified here (items_in_cart is greater than zero) is true. You should assume that the number of the items in the cart has been counted ahead of time and that value stored in the variable items_in_cart. When there are no more items in the cart, items_in_cart will be zero and execution will continue after the Wend statement. It's good style to indent lines that make up a block of code in a loop, so it's clear to humans that they are all grouped together

(Line 6) Assign the value returned by the function `pick_up_item` to the variable `item_id`. The function `pick_up_item` would do some magic, including getting the object out of the cart and identifying it; once identified, that functions should return the item's identification to the procedure that called it.

(Line 7) Use a function called `cost` to look up the price of the item the robot selected from the basket. Tell the `cost` function which item you are interested in by passing the item's id to it as a parameter.

(Line 8) The `bag_item` subroutine puts the item in a bag somehow.

(Line 9) We decrement the variable `items_in_cart` by subtracting one from it and assigning the subtracted value back to itself.

(Line 10) The `Wend` statement completes the loop started on line 5.

(Line 11) You only get to this line when the `While` statement between lines 5 and 10 is finished. This line uses a yet unwritten function called `calculate_tax` to figure the tax on the total cost (which is passed as a parameter) and return that value, which is stored in the variable `tax`.

(Line 12) The variable `total` is computed by assigning it the sum of the cost of the items (`total_cost`) and the tax (`tax`).

(Line 13) The `End Sub` statement completes a subroutine. Access automatically draws a line after it for clarity.

(Lines 14 and 15) This empty function is called a stub; it's included because you need to fill it in later. The keywords `As Integer` tell Access that this particular subroutine will return an integer value when it's run.

(Lines 16 and 17) Another stub. The statement `ByVal id as Integer` means that this function will be passed an integer parameter to work with, and that integer will be called `id` as long as you are in this function. The `ByVal` keyword means that a change to the value of the variable `id` in this function will not affect the procedure that called it.

(Lines 17–21) More stubs.

This relatively simple Access procedure (presumably a standard module) uses most of the elements of VBA code. All procedures look similar to this one.

Modular Code and Reuse   You may have noticed that two of the lines in the grocery robot's instructions are identical. Getting in the car (and closing the door and starting it, presumably) are the same no matter where they're done, and if you write the code correctly, you can reuse it as many times as the robot needs to get in the car. This is called *code reuse*, and reusing your code can save you a lot of programming time.

In this case, you only need to write the instructions for getting in the car once, and the robot could follow those same instructions whenever it needed to do that. Code reuse of this type is common in VBA programming. You might write a procedure that prints a certain report, and reuse it every time you need to print that report. If you think about it, the things that happen whenever you select an option from a menu are just reusing the same code every time you select that option. The code behind the menu items is written modularly and is therefore reusable. ●

Beginning Programming for Your Database Using VBA

Now that you know what modules are and how the Code Builder window looks and works, it's time to get into the details of writing useful code. You're never going to write an Access procedure that buys groceries, but you may well write VBA programs that handle the clicks of command buttons and manage the display of forms on the desktop. Your first VBA programs will probably be short, maybe one or two lines, but as you get more comfortable, they will grow in size and complexity.

One of the nice things about the new VBA in Office 97 applications is that it's standard across the suite. The development environment is a little different in Access than in the other applications, mostly in deference to seasoned Access programmers used to the old environment, but the *object hierarchy* (the way all of the objects in the application interact with one another) is consistent among all of the Office applications. That means that whatever you learn writing code in Access will transfer to Word, Excel, PowerPoint, and Outlook. ■

The process of writing VBA code

Getting code onto the screen involves organizing your thoughts, understanding what your capabilities and limitations are in the environment, and knowing enough about syntax to get started.

Properties, methods, events, and built-in functions

These are the elements that make code fun to write. All are provided by Access to handle the mundane tasks of making objects do things; because they're already written, all you have to do is learn what they are and how to use them.

Writing code that makes decisions

Code that always does the same thing is essentially a macro. The power of VBA lies in its ability, like most full-featured programming languages, to evaluate expressions and change the flow of the program based on their values.

Making sure your code works

Access provides many tools for testing and debugging VBA code.

Writing Code

In Chapter 10, you learned how to open the Code Builder window to write a new procedure. While writing actual VBA code in the Code Builder is a little more difficult than the drag-and-drop method you use to design forms and reports, Access includes a lot of helpers and samples to get you going.

The key to writing compact, efficient code is to have the process you're coding well thought-out. If you don't know exactly what you want the computer to do, you won't be able to tell it. It helps to understand exactly what the computer can do, however; referencing the example in Chapter 10, most PCs can't lift groceries out of a cart or drive a car.

A good place to start is Access help. If you click the Help menu, then select Contents and Index, you'll see a library of help topics. The topic Microsoft Access and Visual Basic for Applications Reference contains hundreds of topics on programming Access, and it's worth browsing to get a feel for what's there. Entire books are written describing every keyword and statement you can write in Access, and we don't have the room for that here. All of the keywords you'll ever need are listed in the help, however.

The best way to get used to writing programs in VBA is to practice. In most programming books, the first example you'll find is a block of code that prints the message "Hello, World!" on the terminal screen. Not to break with tradition, let's do the same here.

To write a dialog box to the screen containing the message "Hello, World!":

1. Open a new standard module (from the Modules tab, click New).

2. Place your cursor in the Procedures section and type "**sub hello**" and press Enter. Access automatically adds a blank line and enters a corresponding End Sub statement for you, capitalizes the keyword Sub, and adds empty parentheses at the end of the line to make it clear that you haven't defined any arguments.

3. Press the Tab key to indent your code between the Sub statements. This is good programming practice; use indentations like this whenever you write a new block of code. It's not required, but it's a good idea for readability.

4. The Access action that creates a simple dialog box is called MsgBox. You can discover this for yourself by searching for "dialog" in Access help. Type **msgbox** on the current line and add a space after the word, and watch what Access does.

5. When you type a keyword that Access recognizes, it automatically displays a syntax reference for that command (see Figure 11.1). This feature is called Auto Quick Info, and it can be disabled by clicking Tools, then Options, then selecting the Module tab, then unchecking the Auto Quick Info box in the Coding Options group if you don't like it.

TIP You can get detailed help on any keyword in Access by highlighting the word and pressing F1. In this case, highlighting the word "msgbox" and pressing F1 brings up specific, detailed help on the MsgBox function, including examples.

FIG. 11.1

The Auto Quick Info box shows the syntax for the action you just typed. The current argument is highlighted in bold, and the highlight moves with you as you enter arguments on the command line.

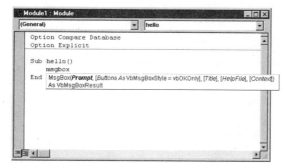

6. Auto Quick Info lists all optional arguments within [square brackets] inside of the parentheses defining this action. In this case, the only required argument is the Prompt, which will appear inside the dialog box you create. All of the arguments should be in parentheses, and the prompt should be delimited by quotation marks. Enter the arguments for the dialog by typing **("Hello, World!")**. Access capitalizes and spaces your statement appropriately when it's finished. Your finished procedure should look like this:

```
Option Compare Database
Option Explicit
Sub hello()
    MsgBox ("Hello, World!")
End Sub
```

7. Save your work by clicking the Save button on the toolbar and name your new module "hello."

After your module is entered, it's always a good idea to have Access check it for errors. You can do this quickly and easily by *compiling* the code. To compile code, either click the Compile Loaded Modules button on the toolbar or select one of the Compile options under the Debug menu. If Access finds any errors in this module (or any other loaded modules, if more than one is open), it will flag them and give you an opportunity to fix them.

Finally, run your code and see how it works. Click the Go/Continue button on the toolbar and your Message Box should appear as in Figure 11.2. There are a lot of elements in this object that you didn't create, like the OK button; Access chooses the default options for this object when you don't specify them.

FIG. 11.2

The dialog box created by the code you entered in this example.

Part

II

Ch

11

When the Auto Quick Info box appeared while you were typing, it showed several additional options you might specify for your message box. You can go back at any time and edit your code to include any options you like, using Auto Quick Info or Access help to determine what they should be. For example, you might change the single executable statement in your procedure to

```
MsgBox "Hello, World!", vbExclamation, "Our First Procedure"
```

which changes the message box to look like Figure 11.3.

N O T E   The syntax of the MsgBox statement is a little different from the first example using this statement. That's because the first example uses the MsgBox *function*, which requires parentheses around its arguments. The second uses the MsgBox *action*, which doesn't. Both produce pop-up boxes to provide information for the user, but they have slightly different syntax. In general, you use the function variant when you want to test the value of a button included in the MsgBox after a user clicks it. ▪

FIG. 11.3

The same message box, slightly modified. Clicking the OK button closes the dialog box. You can select from a number of predefined buttons and icons with standard meanings.

vbExclamation in the code is an Access constant that was supplied by the Auto List Members feature. As you type a statement, if Access recognizes what you're doing, it recommends various options and entries to fill in the blanks. In this case, as you enter the MsgBox statement, Access lists all of the different message box types in a drop-down list (see Figure 11.4). You can choose any of the values in the box and keep on typing. Of course, it helps if you know what each of the options presented actually does; for that, press F1 while entering a statement and Access help will show you the meanings of all of the available values.

 After you've written a procedure, be sure to save it by clicking the Save button on the toolbar so you can edit it later.

You enter code in class modules the same way you enter it in standard modules. The only difference in the process is the way you start writing; to create a class module, first select the control the module should apply to and press <u>V</u>iew, then <u>C</u>ode. The Module Window appears; in it, you can create a new class module rather than working from the Database window. When you save the object the class module is attached to, your code is saved as well.

FIG. 11.4

The drop-down list provided by Auto List Members to help complete the statement. Here you see predefined constants. Access may supply a list of properties for an object or methods for an action.

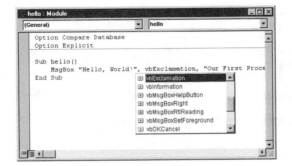

Properties and the Expression Builder

One of the most common things you'll do with code is change the properties of an object. Because all objects have different properties, it would be impossible to list all of the properties you can modify for all of the objects you can reference in Access here, but you can find a list, by object type, in Access help under the topic "Properties Reference."

To write code that modifies the properties of an object, you need to know the name of the object whose properties you want to modify. In some cases, that's easy; if you create a form called My_Form, you can generally refer to it by name. But what about named controls in forms? Or forms within forms? Access provides some help in cases like this; the Expression Builder is available to help you figure out the properties applicable to any object in your database. By starting the Expression Builder whenever you're less than 100 percent sure of the name of an object, you avoid syntax errors and some of the headache of debugging.

 The Expression Builder (see Figure 11.5) is available at any time when you're in the Code Builder by right-clicking in the Procedures section and selecting Build. It's made up of five elements:

- A horizontal window across the top, called the Expression box
- A toolbar below the Expression Box called the Operator buttons
- Three vertical windows called Expression Element windows

The lower-left Expression Element window contains a top-level view of all of the objects in your database, sorted by object type. As you select objects in the leftmost window, the second and third windows are populated with contained objects (if any), elements, or fields to choose from.

To enter a code statement referencing any property of any object in the database:

1. Double-click any folder to open up more folders or objects of that type.
2. Double-click a specific object to see a list of its fields (for tables, queries), controls (forms, reports), or elements (functions, constants, operators, common expressions) in the second Expression Element window.

3. Select any field, control, or element in the second window to display all of that object's properties in the third window.

4. Choose the property you want to modify and click the Paste button to move it to the Expression Box.

Operator buttons   Expression box

FIG. 11.5

The Expression Builder.
If text is selected in your
code when you open it,
that code will appear in
the Expression Box so
you can edit it in place.

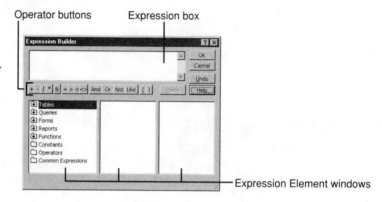

Expression Element windows

After you've selected the object and property you want to modify, you can use the keyboard or the Operator buttons to complete the statement as discussed later in this chapter. Clicking OK returns you to the Code Builder.

TIP If you've got object-referencing code you're unsure of and want to change, select it in the Code Builder before you start the Expression Builder, and select it in the Expression Box before browsing through the objects and properties lists. When you Paste it and click OK, it will replace the suspect code in the correct place in your module.

This example uses the Expression Builder to modify an object's properties, by taking advantage of the Open and Close *methods* of the Form object. Methods are procedures that act on specific objects, and Access includes several hundred methods for all of its object types. Methods for forms include opening, closing, and resizing; methods for queries include executing and deleting. Because Access has procedures that do these kinds of things, you don't need to write them from scratch.

You'll also use a new kind of loop statement, called a For loop. A For loop specifies the starting value of a counter at the beginning of a block of code. When all of the code in the loop has been executed, Access automatically increments the counter and returns to the top of the loop. The For statement at the beginning of the loop tells Access how many times to go through the loop.

In this example, you'll create a new form containing nothing but a simple rectangle, cycle through all of the possible background colors of the rectangle, and delete the form. To do this, you'll need to do the following things:

- Create the form and rectangle
- Set the rectangle's background color property (using the Expression Builder)

- Repaint the screen to make the change visible
- Delete the form after all of the colors have cycled through

You can create the form by using code, but it's a lot easier to do it in Design view. To create the new form for this example:

1. From the Forms tab of the Database window, select New, then Design view, then OK. You don't need to specify a data source.

    Place a rectangle control in the middle of the Detail section of the new form. Resize it so it fills most of the form.

2. Change the BackStyle property of the rectangle from Transparent (the default) to Normal.

▶ **See** "Using Controls in Forms," **p. 61**

3. Close and save the form. Call it color_box.

4. Create a new standard module by clicking New from the Modules tab of the Database window.

5. Create a new subroutine called color_changer by typing

    ```
    sub color_changer
    ```

    in the Procedures section and pressing Enter. Access adds empty parentheses and an End Sub statement.

6. The statement to open a form is DoCmd.OpenForm. The code that will open the form you just created is:

    ```
    DoCmd.OpenForm "color_box"
    ```

    The unusual syntax of this command is due to the fact that the command OpenForm is really a method of the special DoCmd object, which Access provides to perform actions that are normally found on the menu. (See Access help for more information on the DoCmd object; you'll use it often.)

    It would be a good idea to indent this line (and all of the lines after it), because they're part of the subroutine color_changer.

7. The loop that cycles through all of the colors is started by entering the code:

    ```
    For i = 1 To 256
    ```

    This tells Access to set the value of the variable called i to 1 and to stop running the loop when i gets to 256. If you have your display set to more than 256 colors, you might want to try other values for the upper bound.

8. The next line of code needs to set the background color of the rectangle. Because you didn't give the rectangle a name when you created the form, you probably don't know what it's called. Start the Expression Builder by moving to a new line and right-clicking. Select Build from the menu that appears.

9. Find the rectangle in the Expression Element windows by double-clicking Forms, then All Forms, then color_box in the left window. You should see the second and third Expression Element windows fill up with controls and properties.

10. In the second Expression Element window, select the Box0 control. This is the rectangle you created, because the other two options (<Form> and Detail) refer to the form itself and the Detail region, respectively.

TIP Be careful when working in the Expression Window to select objects and properties by single-clicking them. Double-clicking has the effect of pasting the double-clicked object or property into the current expression, potentially replacing whatever text was already selected.

If you accidentally overwrite something critical, press Ctrl+Z to undo the erroneous action.

11. The third Expression Element window fills with properties of the rectangle object you selected. The first property listed is BackColor, which refers to the background color of the object. Select it and click the Paste button to create an expression in the Expression Box. Your Expression Builder window should look like Figure 11.6. Click OK to bring the expression you created back into the Code Builder.

FIG. 11.6

The Expression Builder with the correct property selected. VBA expression syntax puts element names in square brackets, separated by periods.

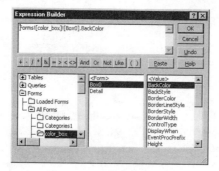

12. You want to set the value of the BackColor property to the counter, so it changes whenever the counter does. By adding two characters to the end of the line, you finish the statement that does most of the work in this code example:

```
Forms![color_box]![Box0].BackColor = i
```

13. To see the changing colors, you need to ask Access to redraw the screen after every change. This is done with the Repaint method of the Form object:

```
Forms![color_box].Repaint
```

14. You are ready to loop back to the top, so close the loop, incrementing the counter.

```
Next i
```

15. You can quit at this point, but pop up a message box to confirm that you're finished:

```
MsgBox "Press OK to quit."
```

16. Close the form. Because the color_box form should be the only thing open when this code is running, you don't need to tell Access what to close. Because this is analogous to selecting File, then Close from the menu, it's a method of the DoCmd object:

```
DoCmd.Close
```

17. Because the End Sub statement is already there, you don't need to enter it. Check your code by clicking the Compile Loaded Modules button.

18. Whoops, an error. You should see a message box reminding you that a variable isn't defined; you used the variable i and didn't tell Access what type it is. In the declarations section at the top of the Code Builder window, enter a new line before the Sub statement:

```
Dim i as Integer
```

19. Try compiling again. This time it works. The code should look like Figure 11.7.

FIG. 11.7

The code to change the rectangle color of the color_box form. The two Option statements at the top are inserted in every module by Access and tell it to use the database defaults to compare strings and to require variables to be dimensioned.

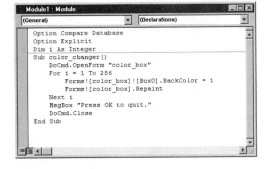

20. Ready to take it for a spin? Place your cursor on the line containing the Sub statement and click the Go/Continue button. Your form should open and cycle quickly through 256 colors, and then display a message box asking you to confirm closing it, as in Figure 11.8.

FIG. 11.8

The color_box form and message box after running this code. In this type of message box, OK is your only choice. Other types of message boxes include additional buttons that you can program.

You'll need to click OK on the message box before you can continue; message boxes are *modal* by default, meaning that they require the full attention and action by the user before they'll go away. For most forms, this behavior is set by the form's Modal property. You should be starting to see that almost any feature of an object's appearance or behavior can be controlled by setting a property. The problem is figuring out which property to set, and you'll have to use the online help for that.

Flow Control

VBA programs, by default, continue from the first line in a procedure straight through until the last line is reached, when control is returned to the procedure (if any) that called the procedure in the first place. While it's theoretically possible to write programs that run linearly, it's pretty inefficient; it's easier to write, maintain, and run code that reuses portions of itself by looping and jumping back as necessary.

Of course, it's easy to have too much of a good thing. Code that jumps all over the place in the name of efficiency at the expense of readability is called *spaghetti code*, because the program flow loops and wraps around itself like spaghetti. You should try to avoid writing spaghetti code at all costs.

VBA provides almost twenty statements that change the linear flow of program statements. Most of these fall into four categories:

- **Statements that cause loops.**   Loops are segments of code that execute circularly, repeating the same statements over and over until an ending condition is met. If code is written so that there is no ending statement (or if the ending statement is never reached), the program can enter an endless loop.

- **Statements that transfer control.**   Branching statements change the flow of code by causing execution of statements that are not directly after the statement being executed. Sometimes branching statements are unconditional, meaning that control always becomes nonlinear after they are executed, or they may be conditional, changing program flow only if a certain condition is met.

- **Statements that stop execution.**   Some statements alter flow by quitting the current procedure or even the application environment altogether. Such statements may be either conditional or unconditional.

- **Statements that evaluate expressions.**   Evaluation expressions change flow by providing options for the program to follow depending on the result of an expression. These differ from loops in that they may only run the chosen option once; they aren't really branches because the options generally follow directly after the condition. Evaluation expressions may result in stopping execution.

Table 11.1 shows a summary of the most useful flow control statements in VBA and the category in the preceding list that each falls into.

Table 11.1 Flow Control Statements and Types

Statement	Loop	Branch	Quit	Evaluate	Notes
Choose			✓		Rare
Do... Loop	✓				Rare
End		✓			Used as "End Function" or "End Sub"
Exit		✓			Used as "Exit Function" or "Exit Sub"
For Each... Next	✓				Rare
For... Next	✓				Increments a counter
GoTo			✓		Unconditional
If... Then... Else				✓	Also "If...Then"
On Error			✓		See "Handling Errors" in Chapter 11
On... GoTo		✓			Rare
Select Case				✓	Simplified "If... Then... Else"
Stop				✓	Doesn't exit the environment
Switch			✓		Rare
While... Wend	✓				Similar to "For... Next"

Several of the most common mechanisms for controlling program flow include:

■ **Exit**. Usually used after an error is detected to get out of a procedure without executing any more code in it. Occasionally, this is used to quit a procedure when error-handling code is included at the bottom of the procedure, but that code is not intended to be executed if no error has occurred.

■ **GoTo**. This unconditional flow statement immediately transfers control to the *label* specified. Labels in VBA are denoted by single words appearing on new lines followed by a colon (:). Most programming experts agree that the readability of code is greatly enhanced by using as few GoTo statements as possible.

■ **On Error**. When Access detects that an error has occurred anywhere in a procedure, an On Error statement near the beginning of the procedure is given control. Usually, On Error is followed by a GoTo statement to clean up after the error and either resume execution or quit.

▶ **See** "Handling Errors and Confirmation," **p. 218**

■ **For... Next**. An integer (called a *counter*) is named on the command line and upper and lower bounds for it are set. With every pass through the block of code between the For and Next statements, the counter is incremented. When the upper bound is reached, control resumes with the first statement after the Next statement. If you need to exit a For... Next loop before the upper bound is reached, use a GoTo statement to jump to a label outside of the loop.

■ **If... Then... Else**. An expression is entered on the line containing the If statement. If the expression is evaluated true, execution continues with the statement following the Then statement. Otherwise, execution continues with the statement following the Else statement. There are several variants on this statement, including versions without an Else, versions that must be on one line, and versions that include several Else statements. Most of these are ended with an End If statement on a line by itself. If you encounter a situation where a lot of Else statements seem required, consider using a Select Case statement instead.

■ **Select Case**. An expression is entered after the Select Case statement that must evaluate to a number or a string. Following the Select Case statement, any number of individual Case statements specify possible values for the expression and include blocks of code to be executed if that case is satisfied. If none of the cases match, a Case Else statement handles every other result. An End Case statement finishes the block. Select Case statements can be nested, as long as each includes an End Case statement.

TIP Case statements in VBA do not "fall through" as they do in C and C++. After any Case statement is executed, control resumes with the corresponding End Case statement.

The following example (see Figure 11.9) from the Sales Reports Dialog form in Northwind illustrates the Exit, GoTo, and Exit statements. You can see this example online by opening the Sales Reports Dialog form in Design view and selecting View, then Code from the menu:

FIG. 11.9

A small block of code that changes flow depending on runtime conditions including errors.

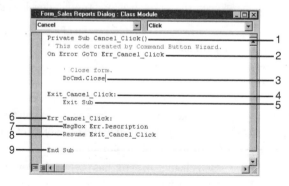

This code is executed when a user clicks the Cancel button on a form. It closes the current form and handles any errors that may come up in closing the form.:

It works like this:

- The On Error statement on line 2 specifies that control should pass to the label Err_Cancel_Click if an error occurs.
- The body of the procedure, line 3, closes the current form. If there are no errors, it proceeds to the next line.
- Line 4 is a label; labels don't affect execution.
- Line 5 exits the procedure. If there have been no errors, this prevents the code from continuing down to the error-handling statements. If there has been an error, the error-handling statements pass control back to this line to exit.
- Line 6 is another label, the one specified in the On Error statement. If there is an error, control passes directly to this line.
- Line 7 displays a message box displaying the Description method of the special Err object, which Access populates with the current error information automatically.
- Line 8 resumes execution at the label Exit_Cancel_Click, line 4, which subsequently exits the procedure. This is really no different than proceeding ahead to...
- Line 9, which ends the procedure.

The following example, modified slightly from Access help, illustrates the use of For... Next loops:

```
1 Dim i,j
2 For i = 10 To 1 Step -1      ' Set up 10 repetitions.
3     For j = 0 To 9     ' Set up 10 repetitions.
4           Debug.Print "Outer loop:", i, ", inner loop:", j
5     Next j      ' Increment counter

6 Next i
```

While this example is a little convoluted, it's descriptive. The individual lines perform as follows:

- Line 1 declares the variables to be used in this routine. The variables i and j are used as "loop counters" and are modified with every execution of each loop.
- Line 2 begins a loop where the variable i is initialized at the value 10 and is decremented by 1 every time the loop is executed.
- Line 3 begins a loop where the variable j is initialized at the value 0 and is incremented by 1 each time the loop is executed.
- Line 4 prints the current values of i and j in the Debug Window. If you have the Debug Window open when you run this code, you will see the variables stream by as they are changed in the loops.
- Line 5 marks the end of the loop incrementing j, and line 6 is the end of the loop decrementing i.

N O T E The use of the variables "i" and "j" as loop counters dates to the 1960s, when the FORTRAN 4 programming language was in widespread use. FORTRAN assumes that variable names beginning with the letters i through n are integers, making them obvious choices for counters. Since common practice dictated that it was more important to write sparse code than to make them readable, using these variable names eliminated the line of code declaring the variables and became common practice.

You can see from this example that For... Next loops can be nested, and can decrement counters as well as increment them. The integer following the optional Step statement specifies how much the counter should be incremented or decremented with every pass through the loop.

The following example of the If... Then... statement is from the Startup module in Northwind (with comments removed for clarity):

```
If Forms!Startup!HideStartupForm Then
        CurrentDb().Properties("StartupForm") = "(none)"
Else
        CurrentDb().Properties("StartupForm") = "Startup"
End If
```

In this example, if the value of the control `HideStartupForm` on the Startup form is true, then the `"StartupForm"` property of the current database (`CurrentDB`) is set to `"(none)."` Otherwise, the `"StartupForm"` property is set to `"Startup."`

This example of the Select Case statement is also taken from the Sales Reports Dialog:

```
Select Case Me!ReportToPrint
        Case 1
            DoCmd.OpenReport "Employee Sales by Country", PrintMode
        Case 2
            DoCmd.OpenReport "Sales Totals by Amount", PrintMode
        Case 3
            If IsNull(Forms![Sales Reports Dialog]!SelectCategory) Then
                DoCmd.OpenReport "Sales by Category", PrintMode
            Else
                DoCmd.OpenReport "Sales by Category", PrintMode, ,
➥strWhereCategory
            End If
    End Select
```

The value of the control `ReportToPrint` on the currently displayed form (`Me`) is evaluated. Depending on the value it's set to, one of four reports is printed. In the case where the control = 3, the value of another control on the same form determines which report will be printed.

All of the flow control mechanisms in VBA are well-documented in the online help, including examples. Search for the topic "Control Flow Keyword Summary" for an overview.

N O T E If you look through the Northwind database for examples of reusable or exemplary code, you'll probably be disappointed. Most of the bells and whistles in Northwind are accomplished through use of Access 97's new usability features, like the aliasing of foreign keys in the Table Designer. Very little is done with code, and most of the code you'll discover is too specialized or arcane to use effectively.

Better examples can be found in the online help; nearly every statement described includes at least one code example using it. These examples tend to be precise and to the point, making them excellent candidates to copy. ▨

Writing Code that Operates on Objects

VBA includes dozens of built-in procedures that are designed to work on specific types of objects. These procedures are available to the programmer as *methods*, and an understanding of the methods available to you for customizing the most common object types can ease your development task considerably.

All objects of a given type share the same methods. For example, the Close method of the Form object works on any form, no matter how the form is customized or modified. You don't need to define or specify any built-in methods at all; they're always there for you.

Similar objects may share certain methods. For example, the Close method also works for all of the basic Access object types (forms, reports, macros, modules, tables, queries). Most methods also work on *collections* of objects; Access includes several object collections with reserved names like "Forms," "Reports," etc. Applying the Close method to the object collection Forms closes all open forms in the database.

The syntax for applying a method to an object is as follows:

objectname.method [argument1] [, argument2] [, …]

where *objectname* is the name of the object or collection you want to the method to act on. If there are arguments to the method, they follow after a space, separated by commas. The syntax for arguments to methods is different from the syntax for arguments to functions in that no parentheses are used.

Methods differ from properties of objects in that they represent procedures that act upon the named object, rather than identify an attribute of the object. You can modify and query the properties of an object, but specifying a method for an object takes action upon it.

Methods are sometimes confused with *actions*, which are also built-in procedures. Unlike methods, actions do not necessarily act on only one type of object at a time; in fact, actions may not apply to objects at all. The commands available in the Macro Builder window for writing macros are all actions. Actions are generally used to perform activities that are outside of the scope of the realm of objects; for example, actions include Beep, TransferDatabase (which imports and exports all or part of a database), and MsgBox.

Part

II

Ch

11

The special object DoCmd is available when you want to use actions inside VBA code. For example, to make the PC speaker sound a tone, you can write a macro that includes the action Beep, or you can use the VBA code

```
DoCmd.Beep
```

to do the same thing. The methods of the DoCmd object correspond to the actions available to macros.

TIP You also can just enter

```
Beep
```

on a line by itself in VBA. When used this way, Beep is a VBA statement, in addition to its other incarnations as an action and a method. There's more than one way to skin a keyboard.

Events

Events are happenings in the life of a database. Whenever the mouse is moved, a button is clicked, or a form is closed, that activity triggers an *event* which can be detected by a program. Events are useful because they allow us to customize the way objects work. A command button without code attached to it is nothing more than a raised rectangle; when code is written specifying what it should do if it is clicked, that code is called an *event procedure* and it is attached to a specific event of that control.

N O T E Access help defines events as "specific action[s] that occur on or with a certain object." This is unfortunate terminology, because we know that "actions" are specific procedures that are used in macros and have nothing to do with events. ▪

Different types of objects are associated with different events. For example, a text box has an associated BeforeUpdate event that is triggered after the data in it is changed but before it's written to the database; because you can't change the data in a label, the label control doesn't have a BeforeUpdate event associated with it. For a complete list of the events associated with each type of Access object, look up the object in the online help (select Help, then Contents and Index, then the Find tab. Type the name of the object you're interested in and press D̲isplay) and click the Events hyperlink at the top of the topic page.

Depending on the type of object involved, Access may trigger several events seemingly simultaneously. However, there is a hierarchy of events that defines which events happen before others. If you're curious as to whether the OnCurrent event for a form occurs before the OnOpen event, the place to find out is in online help.

N O T E Technically, OnCurrent and OnOpen are *event properties* of forms, not events. By associating a macro or event procedure with these properties, you make them act like events. Most events have similarly named event properties associated with them. ▪

You can familiarize yourself with the events that are associated with a given object by examining the property sheet for an instance of that object. For a form, select the form (click the Edit menu, then Select Form) and then view its property sheet (click View, then Propreties). Selecting the Events tab in the property sheet will show all of the event properties for that object. Nearly all objects have events associated with them, but you'll usually be most concerned with events associated with forms, controls, and reports.

There are two ways to make Access do something when an event occurs; you can

- Call a macro from the Events tab of the Property sheet for a given control when that event occurs
- Associate VBA code (event procedures) with the event

To associate a macro with an event:

1. Open the Property Sheet for the object (click the View menu, then Properties).
2. Click the Events tab to see the event properties associated with this object.
3a. Select an event property and choose the name of an existing macro from the pull-down list that appears, or

3b. Select the Builder button and choose the Macro Builder to define a new macro to be associated with this event.

To associate a procedure with an event:

1. Open the Property Sheet for the object (click the View menu, then Properties).
2. Click the Events tab to see the event properties associated with this object.

3. Select an event property and select the special object [Event Procedure]. Then click the Builder button and choose the Code Builder.

Code modules associated with events are usually named by combining the name of the object that they're associated with and the name of the event. This syntax is required and is enforced by the Code Builder; when you create a new event procedure, Access names it for you, including the Sub and End Sub statements. Renaming the procedure will result in it being disassociated with the event, which is a bad thing. A typical procedure name for a control called CancelButton is CancelButton_Click, which is associated with the OnClick event of the control.

The number of events available is astonishing. You can control nearly every aspect of the operation of your application by carefully manipulating events. Some commonly used events for various objects are listed in Table 11.2.

Part

II

Ch

11

Table 11.2 Commonly Used Events

Event Name	When Triggered
Activate	When a form receives the focus and becomes the active window
AfterInsert	After new data is inserted into the underlying data source

continues

Table 11.2   Continued

Event Name	When Triggered
AfterUpdate	After data is edited in the underlying data source
BeforeInsert	Before new data is inserted into the underlying data source
BeforeUpdate	Before data is edited in the underlying data source
Change	When data is changed in a control, but before the Before events
Click	When a control is selected by pressing the left mouse button
Close	When an object is removed from the screen
Current	When the record is changed in the current form
DblClick	When a control is selected by pressing the left mouse button twice in quick succession
Delete	When a record is marked to be deleted, but before it's actually deleted
Enter	Just before the focus is passed to a control by selecting it
GotFocus	When a control is selected, but before the control is activated
Load	When a form or report is opened
NotInList	When a user types a value in a combo box or list box that isn't in the associated list of values
Open	When a form or report is opened, but before a record or print preview is displayed
OnClick	When the left mouse button is pressed while the pointer is over a specific object.
Resize	When an object's dimensions are modified
Timer	When a multiple of certain number of milliseconds have passed since the object was activated
Unload	When a form or report is closed

As an example of the use of an event property, let's examine the use of a typical OnClick event procedure in Northwind's Orders form. The form includes a command button control called PrintInvoice. To view the control's OnClick event procedure:

1. Open the Orders form in Design view (from the Database window, click the Forms tab, then the Orders form, then the Design button).

2. Select the Print Invoices button near the bottom of the form. If its property sheet isn't already visible, open it by clicking the View menu, and then Properties.

3. Select the Events tab. The only event property with an associated event procedure is the OnClick property.

4. Open the associated event procedure by selecting the text box for the OnClick property and clicking the Builder button.

The event procedure for this property looks like Figure 11.10.

FIG. 11.10

A typical event procedure associated with an OnClick event. This one is well-designed in that it handles possible errors in execution as well as the event for which it was designed—an event within an event.

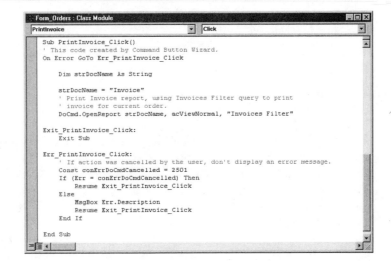

This code, despite its length, opens a report. By itself, it wouldn't be useful (you can open a report from the Database window), but associated with an event and a command button, the user gets concrete feedback that something has happened (the button appears to depress and pop back out) and the procedure is executed without ever allowing the user to see the Database window.

N O T E Figure 11.10 is a good example of the way the Wizards write code. The line that begins with DoCmd.OpenReport is actually the only line you need (in addition to the Sub and End Sub lines) to open this report. All of the other lines declare variables and handle errors and events that might come up during the execution of this routine. It's important to handle errors—there's nothing more frustrating to user and programmer alike than a crashed application—but one has to wonder about the wisdom of writing error-handling code that makes the really functional stuff hard to read. ▪

Built-In Functions

Access includes almost 200 built-in functions that can be used to perform simple arithmetic, calculate interest rates, manipulate strings, run external applications, and so on. Of course, the procedures you write yourself often borrow heavily from these functions. Without them, writing code would be more of a chore than it already is.

You can see the complete list of available functions by searching for the topic "Functions Reference" in Access help. Some, like CreateForm(), require no arguments and perform their task silently; others, like Ipmt(), require several arguments. The only way to tell is to use the online help, or depend on the Auto List Members feature in VBA.

Built-in functions, like the functions you write yourself, return values to the procedure that called them. For this reason, it's especially convenient to use functions (built-in or otherwise) as parts of expressions; the value they return is substituted directly into the expression, which contributes to concise, readable code.

Consider the following example, taken from the class module attached to the Suppliers form in Northwind:

```
Select Case Me!Country
        Case IsNull(Me![Country])
            Exit Sub
```

In this typical Select Case statement, the individual Case blocks check the value of the control [Country] on the current form (Suppliers, which can be abbreviated as Me as long as the form is open). The values checked by Case statements must evaluate to integers or strings, and usually you'll see literal strings or integers entered in them. But in this case, the first Case statement checks for the value of the function IsNull. IsNull returns True (which is an integer constant equal to –1) if its argument is blank, or null. So this Case block (consisting of one line, Exit Sub) is executed if the value of the [Country] field is left blank. It would be pretty difficult to write this particular block without using the IsNull function this way.

Another example of the use of a built-in function is provided in the next Case block of the same procedure:

```
Case "France", "Italy", "Spain"
            If Len(Me![PostalCode]) <> 5 Then…
```

Here the designer has used literal strings as the Case expression arguments, but the next line uses the built-in Len function to evaluate the length of the string entered in the field [Postal Code] on the form. If a user has entered a valid, five-digit ZIP Code, the statement

```
If Len(Me![PostalCode]) <> 5 Then…
is evaluated by the computer to the statement
If 5 <> 5 Then…
```

The computer evaluates the expression "5 not equal to 5," discovers that it's false, and continues without finishing the If statement.

It also is correct to write this code like this:

```
Case "France", "Italy", "Spain"
                zipcode_length=Len(Me![PostalCode])
            If zipcode_length <> 5 Then…
```

but in this case, the reader has an extra line of code to read to figure out what's going on. You'll eventually become familiar with the most common 20 or 30 functions (like IsNull and Len) that reading them in code will be as easy as reading this book.

Variables and Variable Scope

When you use variables to represent data values, you need to tell Access what kinds of data those variables will represent. Because different data types require different amounts of memory to store them, Access generally has to know ahead of time how much memory a given variable will require.

To allocate (also called declare) memory for a variable, you use the Dim statement. The syntax (simplified; there are a lot of special options you'll never use) is

```
Dim varname[([subscripts])] [As type]
```

where varname is the name you'll use to refer to the variable and type is a valid Access data type. If the variable is to be an array, subscripts are the lower and upper bounds of the array (you don't use subscripts otherwise). You can declare more than one variable of the same type in the same statement by separating the names with commas.

▶ **See** "The Code Builder Window," **p. 175**

In most programming languages, you can't automatically assume that a variable declared in one procedure can be used in another. That's because the memory reserved for the variable may be returned to the operating system after its home procedure has finished executing. Variables have *scope* if they are not automatically shared between all of the procedures in a program, and that a variable is *visible* to a procedure if it can be used in that procedure without redeclaring it. VBA is one of those languages that makes good use of the rules of scope.

The following short example shows how scope works. Consider the code in Figure 11.11.

Part
II

Ch
11

Dimensioned variable in the Declarations section (scope
is global within this module, but not outside it)

FIG. 11.11

A simple procedure
illustrating variable
scope. The variable
city_name is declared
in subroutine
number_one, but not in
subroutine
number_two.

Dimensioned variable
outside the Declara-
tions section (scope
is local to the
subroutine in which
it's defined)

This module won't compile. The variable `country_name` is declared in the module's Declarations section, before any procedures, so it has module scope and is visible to both procedures within the module. However, the variable `city_name` is declared within the subroutine `number_one`, and it's invisible to the subroutine `number_two`. When you try to compile this, VBA complains that the variable `city_name` in number_two is undefined.

The scope of a VBA variable is determined by two things: where you declare it in the procedure, and whether you use the Dim, Public, or Private statements to declare it.

Let's first consider variable scope when you declare it using the Dim statement. You can declare variables in two places in a module: in the Declarations section at the top of the Code Builder window, or after the Sub (or Function) statement of a procedure in that module. In this case, determination of scope is easy: variables declared in the Declarations section of a module are visible to all procedures in that module, and variables declared within a procedure are visible only within that procedure.

Things get more complicated when you use the Public and Private statements. The syntax for their use is exactly the same as for the Dim statement, except that you use the word Public or Private instead of Dim (i.e., `Public country_name As String`), but they are generally used in the Declarations section of a module. A variable declared as Public is visible to all procedures in the application in all modules. Conversely, a variable declared as Private is visible only to the module or procedure in which it is declared (the default).

```
Dim country_name As String
Public country_name As String
Private country_name As String
```

You use the Public statement to declare *global variables*, variables that need to be used by all procedures in a database. It's best to avoid using globals if you can, as a variable defined in a different module can be confusing for a programmer to remember when it appears in the module being worked on. Someone reading your code needs to know what they are to make sense of what you've written, but they may not have read the procedure containing the global declarations. If you must use global variables, consider putting them all in a module you call "Globals," or something similar, to make it clear where to find them.

One exception to the scope rules comes into play when a variable is passed as an argument to a subroutine or function. In general, when you list a variable name as an argument, the address of the variable in the computer's memory is passed to the called procedure. This method, called *passing by reference*, means that any changes to the variable's value in the called procedure also change its value for the calling procedure, and it effectively bypasses the scope rules by making that variable visible to the called procedure. This may or not be desirable; to force Access to pass the value of a variable to a called procedure instead of its address, use the keyword ByVal in the declaration of the called procedure, as in this example from Northwind:

```
Function IsLoaded(ByVal strFormName As String) As Boolean
```

In this case, the function may (or may not) change the value of the string passed to it as an argument. To prevent changing the value of `strFormName` in the procedure calling this function, it's declared ByVal to make it clear that a copy of its value should be used by the function for the function's calculations.

Testing Your Code

After you write a module and exit the VBA window, your work has just begun. It's unlikely that most code will work as you intended it the first time it's run, so Access provides several features to help you remove errors (debug) from your code.

When you save VBA code, only a rudimentary error-checking is performed on it. Obvious problems, like the use of undeclared variables, are caught before you even exit the editor; Access turns the offending lines of code red and shows you an error dialog box (if you have the Auto Syntax Check option turned on, which is the default). After you exit the editor and execute your code, Access performs still more error-checking, displaying error dialogs as the code runs. This kind of error is called a *runtime error*; when one occurs, Access stops executing the code and returns you to the code editor at the point where the error occurred. Common runtime errors include specifying the wrong arguments to functions and opening and closing objects that are already open or closed.

The most difficult kind of error to diagnose and fix is the one that produces no error message. Mistakes in logic, incorrect counter values, and unforeseen circumstances all contribute to *stealth* errors like this, and this kind of coding mistake is properly called a *bug*. Fortunately, there are several things you can do to try to find the source and resolution of bugs in VBA.

Breakpoints

VBA code is *interpreted*, meaning that it is evaluated line-by-line as it executes. Access doesn't do any optimizing or rearranging of the code before it runs, so you could theoretically watch as the code executes, tracking the values of variables and seeing which branch of an If block is followed. The problem is that the code isn't normally visible while it's executing, and it's hard to follow when it's invisible.

The solution to this problem is the use of *breakpoints*, instructions to the VBA interpreter to stop when a certain line of code is reached. When a breakpoint is reached, the interpreter stops, the code is displayed, and it's up to you to decide what you want to do next.

To set a breakpoint in code,

1. Open the Code Builder window, displaying the code you want to stop in. You can use breakpoints in any VBA code, including standard and class modules, functions and procedures, and event procedures.

2. Place your cursor on the line where you want to halt and click the Debug menu, then Toggle Breakpoint. The line you selected displays in bold white text on a crimson background, and a circle appears in the left margin of the Code Builder to remind you that there's a breakpoint there. You also can click the Toggle Breakpoint button on the toolbar.

3. Run the code by opening the form or report that makes it run, or by clicking Run, then Go/Continue from the menu. Alternatively, click the Go/Continue button on the toolbar. You can leave the code window open or close it if you like; it will reopen when the breakpoint is reached.

TIP   If your code depends on controls in a form, make sure the form is open when you run the code. You don't have to execute the code from the form as long as the form is open and the controls you need are populated correctly.

If you don't want to (or can't) open the form that runs your code, try running the code from the Code Builder window anyway. When VBA reaches a statement that references a control it can't find (because the form is closed), it will prompt you for a value for that control. You may be able to debug effectively by filling in the prompts as the code runs.

4. When the interpreter reaches your breakpoint, it will stop executing before it executes the code in the breakpoint. At this point, you have several options, described in the sections that follow.

To clear a breakpoint, follow the same process you used to set it in the first place. The breakpoint is toggled on and off whenever you need it. You can set as many breakpoints as you want in as many modules as you need.

You can clear all of the breakpoints in your modules by clicking Debug, then selecting Clear All Breakpoints from the menu.

Breakpoints aren't saved with your code, although they persist until you close the current database or clear them manually. See the section "When All Else Fails," for some ideas on setting stops that remain after code is saved.

There's one additional way to stop code execution without modifying code: You can place your cursor on any line of code in a module and click Debug, then select Run to Cursor from the menu. Execution of the module begins immediately and stops *after* the code on the line containing the cursor is reached.

Auto Data Tips, Watches, and the Value of Variables

After your VBA code stops at a breakpoint, how can you check on the status of the code? Access 97 provides several useful features for seeing what's going on when code execution is halted.

One of the nicest new features in Access 97 is called Auto Data Tips (see Figure 11.12). This improvement automatically displays the value of a variable when you hover (stop moving) the mouse over the variable when code is stopped. You quickly can check the values of all variables in your modules without any clicking or typing at all; after a breakpoint is reached, just move your mouse around the Code Builder window to see the value of all variables.

If you want a little more control over the display of variable values, such as you might need to trace the value of a variable throughout a program, you can use the Debug and Watch features of Access 97 to follow as many variables as you need while they change. You can use the Debug window to interactively work with variables during the execution of code. Included with the Debug window is a facility for "watching" variables; after you set up a *watch* for a variable, you can inspect its value at any breakpoint in the Debug window.

FIG. 11.12

The cursor is over the variable blnReturnValue and its current value is shown in a small box beneath the variable name (from Northwind, module Startup).

An Auto Data tip

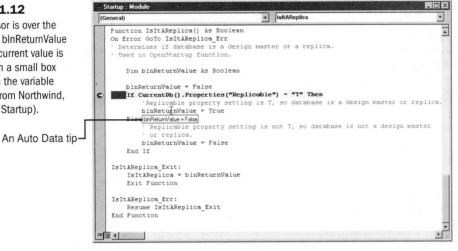

To view the Debug window, select View, then Debug Window. The two sections of the Debug Window shown in Figure 11.13 are used to view the values of variables at any point when executing code. The top pane, called the Locals Pane, shows the values of variables with watches set. The bottom pane, called the Immediate Pane, is used to interactively type expressions for immediate evaluation (such as print country_name).

FIG. 11.13

The Debug Window in the middle of a debugging session.

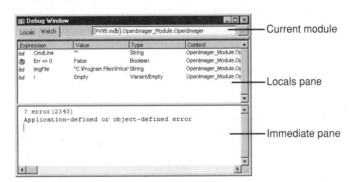

Current module

Locals pane

Immediate pane

There's a tab on the Debug window marked Locals, which is selected by default. While code is running, you can use the Debug window with this tab selected and see the values of all variables in the current procedure. This will suffice for 95 percent of the watches you need, without going through the Add Watch procedure detailed here.

To watch a variable,

1. Click the Debug menu, then select Add Watch. The Add Watch dialog box (see Figure 11.14) appears.

Part

II

Ch

11

FIG. 11.14

The Add Watch dialog box, showing the defaults. There's not a lot of sense in using this feature in Northwind, because there's so little code to watch there.

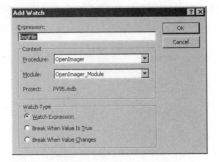

2. In the Expression box, type the name of the variable or expression you want to watch.

 TIP If you select the name of the variable you want to watch before opening the Add Watch dialog box, it will be entered automatically in the Expression box for you.

If you only want to watch the value of this variable (and don't want to write an expression using it), you can use the Quick Watch feature. Just click the variable name in the code, select Debug, then Quick Watch from the menu, and click Add in the dialog box that appears. The variable is added to the watch list.

3. Several options are available in this dialog box:
   - You can select the procedure and module in which you want to watch this variable or expression. If you want to watch it in all procedures or modules, select (All Procedures) or (All Modules) from the pull-down list.
   - You can choose from three types of watches:
     - **Watch Expression**, the default, adds the variable or expression to the Debug Window and displays its value whenever the execution of code is stopped by a breakpoint;
     - **Break When Value is True** has the effect of setting a breakpoint whenever the expression or variable evaluates as true. This option is especially useful when used with expressions like Err <> 0, which causes a breakpoint whenever an error occurs and shows the value of the error in the Debug Window;
     - **Break When Value Changes** stops execution when the expression or variable is changed. This option also breaks when the expression is initialized, so you're guaranteed of at least one break with this option.

   Select the appropriate options and click OK to continue. The Debug window appears.

4. The watch you set appears in the Debug window in the top pane under the Watches tab. You can set as many watches as you like. The vertical scroll bar allows you to view them all.

5. Close the Debug window if you like; the watches stay in effect until you remove them (by selecting the watch to delete in the Debug window and pressing Delete) or you close the database.

There are a couple of additional features in the Debug window. The bottom pane of the window is called the Immediate window, and it's used to enter expressions for instant evaluation. The most common use of this window is to perform a one-time watch; you can type

```
print expression
```

(where `expression` is a valid variable or expression) in the Immediate window, and Access displays the value of that variable or expression, regardless of what's going on in the code. This is useful when trying different values as arguments to built-in functions; you can try out a statement as many times as you like before pasting the statement into the code window.

 TIP In a nod to old Basic programmers, you can use "?" as a shortcut for "Print" in the Immediate window.

 The Debug window also is available from the toolbar while code is visible.

 TIP You can do more than view the values of variables in the Immediate window. You also can set them, by typing "**varname = x**," or even execute methods and SQL statements (" DoCmd.RunSQL " Insert x into Personnel where...).

 TIP You can see the Debug window without adding a watch by clicking the <u>V</u>iew menu, then <u>D</u>ebug Window whenever code is visible.

Stepping

It's one thing to watch the values of variables change as code proceeds, and another to watch the code itself. You can actually follow the execution of code, line by line, by using the stepping features. You can even set the next active line of code, causing Access to skip whole blocks of code if you don't want to execute them while stepping.

To step through code:

 1. Set a breakpoint at the beginning of the code you want to inspect.

2. When the interpreter stops at the breakpoint, continue from there using one of the following options, all available from the toolbar:

 • **Step Into**.   Clicking this button executes the next line of code and stops the execution of the running module. If the next statement is a procedure call, that procedure is opened for viewing and you can continue to step through it.

- **Step Over**. Clicking this button executes the next line of code and stops. If the next statement is a procedure call, that procedure is executed without opening it and executing stops with the first statement after the procedure call.

- **Step Out**. Clicking this button executes the rest of the current procedure, returns to the calling procedure, and stops. This is useful for continuing from within a procedure you've accidentally stepped into.

- **Continue**. Clicking this button executes the rest of the code until the next breakpoint or end.

- **End**. Clicking this button stops the procedure at the current line. To continue, you'll have to restart.

You can change from Break Mode (where the next line of code is ready to be executed immediately) to Stop Mode (where you'll have to restart the entire procedure) by clicking the Reset button while the code is stopped in progress. This is sometimes necessary to close forms with attached code before the code can be restarted.

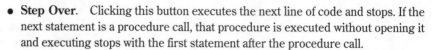

TIP The Step options also are available from the Debug menu; Continue, End, and Reset are available from the Run menu.

If, after stopping for a breakpoint, you want to skip a block of code, you can place your cursor at the next statement you want to execute and select Debug, then Set Next Statement from the menu. This has the effect of skipping all lines between the current statement and the cursor position. You only can use Set Next Statement in the current procedure. A related command is Show Next Statement, which returns the cursor to the next executable statement when you've stopped and wandered off into the code.

When All Else Fails: Some Final Tips for Debugging Code

The features Access provides to debug your code are a boon to programmers by easing the task of writing reliable code. You still have a couple of age-old tricks up your sleeve, though, and they sometimes work when all else fails.

- Don't be afraid to use message boxes to tell you what's going on in your code while you debug it. Consider placing message boxes strategically throughout your code, showing the values of variables as the code executes. This has the effect of causing a breakpoint whenever a message box displays; if you display the Code Builder while a message box is up, you can start stepping from the statement generating the message.

- Use the Stop statement in your code to cause it to halt execution without clearing all variables and calls. You can continue from a stop just as you would a breakpoint.

- The Debug.Print method is useful for showing the process code goes through as it executes without interfering with the interface. Debug.Print commands cause the arguments provided to write to the Immediate Window only, where they stay until cleared. You can load a program with Debug.Print statements displaying variables and status messages, run the code, and inspect the entries in the Immediate Window later.

Miscellaneous VBA Tools

There are three additional Code Builder features that you may find useful, especially as you develop applications in Access:

- **Definitions.** By clicking the View menu, then Definition while the cursor is in the name of a variable, procedure, method, or action, you can cause Access to display the object's definition in the form of its declaration (for variables) or syntax (all others). A useful shortcut for this command is available when you right-click one of the supported object names in the code.

- **The Object Browser.** A quick reference for all of the methods, properties, and actions of every object in a database is available by clicking the View menu, then Object Browser. This dialog box (see Figure 11.15) provides a complete reference for all objects in all loaded libraries, permits keyword searches of the entire object hierarchy, and brings up context-sensitive help when a particular object or method is selected. It makes for great browsing and can be a useful tool after you get used to its depth and master its interface.

FIG. 11.15

The Object Browser, showing various class modules, standard modules, properties, and events. You can infer the type of each object shown (module, macro, etc.) by looking at the icons to the left of their names.

- **The Call Stack.** This dialog box, displayed by selecting View, then Call Stack when code is stopped, shows all of the procedures above this one in the hierarchy of calls. As procedures call procedures, more and more appear on the call stack for display here.

Database Applications: Advanced Topics

CHAPTER 12

Additional Programming Topics Using VBA

There are some features available in VBA that you may never need to use in your applications. On the other hand, you may find that there's no way to accomplish what you need to do without them. Want to use a custom help file from a menu item? Trap and handle errors before users see them? What about working with databases created in Access 2.0 or Access 95?

Most of the topics covered in this chapter cannot be demonstrated using the Northwind database, because there are no examples of their use provided. ■

Intercepting errors and confirmation messages

Do you really want your users to see Access' built-in messages, like You are about to delete one record ? You can turn them off, or create messages of your own.

Converting from Access Basic

The syntax and structure of code written in previous versions of Access, especially Access 1.0 and 2.0, is slightly different than the syntax in Access 97.

Handling Errors and Confirmations

There are times when a running Access program will detect an error and look to the user for help in surmounting it. Errors occur in all phases of program execution and in the best programs; they are a fact of life, not an admission of coding inefficiency. For example, your program may expect a user to enter a number in a given form field. If the user enters a character string instead, an error may be generated. If you don't detect and handle the error (called *trapping* the error), your program will crash.

You could take the "all-or-nothing" approach and try to anticipate every error that may occur during the running of a given program. This tack is ultimately futile, however; no human can conceive of all of the things that can go wrong in the execution of a computer program. A better approach is to expect that errors will occur and write code to handle them gracefully. The parts of programs that perform this function are called *error handlers*.

When a running Access program generates an error, an Error event is generated. Instead of passing those errors on to your users, you can (and should) write special procedures called error handlers to manage and correct the error, rather than allowing the errors to crash your application. There are several ways to write error handlers, but all of them make use of the special Err object.

N O T E If you're familiar with programming in C or C++, you can think of the Err object as a struct with various members and functions. Some of those members are read-only, and some can be written to.

VBA includes a special object called Err to contain information about errors; the properties of this object are automatically populated whenever an error occurs. The Err object includes the following properties and methods, which you can inspect when an error is trapped:

- **Err.Number**.   The default property, this number (0–64K, not all numbers used) represents a specific runtime error that has occurred. The number property is useful when you use a Select Case statement to handle certain, expected errors that occur within an application.

- **Err.Description**.   This property contains a brief text description of the error associated with Err.Number. When you allow Access to display an error message to a user, this is the text it displays. If Err.Number contains a number with no associated Access error, the Description property contains the string `Application-defined or object-defined error`.

- **Err.Clear**.   This method removes all error information from the Err object. If you write error-handling code that corrects the condition that caused an error, it's a good idea to clear the error condition using this method.

- **Err.Raise**.   This method causes an error. It's most often used when a subroutine includes error-handling code, but can't handle a particular, usually unexpected error. By re-creating the error condition after trying to handle it, the subroutine can force the next-higher procedure in the call tree to try to handle it. This technique is especially useful if you include one master error-handling procedure at the top level of an application; each called procedure can pass errors back to the top-level error handler.

You can create a program guaranteed to create an error; this will allow you to follow along in this chapter. Enter the following text in a new module (from the Database window, select Modules, then New):

```
Sub create_error()
Err.Raise 1000
End Sub
```

Save this procedure by closing the Code Builder window and name it create_error. You can execute it by opening the module in Design view, placing the cursor on the first line of the procedure (the sub line), and clicking the Go/Continue button on the toolbar. In this case, execution will stop with an error 1000 almost immediately.

N O T E The choice of the error code 1000 in the example code is arbitrary. You can choose any number, including numbers usually used by Access for internal errors. ∎

To examine the error condition from the Code Builder window after execution has stopped due to a runtime error:

1. Open either the Debug window (click the View menu, then Debug Window) or click the Immediate Window button on the toolbar.

2. In the Immediate window pane of the Debug window or anywhere in the Immediate window, type the following ? Err.

3. The number corresponding to the current error appears. If you need more information, you can either print individual properties (Err.Description, and so on) or you can add a watch on the Err object and use the Debug window to view all of its properties.

T I P If all you need is the descriptive text of an error, it's easiest to type ? error in the Immediate window. This runs the built-in Error function, which returns the descriptive text from the Err object.

The On Error Statement

Printing information about the current error is fine, but it's more important to trap, correct, and handle errors before they're visible at all. Writing error handlers is something of an art, but you can do a good enough job if your goal is to fix problems before the user sees them.

Access provides the On Error statement to permit you to manage errors. The bottom line is that a procedure with an On Error statement announces to the interpreter that it, not VBA, gets first cut at errors. Depending on the way the On Error statement is written, several different actions can take place when an error occurs.

One of the uses of the On Error statement is redirecting program flow to a statement that's not the next line in the order of statements. These variations use a GoTo statement in conjunction with a *line label*. Line labels are strings that appear on a line by themselves, followed by a colon (:), as in

```
OnClick_Error_Handler:
```

Line labels don't affect program flow, except to give transfers of control somewhere to go.

On Error GoTo Line   When you include the statement On Error GoTo *line* in your code, where *line* is the name of a line label, Access transfers control to the specified label when an error occurs. This is the most common way to *trap an error*; by jumping out of the normal program flow, you have an opportunity to handle the error in a corral of sorts, correct the problem, and pick up where you left off.

In a typical example of this kind of error handler, the code to trap and handle an error looks like this (line numbers added for illustration only):

```
1 Sub create_error()
2 On Error GoTo error_handler
3 Err.Raise 1000
4 Exit Sub
5 error_handler:
6 MsgBox "Error trapped:" & Err & "."
7 End Sub
```

Lines 1, 3, and 5 are the error-creating code from the previous example. The additional code in this example is the error handler. Line 2 tells Access what do to if it detects any error during the execution of this procedure; in this case, Access should transfer execution to the line labeled error_handler.

Line 4 ends the portion of the module that is executed when no error occurs. The program must exit before it continues to the next line, which begins the error handler; you use the Exit Sub statement to leave a procedure before the last line.

Line 5 is a label identifying the beginning of the error handler and the point to which the program should jump when an error is detected. Line 6 defines what to do when the error is trapped (raise a Message Box and identify the error), and line 7 leaves the procedure.

It's important to note that the installation of an error handler disables Access' handling of errors. Since an error handler exists in this procedure, it will continue executing after the error is detected and handled. If Access were allowed to handle the error, it would stop execution at the point where the error occurred.

Most error handlers use this variation on the On Error statement. When you create a command button on a form using the Control Wizards, Access automatically includes an error handler of this type in the On Click event procedure of the control. It doesn't do anything but display the error, but at least the error is handled.

Figure 12.1 shows an example of a typical use of the On Error GoTo (line) statement. The error isn't really handled, but at least it's trapped. Notice the way the Exit Sub statement comes before the error handler. This way, if there's no error, the procedure is exited before normal program flow gets to the error handling code. You can't just put the error handler in a separate subroutine, because there's no On Error GoSub... statement in VBA.

FIG. 12.1

The most common use of On Error is to transfer control to a new line outside of the normal program flow.

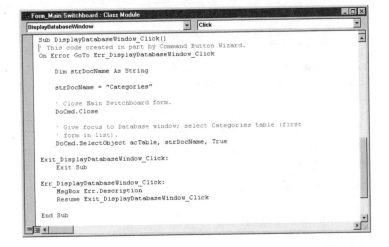

```
Form_Main Switchboard : Class Module
DisplayDatabaseWindow                     Click

Sub DisplayDatabaseWindow_Click()
' This code created in part by Command Button Wizard.
On Error GoTo Err_DisplayDatabaseWindow_Click

    Dim strDocName As String

    strDocName = "Categories"

    ' Close Main Switchboard form.
    DoCmd.Close

    ' Give focus to Database window; select Categories table (first
    ' form in list).
    DoCmd.SelectObject acTable, strDocName, True

Exit_DisplayDatabaseWindow_Click:
    Exit Sub

Err_DisplayDatabaseWindow_Click:
    MsgBox Err.Description
    Resume Exit_DisplayDatabaseWindow_Click

End Sub
```

The first executable statement in this procedure is an On Error statement, nipping any loose errors in the bud. When an error occurs, control passes immediately to the improbably named label `Err_DisplayDatabaseWindow_Click`, which displays the error message and keeps going from where the error occurred. In real user code, it might be more useful to include a Select Case statement like Figure 12.2.

FIG. 12.2

Here is a better way to handle errors than just displaying the message. Anticipate what might happen, and try to fix it.

```
Form_Main Switchboard : Class Module
DisplayDatabaseWindow                     Click

Err_DisplayDatabaseWindow_Click:
'    MsgBox Err.Description
    Select Case Err.Number
        Case 11 ' Divide By Zero
            'fix calculation or warn user here
        Case 53 'file not found
            ' search for file or give user a chance to retry
        Case 482 'printer error
            ' ask user to check printer status
        Case Else
            MsgBox Err.Description
    End Select
    Resume Exit_DisplayDatabaseWindow_Click

End Sub
```

The Case statement illustrated in Figure 12.2 handles three specific errors (11, 53, and 482) and all other possible errors in a catch-all Case Else statement. It's extremely unlikely that any real error handler would handle these specific errors, since they're unlikely to be caused by the same piece of code, but you can extend and modify this example to any procedure you might write. Use the actual error numbers of the errors that you see often, and handle the exceptions with a Case Else statement.

Part

III

Ch

12

Want to know what all of the error codes in Access are? Look for the topic "Determine the Error Codes Reserved by Microsoft Access and the Microsoft Jet Database Engine" in Access help; this topic includes a procedure that you can paste into a new module. When run, this procedure creates a table that contains all of the error codes and descriptions from 0 to 4500; you can extend it past 4500 if you like. The code itself also is worth inspecting for technique.

On Error Resume Next   This form of the On Error statement says, "Ignore any errors that occur in this procedure." Because your program almost certainly won't work correctly if you just ignore a runtime error, this version is most useful when the error handler is directly after the line causing an error in the code. This is an elegant solution if you know where the error will occur, because it doesn't detract from program flow. Your Select Case statement handling errors just needs to include Case 0 (no error) in case the troublesome statement doesn't actually cause an error.

Modifying your earlier example slightly, you have

```
1 Sub create_error()
2 On Error Resume Next
3 Err.Raise 1000
4 End Sub
```

This example eliminates the error handler code (lines 5–7 in the previous example), because it would never be executed. After the error is detected in line 3, Access will resume execution immediately with line 4.

On Error GoTo 0   This form of the On Error statement doesn't really transfer control to line 0, even if there is one. It disables any currently installed error handler, and is rarely used. An example:

```
1 Sub create_error()
2 On Error GoTo 0
3 Err.Raise 1000
4 End Sub
```

As in the previous example, this version of the code essentially ignores the error and continues with the next line.

The Resume Statement

After you've trapped and handled an error, you need to return to the previously scheduled program. This is accomplished with the Resume statement, which, like the On Error statement, comes in three flavors:

■ Resume 0 returns control to the line that caused the error. If your error handler has fixed the problem, this is one way to pick up from where you left off. It's especially useful when the error is caused by a statement requiring user intervention, like a message box, because it gives the user another chance to execute the action that caused the error in the first place once the problem has been fixed.

- Resume Next is the most common way to exit from an error handler; it picks up with the line *after* the one that caused the error. This is used when the error handler corrects the problem and performs the function the errant statement was supposed to.

- Resume line continues executing at the line specified. You can either use a line label, as described previously, or a line number (which is much less clear to human readers).

You can't use a Resume statement in a procedure without an error handler. If a Resume statement is encountered, but no error condition exists, the Resume statement acts like a GoTo statement.

Confirmation Dialogs

Access generates annoying confirmation messages before it deletes or changes records in a table or completes an action query. While these messages may be useful in interactive sessions with simple databases, they're distracting when they occur during application execution.

There are two ways to turn them off. The first method changes Access defaults directly: Click the Tools menu, and then select Options. Then click the Edit/Find tab, and clear the check boxes next to the labels "Confirm Record Changes," "Confirm Document Deletions," and "Confirm Action Queries."

The second method works through code. In a VBA module, include the statement:

```
DoCmd.SetWarnings False
```

The major disadvantage to the first method is that it only applies to the current copy of Access. If this database is used on another machine, the warnings will still appear. By modifying the SetWarnings method (the second method shown here) of the special DoCmd object, your code will turn off warnings wherever it's used. This setting remains in effect as long as the current database is open, but it does not actually change the options for the current copy of Access (so it won't affect other databases or applications run on the same machine).

Part

III

Ch

12

> **CAUTION**
>
> It's easy to turn warnings off and forget they're disabled, which can make debugging really difficult. Consider leaving warnings on until you're sure your code is debugged and ready for users. If you're ever debugging a particularly difficult bug and can't find the cause, check to see if warnings have been disabled (either in VBA or in the Options dialog box).

Converting Access Basic to VBA

There are many reasons why you might want to convert an Access database created in an older version of Access to Access 97. These reasons include better performance and additional features. However, before embarking on a conversion project, you need to consider why you might not want to convert an old-style database to Access 97; if it's being used by people who don't have Access 97, converting it will lock them out. While Access 97 can read and edit data in databases created by older versions of Access, the reverse is not true. If you convert an older database to Access 97, users with Access 1.0, 2.0, and Access 95 won't be able to read it.

Partially Converting Databases

If this is the case, however, you can convert part of the database to Access 97 and leave the data in the tables generated by the earlier version. This method takes advantage of Access 97 interface features without preventing users of older versions from storing and editing data. To partially convert a database made in an older version of Access to Access 97:

1. Make a copy of the earlier version database. In Access 97, open the copy of the old database. When prompted, choose to Convert it to Access 97.

2. If the conversion is successful, continue with step 3. If not, try the techniques in the rest of this chapter to finish the conversion before continuing.

3. Use the Database Splitter utility provided in Access 97 to separate the interface and underlying data into separate databases. To run the Database Splitter, click the Tools menu, then select Add-Ins, then Database Splitter.

4. When prompted, select Split Database. You'll be asked for a new name for the "back-end" (which will contain the tables) database; you can select the default. Click Split to continue.

5. The wizard removes all of the tables to another database file and links the tables to the database file containing all of the other elements. The arrows next to the names of the tables indicate that the tables are stored in a separate file and are "linked" in. Of course, the new back-end database is an Access 97 database, and you want to use the database created in an older version of Access. The newly converted Access 97 tables will not be used and can be safely ignored. Click the Tools menu, then select Add-Ins, and then the Linked Table wizard.

6. The linked tables just created by the Database Splitter appear, linked to the new back-end database. You want to relink them to the older version database; click Always prompt for new location, then Select All, then OK.

7. A file selection dialog box appears; select the name of the old, pre-Access 97 database and click Open. Access relinks the tables from the old database to the interface created in Access 97, which you can now use in Access 97 (enjoying new functionality and speed) while users on older systems can continue to use the old version. Click OK and then Close to exit the Linked Table wizard.

Converting Entire Databases

If you decide that you want to convert an entire database to Access 97, Access will do the conversion for you automatically when you open the old database file in Access 97 and select Convert Database from the options that appear. However, only the simplest databases convert correctly the first time; in most cases, Access 97 returns a message after attempting the conversion that The database is not saved in a compiled state. This is a sure bet that there were problems converting the code, and you'll have to complete the conversion yourself.

To check converted code for errors:

1. Open any module and click the Debug menu, and then Compile and Save All Modules. If you use the Compile Loaded Modules button on the toolbar, your compiled code will not be saved until you exit the Code Builder.

2. The compiler breaks at any line in any standard or class module containing an error. Correct the error and try compiling again.

3. Repeat steps 1 and 2 until the code compiles and saves correctly.

The most common code conversion error, by far, is the conversion of statements containing the DoCmd object. In Access 1.0 and 2.0, DoCmd was an action, so its syntax separated the keyword DoCmd and its argument by a space. In Access 95 and 97, however, DoCmd is an object with methods corresponding to the old arguments, so the correct syntax includes a period (.) between the keywords DoCmd and its methods instead of a space.

A common conversion problem that won't appear on initial conversion is the conversion of custom controls. If you've used any custom controls on forms or reports created in previous versions of Access, they will not work correctly (although they may seem to convert) in Access 97. The only solution is to delete them and re-create them in the new version of Access. This caveat includes the Tab and Calendar controls, which are not custom controls in Access 97 (but were in previous versions). ●

CHAPTER 13

Managing Database Security

Access includes complete user-level security for your databases. Whether you're interested in protecting your design from unintended modifications or you're fending off prying eyes, the robust (maybe too robust) security features available in Access 97 should prove more than enough for your needs.

How security works in Access

An overview of security levels and features. It helps to know what kind of security is available before you start altering it.

Creating users and groups to manage security levels

Every object in a database can have various permissions assigned to it, and those permissions can be limited to certain users or groups of users.

Implementing security for your database

You can enable security at many levels, from no apparent restrictions to the most stringent security possible for the entire database. No security scheme is perfect, though; we'll talk about the limitations of Access security.

NOTE The topic of system security is so detailed that it can (and does) fill books all by itself. For more information on the implications of security in Access, consider one of the following resources: *Special Edition Using Microsoft Access 97* (Que, 1996), the *Microsoft Access 97 Developer's Handbook* (Microsoft Press, 1997), or the Access Security FAQ (available at **http://www.wji.com/access/w7365.html**). ▪

An Overview of Access Security

Access 97 includes two separate security models. The first, called *share-level security,* is the simpler, but is limited in its flexibility. The second, called *user-level security,* permits an administrator to set *permissions* on database objects, and privileges for users and groups of users. Depending on the kinds of limitations you want to set for your database, you can choose to implement either of these security schemes or none at all.

The "No Security" Option

Even if you don't take any positive action to secure your database, some level of security is provided depending on how you install Access on your PC. Some things to consider include:

- Both Windows 95 and Windows NT provide reasonably reliable user-level protection in the operating system itself; if this is sufficient, you may not need to use Access' security features at all.

- Many newer PCs permit the setting of a password in the CMOS, which prevents the machine from even booting unless someone knows the correct password.

- In Windows NT, the default settings require each local user to have an account and password, and these accounts can be tailored to prevent changes to certain directories on the local storage devices.

If you are the only user of your database, and nobody else has physical access to your machine, you may not need Access security at all. Even if others do have access to the machine, you can make it very difficult for them to view your database files unless you establish accounts for them.

If your PC is attached to a network, your options become a little more varied. Because Windows 95 and NT machines attached to a Windows NT network may permit access to remote users if they belong to a machine in the same *NT domain,* a user with Administrator access on the server machine may be able to gain access to your PC if they can get to the console. If they can be kept away from the console, and you don't share the directory containing the database, it is unlikely that a remote user will be able to access your database.

If all you want is to keep users from redesigning your forms and viewing your code, Access 97 gives you the option of creating an MDE file, which solves the user access to Design view problem by not including the design elements in the file. You can give an MDE version of your database to anyone and they can run queries, print reports, and change data as much as they like, but they can't view your code or modify the design of anything. To create an MDE file from the Database window:

1. Click the Tools menu, then select Database Utilities.
2. Choose Make MDE File… and enter a name for the file in the dialog box that appears.
3. Click Save to create the file.

MDE files have the added advantage of running marginally faster than "normal" MDB files. If you choose to use MDE files, remember to keep a copy of your original MDB for changes and editing; you won't be able to edit the MDE file, and you can't convert it back to an MDB.

The "no security" option, while seemingly trivial, is worth considering because Access security is powerful magic. If you set a critical password and forget it, there is little you can do (and nothing you can do for free) to get your data back. If you don't need ironclad security, maybe no security at all is good enough. Or maybe you should consider quasi-security, in which you use a sequence of forms and VBA code to track users and use forms/tables they can access without using the built-in security features Access provides.

Share-Level Security

If you need more security, but don't want to deal with the administrative burden of defining and maintaining users and groups, you can effectively limit access to your entire database by setting a database password. To set a database password:

1. Start Access and open the database you want to protect exclusively (make sure the Exclusive check box is checked before you click Open).
2. Click the Tools menu, then select Security, then Set Database Password.
3. Enter a password in the first box, and re-enter it in the second box to verify it. Click OK to set the password.

Anybody trying to open this database will be prompted for the password you entered. You can only have one database password at a time, and users knowing it will have complete access to your database (unless you've set additional limitations with user-level security, discussed later in this chapter).

> **CAUTION**
> Don't use backslashes (\) in your password. A bug in Access 97 forces you to enter the backslashes twice when trying to open the database, and this can get confusing quickly.

You can remove a share-level password by clicking the Tools menu, then Security, then Unset Database Password. Click OK after entering your old passsword and share-level security is removed.

User-Level Security

If share-level security isn't good enough, consider user-level security. Going to this extreme allows you to define specific privileges for each object in the database (including the database itself) and permissions for every user. While this level of control is nice, it comes with a price—there's significant effort required to plan and implement this kind of security, and if you forget the Administrator password, there's nothing you can do about it. When implementing user-level security, take your time, take copious notes of the settings and options you select, and save an unsecured, backup copy of your database somewhere offsite in the unlikely event that you need it.

Access objects (tables, queries, reports, forms, macros, or modules) can have various combinations of security permissions set for them, and different objects have different permissions available. Table 13.1 illustrates the various permissions available for each type of database object:

Table 13.1 Available Permissions for Access Objects

Permission	Tables	Queries	Forms	Reports	Macros	Modules	Database
Open/Run			✓	✓	✓		✓
Open Exclusive							✓
Read Design	✓	✓	✓	✓	✓	✓	
Modify Design	✓	✓	✓	✓	✓	✓	
Administer	✓	✓	✓	✓	✓	✓	✓
Read Data	✓	✓					
Update Data	✓	✓					
Insert Data	✓	✓					
Delete Data	✓	✓					

By setting and clearing various combinations of these options for a database, you can limit access to levels appropriate for every group you define. The only item in Table 13.1 which may not be self-explanatory is "Administer"; granting the Administer permission for a database object permits the grantee to set permissions on the objects. Granting Administer permission for a database allows the grantee to set startup and security options for the entire database.

Access uses the popular users/groups scheme of permissions, in which certain permissions can be assigned to individual users, groups, or both. If a user has more than one level of security set for a given database object, the more permissive security level is permitted. For example, if a certain user has permission to change a certain table as an individual, but the group to which that user is assigned does not, the user will be able to modify the table despite the group permission set. Conversely, if a user's individual permissions are more restrictive than the group's, the user will be able to use the group's less-restrictive settings.

For this reason, it's almost always best to restrict yourself to assigning permissions to groups, not users. If a user belongs to a group with less-restrictive permissions than his own, you can tighten the screws around him as much as you want, but the more-permissive group permissions will always allow him to roam free. The additional overhead required to maintain individual users' settings becomes prohibitive once a system's user community grows beyond a few people.

Managing Users and Groups

When you use Access without initiating user-level security, you're really running as the user "Admin," who is a member of the group "Admins." This user and group are built into Access and have all permissions on all objects. There also is a group called "Users" set up by default, and it has no members.

When you initiate share-level security by setting a database password, you do so as the user "Admin," who has Administer permissions on the current database by default. Setting a database password does not create any new users or groups, but security is enabled, nonetheless.

Things get interesting when you enable user-level security by modifying the password for the built-in user Admin. This action makes Access security come out of the woodwork and causes Access to begin asking everybody who tries to use the current database for a password. Until you change the Admin password, everybody is, in effect, the user Admin with unlimited rights. Once that password is changed, everybody needs a user ID and password.

The Workgroup Information File

When you first install Access (probably as a part of Office 97 Professional), you're prompted for a name and organization. This information, in addition to being stored in the Windows Registry to identify you, is used to create a special file that contains information about the users and groups authorized to use your copy of Access. This means that, for all practical purposes, a workgroup information file (sometimes called a *system database*) can't be used with any installation of Access other than the one that created it.

Unfortunately, it's relatively trivial to re-create a workgroup information file, since your name and organization are relatively easy to guess. If you secure a database using the default workgroup information file and a malicious user manages to figure out what user name and organization name you used to install Access, they can create an identical workgroup information file containing a user ID with full access to your database, install it on your machine, and gain access to your database.

To prevent this from happening, it's a good idea to create a new workgroup information file (not based on your name and organization) before populating it with all of the users and groups you want to set up for your database. To do this, you use the Workgroup Administrator, a separate application from Access that's installed with Access.

To create a new workgroup information file:

1. Exit Access.
2. From the Start menu, select Programs, then Microsoft Office, then MS Access Workgroup Administrator.

Part
III

Ch
13

3. A dialog box appears identifying your name and organization, and the name of the current workgroup information file for your copy of Access (probably C:\Windows\System\system.mdw). If there is another workgroup information file on your system (presumably created earlier) that you'd like to switch to, you could select it now, but you are going to create another file. Click Create.

4. You're asked to specify a new name, organization, and optionally a Workgroup ID of as many as 20 characters. Enter a name and organization, and enter an arbitrary Workgroup ID. *Write all of them down on a piece of paper you can lock up.* Click OK to continue.

5. Next, you'll be asked to give a name to your new workgroup information file. You can replace the default name, or use any name you like for the file. After you create a new file, any users or groups you create will be added to it until you either create or join a new workgroup.

The practice of writing down the unique IDs and names you use to create a workgroup information file (and, less critically, users and groups) is for self-protection. If the workgroup information file is ever corrupted or lost, you can re-create it by using the information you've written down. Because a new workgroup information file is automatically created with an Admin user, you should be able to gain access to a secured database with a brand-new workgroup information file if you know the strings used to create it.

Creating, Deleting, and Assigning Users and Groups

If you need to implement user-level security, you'll want to develop a security plan, which details the groups you'll establish and the permissions each group will need. Remember that Access automatically establishes two groups: Admins and Users. While these two groups (which you can't delete) imply a certain level of security for their members, there's no requirement that you use them that way. In fact, it's highly advisable that you remove the user Admin from the group Admins; see "Securing a Database" later in this chapter.

After you've decided what the groups and users are to be, at least initially, you can start creating them. Most of the work involved in managing user and group accounts is accomplished from the User and Group Accounts dialog box (see Figure 13.1).

FIG. 13.1

The User and Group Accounts dialog box, showing the default user Admin as it is assigned when setting up security for the first time.

To create a new group:

1. From the Database window, click the Tools menu, then Security, then User and Group Accounts.

2. The User and Group Accounts dialog box appears (refer to Figure 13.1). Select the Groups tab. A pull-down list of existing groups is shown; to create a new group, click the New button.

3. In the dialog box that appears, enter the group's name in the Name box and an arbitrary string of your choosing in the Personal ID (PID) box. Write the name and PID you chose on a piece of paper, taking care to get the case and spelling correct.

4. Click OK. Your group is created, and you are returned to the User and Group Accounts dialog box. You can then create more groups or click OK to exit.

Creating users is just as easy. To create a user:

1. From the Database window, click the Tools menu, then Security, then User and Group Accounts.

2. The User and Group Accounts dialog box appears. If it isn't already selected, click the Users tab.

3. In the region at the top of the User dialog box, click the New button to create a new user.

4. In the dialog box that appears, enter the user's name in the Name box and an arbitrary string of your choosing in the Personal ID box . Write the name and Personal ID you chose on a piece of paper, taking care to get the case and spelling right.

5. Click OK. Your user is created, and you are returned to the User and Group Accounts dialog box. You can then create more users, or click OK to exit.

To remove users or groups, click the appropriate tab in the User and Group Accounts dialog box, select the user or group you want to delete from the pull-down list, and click the Delete button.

Assigning users to and from groups is accomplished with the same dialog box. After the user and group accounts are established, the bottom half of the User and Group Accounts dialog box (refer to Figure 13.1) is used to assign a user to as many groups as necessary. Remember that the least-restrictive permissions apply to any user who is assigned to more than one group.

The pane at lower left shows all of the groups available, and the pane at lower right shows all of the groups to which the current user (the user selected in the Name pane of the User and Group Accounts dialog box) is assigned. To assign a user to a group, select the name of the user you want to modify, then select the group name in the lower left pane and click Add. To remove a user from a group, select the group name in the lower right pane and click Remove.

Clicking the button marked Print Users and Groups starts the Database Documentor Wizard, which offers you the option of printing the user information, group information, or both. You can select the option you need and click OK to send a report directly to your printer.

Part
III

Ch
13

You can't send the report to the screen, but you can set up a Generic/Text Only printer in Control Panel to save the output to a file. Make this printer the default before clicking the Print Users and Groups button and you'll get a formatted text document ready to edit or to include in documentation.

Setting and Removing Permissions

You can set any or all of the permissions identified in Table 13.1 for any user or group in any workgroup information file to which you have Administer access. If you haven't yet secured your database (see "Securing a Database" later in this chapter), you should have an Admin user with Administer permission by default.

To set or remove permissions from existing users or groups:

1. Click the Tools menu, then Security, then User and Group Permissions

2. The User and Group Permissions dialog box appears (see Figure 13.2). In the List area of the dialog box, choose either Users or Groups option; the Users view is selected by default. Choose the Object Type by clicking the drop-down list containing all of the object types for which you can set permissions and making your selection. You should see a list of all of the modules in the database in the Object Name pane at upper right.

3. Select a user or group name and an object in the two panes at the top of the dialog box. Depending on what type of object you select, certain permissions (see Table 13.1) are available. In the Permissions area, click the check box next to the privileges you want assigned. Click the check box again to clear the check mark and remove the privilege. You can set any combination of permissions for any combinations of users and groups on any objects.

FIG. 13.2

The permissions available for each type of object are different; these are the permissions available for forms.

You can set permissions for objects not yet created by selecting the first object in any of the lists, "<New *object*>." The only object you can select for the Database object types is "<Current Database>," which makes sense.

4. Click the Change Owner tab. You'll see a similar list of objects and users/groups, designating the "owner" of each object in the database (see Figure 13.3). Ownership of objects is important because the owner of an object (usually the user ID that created the object) can change permissions on that object. If you secure your database properly, this isn't really a security hole, but if you allow users to create new objects, they can then control who has access to them. To prevent this potential problem, change ownership of all objects in a secure database to Admin (or another administrator) by selecting the object and the name of the new owner in the New Owner box. Then click Change Owner to make the change.

FIG. 13.3
Every object in the database is "owned" by a user, and you can change ownership by using this dialog box.

5. When you're done changing permissions and ownership, click OK to return to the Database window.

Securing a Database

Creating users and groups and modifying their default privileges is an effective way to control access to particular objects in a database. However, the way Access security works is sufficiently well-understood that typical security measures will generally succeed in making unauthorized access inconvenient, but not impossible. We've already seen how a re-created workgroup information file, created knowing only the developer's name and organization, can thwart security; several other techniques can be used to intentionally gain access to a secured database if it hasn't been secured adequately.

With the advent of Access 97, Microsoft has provided the User-Level Security Wizard (discussed later in this chapter), which does most of the work required to secure your database. You can use only the Wizard to set your system security, but an additional few steps (described here) can enhance system security, as well as help you develop insight into the limitations of the Wizard. That insight may help you someday restore access to an accidentally locked database, or help you envision ways to enhance your security further.

These steps are well-known and are published in various books and journals; in the interest of good programming practice, you should use them and encourage their use. You'll need to use the techniques listed earlier in this chapter to create a workgroup information file, users, and groups, and to set permissions, so become familiar with those techniques before continuing.

Part
III

Ch
13

To manually secure an Access database:

1. Create a new workgroup information file. Write down the strings you use to create the file.

2. Open the database you want to secure, create a new user to act as the Administrator (not Admin), and add this user to the Admins group. Write down the user name and PID you choose. You'll set the password for this user ID the first time you log in with it.

3. Remove the user Admin from the Admins group. You can't delete the Admin user ID, but you can remove it from the group that gives it far-reaching permissions by selecting Admin in the Name pull-down box and clicking Remove. By doing this, you prevent someone from gaining access to your database by using the Admin ID (because the new user ID will be unknown to anybody but you). Note that you have to have created a new Administrator before you can do this; there must always be at least one member of the Admins group.

4. If you haven't changed the password for the user Admin, do so now to enable system security. Until you do this, anybody running the database is assumed to be Admin. There's no advantage to creating and using different User IDs until you enable system security, since all users have full rights to the database. The value of the original Admin password is likewise moot, because you have to change it to make use of it.

5. Exit Access and restart it, this time using the new administrator ID you just created. Assign a password to this ID.

6. Run the Wizard by clicking the Tools menu, then Security, then User-Level Security Wizard. The Wizard consists of one dialog box (see Figure 13.4), which verifies your identity and asks which objects in the database you want to enable security for. Because you can control permissions for any object in the database, you may as well secure them all, which is the default. Click OK to continue.

FIG. 13.4

The User-Level Security Wizard. You probably don't want to do this as Admin; use the user name you created.

7. The Wizard creates a new, encrypted database (you're asked to specify a name for it) without affecting the current database file. The new database still includes Administer permission for any members of the group Admins, but members of the group Users have no permissions at all. This process may take a few minutes depending on the size of your database and the speed of your PC.

8. Save the unsecured version of your database, along with the paper you used to write down the workgroup information file ID and the name and PID for the Admin user, in a

locked container somewhere far away from your secured database. Quit Access, delete the unsecured version of the database, and clear your Recycle Bin.

 Really crafty data thieves could conceivably scan your hard drive for fragments of deleted files and find the old workgroup information file or deleted unsecured database. If this is likely to be a problem for you, consider commercial software that reliably deletes files by overwriting them with garbage characters. Remember that no security scheme is 100% secure, no matter how careful you are.

9. Open the secured version of your database as the Admin user and add users and groups as appropriate. Remember that every user is a member of the Users group, so granting permissions to the Users group grants them to everybody.

To increase the annoyance level for someone trying to get into your database, you can do one more thing to keep your data private: Set a database password (click the Tools menu, then Security, then Set Database Password). Users will be prompted for a user ID and password when they start Access, then another password to get into the secured database. ●

CHAPTER 14

Network-Enabling Your Database Using Replication

Greatly enhanced in Access 97, replication enables you to maintain a master database (a Design Master) and farm out replicas of it (or parts of it) to other users on your network. This feature allows you to minimize network traffic as remote users work on their own copies of a database, but gives you a way to ensure that the data in all of those remote copies is periodically synchronized with a master copy. Remote users aren't allowed to change the structure of the database, but you can make changes to the master and "replicate" your changes throughout all of the replicas. Changes to data made at the replica level can be shared among all of the replicas and the master via a process called *synchronization*. ∎

What replication is and how it works

The replication model is an efficient way to distribute a database among a large group and still maintain some control over the design and data.

How to create a Design Master and replicas

You can use Access to do this, or you can use the Briefcase application in Windows. Both work the same way.

Synchronicity

The real advantage to using replication is the ability to let the copies get "out of sync" and bring them back again.

Wizards to help make databases network-friendly

Another way to distribute a database across a network uses the Linked Table Manager and Database Splitter Wizard. It's a little easier, but not as comprehensive.

Replication Overview

There are times when you may want to permit different users to use individual copies of a database: maybe they're travelling with a laptop, they're on a slow network connection, or maybe they need to make local changes that don't affect everybody else. In previous versions of Access, you'd have to find a way to merge the tables modified by these disconnected users, and with a database of any size, that task quickly became overwhelming.

Access 97 includes built-in support for *replication*, the loose coupling of different versions of the same database distributed across many machines. When you make a database replicable, you create two copies of the original database: a Design Master, which acts as the central arbiter of all changes to data and enables changes to structure, and a replica, which can be installed on a remote machine. A replica differs from a Design Master in that any data modifications made in the replica can be updated in the Design Master, but design changes cannot.

TIP You can't make a database with a password replicable, so remove any database passwords (click the Tools menu, then select Security, then Unset Database Password) before trying to create a Design Master. User-level security should continue to work in replicas.

Creating and Deleting Design Masters and Replicas

After a database is sufficiently complete to distribute to endusers, the act of making it replicable is relatively straightforward. Access provides two methods for creating Design Masters and replicas: through the Replication menu, and in conjunction with the Windows Briefcase. The two processes are similar, although it's conceivable that you might want to use the Briefcase to control distribution of a database without replicating it.

NOTE There's actually a third way to create replicas, by using DAO and writing a procedure using the MakeReplica method on a Database object. That process is outside of the scope of this book, but you can read about it in the online help topic "Create Partial Replicas." ■

Replication Using the Replication Menu

To make a database replicable, you'll need to create a Design Master and a replica, which you can copy to as many remote machines as needed. To convert a database into a Design Master:

1. Back up the unreplicated database. Unlike the process followed by some other wizards, the default Design Master creation process actually changes the selected database into a Design Master. Because it's difficult to convert a Design Master back into a regular database, it's best to back up the original before you convert it.

NOTE Changes you make to the Design Master after conversion will not be reflected in the original, unreplicated database. Likewise, changes you make to the unreplicated original will not be reflected in the Design Master. In general, you should make changes to the Design Master and periodically make the same changes to your backup manually. This process, while tedious, ensures that you can always recover from a crashed database and pick up from more or less where you left off. ■

2. In Access, open the database you want to replicate and click the Tools menu, then select Replication, and then Create Replica. A dialog box appears informing you that the database must be closed before beginning; click Yes to close it.

N O T E You have to have the database open to use the Create Replica menu option, but the first thing Access does is close it. ■

3. If you didn't make a backup of your database before starting, you have an opportunity to do so with the next message box, which asks if you want a backup created. Click Yes to create one and continue, or No to continue without creating a backup.

4. The database you originally opened is converted to a Design Master and a file selection dialog box appears. This dialog box is used for designating a name for a replica, not the newly created Design Master. Enter a filename in the File Name box (or use the default, Replica of…) and click OK to continue.

5. A replica is created and a dialog box appears confirming that your database is now a Design Master and that a replica has been created. Click OK to work in the Design Master.

You'll notice that the Design Master looks the same as the original, except that the name of each object in the Database window has a yin-yang-like symbol next to it (see Figure 14.1) to denote that it's replicated. If you open any of these objects in Design view, you'll see that the object's title appears as *ObjectName* (Replicated) as a reminder. The replica of this Design Master now resides in the same directory as the Design Master, but under the filename you specified in Step 4.

FIG. 14.1

The Database window, showing the replication symbol next to the object name.

After you create a Design Master and replica, several changes are made to the tables in the replica. Fields are added to each table to manage the synchronization of the data between the replica and the Design Master, and a few new tables are added. These changes are transparent

Part

III

Ch

14

to you unless you have enabled the display of system objects (click the Tools menu, then select Options, then the View tab, then System Objects). They're only worth knowing about in the event that you later decide to change a replica into a "normal" database.

If you decide at some later date that you don't want this database to be replicable, your best bet is to restore the backup you made before making the database replicable (rename the .bak file created during the creation of the Design Master to .mdb). If that's impossible or not feasible, you can make a replica into a regular database following the instructions in the online help topic "Make a replicated database a regular database," which involves importing all of the nonreplication objects from a replica into a new database. You'll have to manually avoid importing all of the new system objects and fields created when the replica was born by using queries to import the tables; the online help discusses how to do this.

Making a single replica enables you to distribute a copy of your database to one remote user. If more than one remote user needs to use the database, you'll need to create more replicas. Since each replica maintains information in hidden tables that identifies it uniquely, you need to create individual replicas for each remote user. To create another replica, you have three options:

- Open the Design Master in Access and click the Tools menu, then Replication, then Create Replica, exactly as you did when creating the first replica.
- Open any replica in Access and click the Tools menu, then Replication, then Create Replica.
- Copy any replica into a new file.

All of these options work, and Access keeps track of the fact that all of these replicas are related by maintaining certain information in the hidden system tables mentioned earlier. The original Design Master and all replicas created from it (or from replicas created from that Design Master) comprise a *replica set*, and it's in this replica set that changes to the Design Master tables are coordinated when you synchronize the replicas (see "Synchronizing Replicas" later in this chapter).

Replication Using Briefcase

If you installed Briefcase on your system when you installed Windows 95, you can use it to help automate the replication process. To create a replica using Briefcase:

1. Drag a database file from the Windows desktop (or from Explorer) onto the Briefcase to begin the Design Master/replica creation process.

2. A message box appears, asking whether you want to continue; click Yes.

3. Another message box appears and asks if you want to make a backup of your database before you convert it. In this case (unlike the process from within Access), you have to choose a backup filename. Click Yes to continue.

4. The backup is created and the conversion begins. When it finishes, a dialog box appears and asks whether you want to put the Design Master or the replica in the Briefcase. The default (Original Copy) puts the replica in the Briefcase, effectively permitting data

changes but not design changes when you're on the road. The other option (Briefcase Copy), permits formatting changes in the remote copy but only data changes in the desktop. You might choose this option if your desktop is used by someone else while you're away. Choose an option and click OK to complete the process.

TIP The problem with using a Design Master/replica scheme with the Briefcase is that you may be in the process of designing the database and you don't want to use replication at this point; you just want to get a copy in the Briefcase so it's easy to take it on the road with you. Although Windows assumes you want to use replication when you drag a database into the Briefcase, you can foil this behavior by changing the file extension to something other than .mdb or .mde before dragging it into the Briefcase.

If you copy a database into the Briefcase which is already a replica, Access doesn't try to make it a Design Master.

Synchronizing Replicas

Coordinating the updating of data among all of the replicas in a replica set can be tricky, especially if the same record has been modified in more than one replica. This is called a *conflict*, and it has to be resolved manually before all of the data can be collected back in the Design Master and reflected to all of the replicas.

When you synchronize two replicas, any changes that have been made to tables in either replica are reflected in the other, making them identical after synchronization. If you synchronize a replica with a Design Master, the data tables in both are made to agree and any changes to the database structure made in the Design Master since the replica was created are copied to the replica. It's easy to see that several synchronization passes may be required among all of the members of a replica set before all are properly synchronized; for large replica sets, it's advisable to consider buying the Microsoft Office 97 Developer Edition (ODE) and using the Replication Manager, discussed later in this chapter. For small replica sets, you can probably manage the synchronization problem manually.

Synchronization Using the Replication Menu

To synchronize two replicas or a replica and Design Master from within Access:

1. Open one of the replicas or the Design Master in Access.
2. From the menu, click the Tools menu, then select Replication, then Synchronize Now.
3. The Synchronize Database dialog box appears asking for the filename of the database with which you want to synchronize. Type the file's full path or click Browse to choose a file from a file selection dialog box. When the correct file is entered, click OK.

Part III Ch 14

TIP Should your Design Master ever get corrupted, you can make a replica into a Design Master by clicking the check box in the Syncronize Database dialog box labeled Make '*filename*' the Design Master. You should only have one Design Master per replica set.

CAUTION

If you choose to make a replica into a Design Master and a Design Master for this replica set already exists, it will be replaced without warning by the new Design Master. Any changes you have made to the original Design Master since the last synchronization (when changes were passed to all of the replicas) will be lost.

4. Synchronization proceeds; if it's entirely successful, a dialog box appears asking if you want to close and reopen the database. Click Yes to complete the process. If synchronization did not complete successfully, you may see an error dialog box; synchronization errors are discussed in "Managing Conflicts Between Replicas," later in this chapter.

5. Even if you don't see an error dialog box, you should check to see if there were any problems during synchronization by clicking the Tools menu, then selecting Replication, then Resolve Conflicts. If Access reports any problems, correct them as described in "Managing Conflicts Between Replicas" later in this chapter.

Synchronization Using Briefcase

To synchronize a replica in the Briefcase and a Design Master on a desktop machine when you're using synchronization in conjunction with Briefcase:

1. Copy the modified replica into the Briefcase on the desktop machine.

2. Double-click the Briefcase to open it. Right-click the name of the replica; a menu appears.

3. Click Update to start the synchronization process. As with any Briefcase document, if the database in the Briefcase is newer than the one on the local disk, a dialog box (see Figure 14.2) appears asking whether you want to overwrite the local copy. You'll usually choose Update to copy the newer file to disk.

FIG. 14.2

The dialog box that appears when a document in the Briefcase is newer than the one on disk that was copied into the Briefcase.

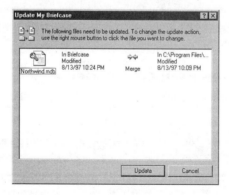

4. The rest of the synchronization process happens behind the scenes. To see if there were any problems with the synchronization, open the Design Master and check for conflicts

(click the Tools menu, then select Replication, then Resolve Conflicts) as described in "Managing Conflicts Between Replicas" in the next section.

If you originally placed a replica directly in the Briefcase, rather than creating a new replica by dragging the Design Master (or an unreplicated database) into the Briefcase, the Update process will not attempt synchronization. You should open Access and manually synchronize the replica as described in "Synchronization Using the Replication Menu" earlier in this chapter.

Managing Conflicts Between Replicas

When a record is changed or deleted in one replica that contains data another replica (or the Design Master) depends on, a problem is created that will have to be resolved before continuing synchronization. There are three kinds of problems that typically appear during the synchronization process:

- Conflicts occur when the same record is modified differently in two replicas.
- Design errors occur when a change is made to the design of a database object in the Design Master that will cause a loss of data in a replica.
- Data errors occur when a change is made to one replica that creates a data integrity problem in another.

▶ **See** "Understanding Table Relationships," **p. 36**

When you begin synchronizing two databases, Access checks for conflicts and data errors and notifies you if it finds any. Any records that are not in conflict are synchronized appropriately, but you'll have to manually resolve the data error or conflict using the instructions in the error dialog box, which automatically appears as Figure 14.3 or 14.4 depending on the type of error encountered.

The resolution of the various problems that can arise during synchronization depends on the kind of error generated and its severity. Data errors (see Figure 14.3), for example, can be very difficult to resolve and may require a significant amount of digging in tables looking for deleted records.

FIG. 14.3

A data error caused by deleting a record in the Customers table of one replica while it still had active records in the Orders table of another replica.

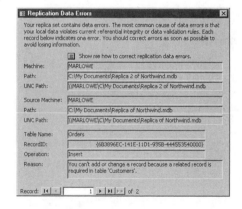

Conflicts, on the other hand (see Figure 14.4), are handled through a simple dialog box that permits the selection of one option or the other to take precedence. For each conflict discovered, you have only two options: keep the existing record as displayed, or replace it with the conflicting record from the other replica. After one button or the other is clicked and all conflicts are resolved, the synchronization process runs to completion.

FIG. 14.4

A conflict ready to be resolved. If there were more conflicts to resolve, you could use the navigation buttons at the bottom of the dialog box to view them.

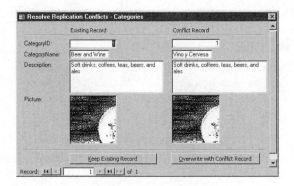

 You can choose to resolve conflicts in code, if you prefer, by devising an algorithm to decide which record should be accepted (usually the more recent change) and using the ReplicationConflictFunction property of the Document object (which you'll have to create) in DAO. It's not easy, but if the operation of your system depends on the automatic resolution of conflicts, you'll be glad it's there. See the online help for details.

You can choose to defer correcting conflicts and data errors until later, if that's convenient; the affected records won't be synchronized until you correct the problem. To view the list of errors previously discovered and not yet cleared, click the Tools menu, then select Replication, then Resolve Conflicts. A dialog box appears (see Figure 14.5) that enables you to select one of three buttons (Resolve Conflicts, View Design Errors, or View Data Errors) to resolve the conflict.

FIG. 14.5

The Resolve Replication Conflicts dialog box appears when you ask to resolve conflicts after you've already tried to complete a synchronization.

Replication Manager (ODE)

If you find yourself creating a lot of replicas, it may be worth a few hundred dollars to obtain the Microsoft Office Developer Edition (ODE) just for the included Replication Manager. The online help in the basic version of Office Professional briefly describes the ODE's features, they include:

- Synchronizers, virtual machines which automatically schedule and perform synchronization among all of the members of a replica set at a time you set. This feature alone is worth the purchase price of the ODE if you have more than four or five replicas to manage.

- A graphical representation of all of the members of a replica set. Without Replication Manager, you have no easy way to know how many members there are in a replica set and whether they've been synchronized.

- A way to create replicas and Design Masters without opening Access.

- A way to synchronize replicas located on machines connected to the Internet. The Replication Manager can use the TCP/IP network protocol to pass synchronization information to and from a remote replica to keep it synchronized.

Replication Manager is a standalone application tightly integrated with Access (you can open a table in Access directly from the Replication Manager) and its graphical display (see Figure 14.6) of the replica set, schedule, and properties is invaluable in managing widely distributed replicas. The online help included with the application is a little sparse, but it's enough to get started; Microsoft's telephone support is available for the ODE and includes an unlimited number of calls on the implementation of the ODE tools, including Replication Manager.

FIG. 14.6
A typical Replication Manager session.

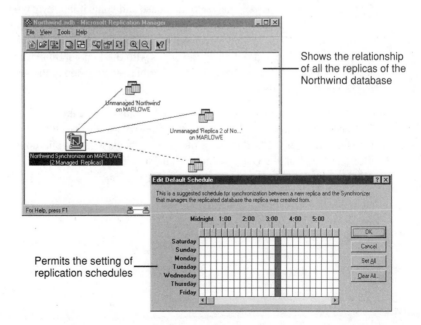

Shows the relationship of all the replicas of the Northwind database

Permits the setting of replication schedules

Part

III

Ch

14

Using the Database Splitter and Linked Table Wizard

If you want to distribute a database across a network but don't want to go through all of the hassle of the replication process, you may want to consider using the Database Splitter and the Linked Table Wizard to ease the task of coordinating changes.

In the replication model, every user has a local copy of the database interface (forms, reports, queries, macros, and modules) as well as the database tables. When a change is made to the data in a replica, the act of synchronizing the replica with a remote Design Master merges the changed data more or less automatically.

In the linked-table model, however, users attached to a local area network share a single, central database containing the data and use local copies of the interface to speed up execution. Access includes decent record-locking facilities that prevent one user from changing data while another user is working on it; while this model is not appropriate for large workgroups and busy databases, it may well suffice for small groups and infrequently accessed tables. The description of this approach is described in this chapter even though it's not related to "replication," per se, because it accomplishes the same goal of effectively distributing access to data across the enterprise.

The key to making this scheme work lies in the developer's ability to separate the interface and tables into different files. Once separated, the tables are linked into the file containing the interface, which can then be distributed. The tables remain physically where they began, but anyone using the interface with the linked tables actually modifies the remote tables when they access the data.

It's not hard to do this manually, but Access provides a couple of tools that make it easier. The first, the Database Splitter, analyzes a database and splits it into two: one contains the interface, and the second contains only the data tables. This is the first step in using this approach to distributing data. The second step involves moving (or copying) the interface file to another machine or location and re-linking the tables with the Linked Table Manager. The Database Splitter and Linked Table Manager are described step-by-step in the section "Partially Converting Databases" in Chapter 12.

When you move the interface to a new machine, use the Linked Table Manager as described in Chapter 12 to relink the tables from the server where they're stored to the new location of the interface. You'll need to make sure the shared database is in a shared folder on the server machine (and that the Guest account is enabled, if the server is running Windows NT) before relinking the tables. ●

CHAPTER 15

Building Applications with Access

Access databases become applications when user interfaces and VBA code is added to them to make them more than databases. While building an application, you may find that some of Access' default behaviors don't suit your coding style; many of these can be changed. After an application is built, however, there's still plenty to do; it needs to be documented, tested, and distributed. And after it's out the door, there will be bug fixes, user modifications, and future releases. ■

Modify Access' defaults

The Options dialog box enables you to change the way Access appears, what values it chooses for defaults, how the Builders work, and more.

Save a record of your database design

The Documenter add-in examines every object in your database and writes detailed definitions to a report.

Distribute your code

Want to keep users from prying into the way your database is built? Consider using an MDE file, which prevents users from viewing or modifying the database's design.

Learn what's in the ODE

The Office 97 Developer's Edition contains various tools to ease the distribution of your code, as well as a runtime license to give a copy of Access to anybody you like.

Get help

There are hundreds of books and Web pages containing information for the Access developer; some of the more useful are listed here.

Database Options

There are several dozen customizable options you can set that pertain to your local copy of Access. While the defaults are satisfactory for most work, you may find that modifying some of these options makes you more efficient as a developer. For example, the option to perform Auto Syntax Checking is turned on by default. However, if you're prototyping VBA code and you don't intend that the code you write should be perfect the first time through, turning this setting off will eliminate the annoying error messages that appear whenever you finish a line and it's not syntactically perfect. As another example, consider creating a series of tables that will contain mostly numbers. The default data type set for new fields in tables is Text, but you can change it to Number in the Options dialog box and save yourself the trouble of changing every field you create to Number from Text.

To set database options:

1. Click the Tools menu, then select Options from the menu. The Options dialog box appears (see Figure 15.1).

FIG. 15.1

The Options dialog box, showing the Datasheet tab. Changes made in this dialog box stay with the copy of Access making the changes and can't be distributed with the application.

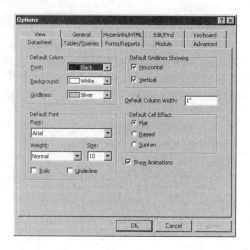

2. Select one of the ten tabs available to display a different pane of options to set. Depending on the option you want to change (see Table 15.1), you may need to fill in a text box, click a check box or radio button, or make a selection from a pull-down list. Navigate through the panes by selecting different tabs and changing the settings you need to change.

3. Click OK to commit your changes to the database.

Some options you may find convenient to change are noted in Table 15.1.

Table 15.1 Common Database Options

Tab/Option	Settings (default bold)	Comments
Datasheet		
Default Colors	Any color in the palette	You can change the background color to provide more contrast, or make the gridlines lighter.
Show Animations	**On**, off	Turn this off on slower machines to make Access faster.
Tables/Queries		
Default Field Sizes	Text – 50, numbers – Long Int	Making these smaller may save disk and memory space.
Default Field Type	**Text**, memo, number, etc.	Change to the field type you use most.
Forms/Reports		
Selection Behavior	**Partially enclosed**, Fully enclosed	Affects the way dragged marquees work to select controls.
Always Use Event Procedures	On, **off**	Turning on appends an empty procedure to every form or report. This was the default in earlier versions of Access.
Module		
Tab Width	**4**	Set to fit your editing preference.
Coding Options	**On**, off	These helpers may slow you down while typing or if on a slower machine.
View System Objects	On, **off**	Turn on to view system tables and macros; useful for replicated databases.
General		
Default Database Folder	**C:\My Documents**	Change to disk location for your project(s) to make saving and opening easier.

continues

Table 15.1 Continued

Tab/Option	Settings (default bold)	Comments
HYPERLINKS/HTML		
HTML Output	Various	These settings are usually modified using the Save as HTML Wizard, but you can do it here instead.
Edit/Find		
Confirm	**On**, off	Confirmations of action queries, changes, and deletions. If you never delete by accident, clear this option.
Keyboard		
Move After Enter	Don't Move, **Next Field**, Next Record	Enter key behavior.

Using the Documenter

When you create an application using Access, there's more to it than a database. You'll generally want to include user-level documentation that describes the system requirements for Access, how to install the system, how to start and run the application, and so on. You also should consider documenting the application for the benefit of system administrators and programmers that come after you.

As you design and develop your database, you should have been making use of the various documentation features that are built into the system. The design environments for tables and macros include room for descriptions of fields and comments for macro actions; in modules, you can (and should) include comments (lines beginning with apostrophes) as often as is necessary to make it clear to a human reader what your code is doing.

One useful way to help document your code is to include a *block comment* at the beginning of each standard and class module that describes several things about it:

- The name of the module
- The name and contact information for the author
- The date it was originally written and a record of changes to the code listed by date
- A description of what the module should do
- A list of any arguments the module requires and an explanation of any values it returns

While this sounds like a lot of work, the time you save yourself and programmers that follow you by doing this far outweighs the time and effort it takes to actually create these block comments. They're easy to spot in the code, and they have the added benefit of giving you more text to search through (using Access' search mechanism; click the Edit menu, then Find, then select the Current Database radio button to perform a full-text search of all modules in a database) when you're trying to find the function that you changed on a particular date or for a certain reason.

One useful technique that you can use with this kind of documentation is to write a procedure that looks for these block comments in all of your modules and writes them to a file (or even to a new table). Your code becomes self-documenting.

Consider the function IsItAReplica() in Northwind. The beginning of the module, as written, looks like this:

```
Function IsItAReplica() As Boolean

On Error GoTo IsItAReplica_Err

' Determines if database is a design master or a replica.

' Used in OpenStartup function.
```

Someone experienced in using VBA can look at this short function and see what it does, but it's hardly well-documented. You can infer that it returns True if the current database is a replica, but you'd have to read it to know that for sure. To make this function self-documenting, you might make it look like this instead:

```
Function IsItAReplica() As Boolean

'- - - - - - - - - - - - - - - - - - - - - - - - - - - - - - - - - - - - - -

' Function IsItAReplica() as Boolean

' J. E. Hammond, J. St. George, M. Sparkman, 10/96

' Change History:

' 10/2/96Initial version

' 10/11/96Added error handler (JEH)

' 11/4/96Peer review (MPS)

'

' Returns True if current database is a replica; False otherwise.

' No arguments. Used in OpenStartup function.

'- - - - - - - - - - - - - - - - - - - - - - - - - - - - - - - - - - - - -

On Error GoTo IsItAReplica_Err
```

Whether or not you choose to use block commenting in your modules, Access includes a tool that helps document your database. It's no replacement for well-written system documentation, but it's useful as part of a formal deliverable. The Documenter examines the current database and writes a full description of the fields, properties, controls, and permissions of any or all objects in the database. Depending on the options you select, you can create anything from a simple list of the major objects to a complete dump of every attribute and property of everything in the database.

To use the Documenter:

1. From the Database Window, click the Tools menu, then select Analyze, then Documenter.

2. The Documenter dialog box (see Figure 15.2) appears; by selecting the tabs at the top, you can select individual objects of various types, or you can use the All Objects tab to work with all of the objects in the database in one pane. Clicking next to the name of an object makes a check mark appear and makes that object's information appear in the final report. Buttons on the right enable you to Select All or Deselect All of the objects in the currently displayed pane. All of the panes except the Database pane have the Options button enabled; clicking it displays a dialog box (see Figure 15.3) of specific features appropriate to the currently displayed type to choose from for inclusion in the report. Choose some objects and options and click OK to continue.

3. The Documenter starts, analyzing the objects in the database. If you don't have Read permission for any object, an error will be displayed and you are given the option to

FIG. 15.2

The Documenter dialog box for the All Objects pane. These dialogs are modal; you can't do anything else in Access while they're open.

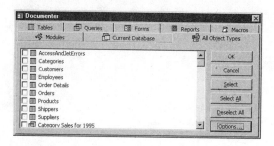

FIG. 15.3

The Print Table Definition dialog box for the Documenter enables you to select various properties and fields to include in the printed report.

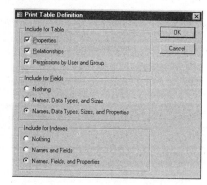

continue without documenting that object. When it finishes, it displays a formatted report in Print Preview (see Figure 15.4). You can print the report (Northwind, with all objects and all properties selected, takes almost 500 pages), view it online, or return to the Database window by using the buttons on the Print Preview toolbar.

FIG. 15.4
A typical Documenter report in Print Preview. You can set your default printer to "Generic/Text Only" with its port to "File" to save this report as a text document.

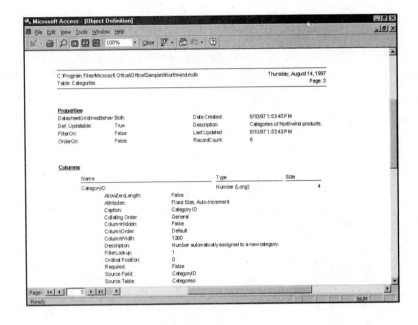

MDE Files

Access 97 gives developers the option to distribute a database without permitting end-users to modify it or disassemble any code it might contain. While this was technically possible under earlier versions of Access, this kind of protection always required setting stringent database security and distributing appropriate security-related files with an application. These measures are no longer necessary if all you need is to prevent the people you distribute a database to from taking it apart or changing it.

▶ **See** "Managing Database Security," **p. 227**

These special unmodifiable databases are called MDE files in reference to the file extension Access appends to them (.mde). Several things are different about an MDE file from a conventional Access database:

■ The code in MDE files is compiled. No readable code is included in the MDE file, so it's impossible for users to view or change it.

N O T E Visual Basic for Applications (VBA) code is never really compiled in the traditional sense in Office applications; the word "compiled" as used by Microsoft really means "syntax-checked and converted to a machine-readable format." There's no optimization of the code, nor can the "compiled" object files be used anywhere except in the database where they were created. ■

- Users can't change the design of any form, report, or module in the database, and they can't change the name of the database in Options (described later in this chapter).

- Users can't import or export reports, forms, or modules. They can, however, export tables and macros to other databases, or import those objects into another database from the MDE file.

To create an MDE file from a typical Access database, click the Tools menu, then select Database Utilities, then Make MDE File from the menu. You are prompted for a file name; click OK to save the file. After saving it, you are returned to your MDB file to continue working.

N O T E   You can't make an MDE file from a replicated database. If you're following along with the examples in this book and converted your copy of the Northwind database to a Design Master in Chapter 14, make sure you restore the original (from the backup you made) before continuing with any of these examples. ▪

CAUTION

Make sure you always save an MDB version of a file you intend to distribute as an MDE. There's no way to convert an MDE back to an MDB, and you won't be able to change forms, reports, or modules in the MDE after you create it. Furthermore, Microsoft has stated Access 97 MDE files won't work with any future version of Access, so you'll need to re-create them from the original MDB if you ever upgrade.

You may see a minor performance improvement using MDE files, especially when compared to using the equivalent MDB. This is because the MDE files are compacted (requiring less disk space and time to access) and because some optimization of the way Access will use memory to run the database is performed when the MDE file is saved.

Distributing Applications (ODE)

The Office 97 Developer's Edition (ODE) takes the place of the Access Developers Toolkit used with earlier versions of Access. You can purchase the ODE together with Office 97 Professional (the package contains two CDs: one containing Office and one containing the ODE), or by itself. If you already have a copy of Access 97 and all you need is the additional functionality of the ODE, you can save a few hundred dollars by purchasing the ODE upgrade, although it can be hard to find.

Although the ODE ostensibly contains developer tools applicable to the entire Office 97 suite, it's primarily a resource for Access programmers. When you purchase the ODE, you receive:

- A distributable, runtime-only version of Access 97. If you're writing applications in Access, people running your applications will require a copy of Access 97 on their desktops to use them. By giving them a runtime version of Access, you enable them to execute your applications without buying Access.

N O T E The runtime version of Access doesn't allow users to work in Design view or to use any built-in toolbars. It's really only useful for running already-written database applications.

You need a full copy of Access to distribute the runtime version, because it uses some files from your full installation. The Developer's Edition upgrade (one CD) doesn't include a full copy of Access (or any other Office 97 application). ▪

- ■ An unlimited license to distribute your code and the runtime executable. While there aren't any legal ramifications to distributing your application, there may be restrictions placed on the distribution of any custom controls you use in the application. With this license, you can distribute any Microsoft customer control along with your application and the Access runtime engine to as many people as you like.

- ■ The Setup Wizard, an Access wizard that manages the creation of file archives that can be used to install and configure Access and your application on a client's machine. The Setup Wizard includes everything you need to produce a professional distribution package for your applications, including the familiar Microsoft Office-like setup screens, progress meter, and installation options. You can even use it to create individual disks for installation and to register custom controls with the operating system when the application is installed.

- ■ The Replication Manager, which schedules and controls the synchronization of replicated databases across local network and the Internet. If you're depending on replication for an enterprise-critical system, this feature alone is worth the purchase price.

- ■ Help Workshop, a help compiler that builds standard Windows Help files from text files you can create in Word.

- ■ Source code control facilities, useful if you use Microsoft SourceSafe to manage version control in your applications.

- ■ Additional ActiveX (custom) controls for use in your applications.

- ■ The Win32 API viewer, which provides syntax definitions for all public Windows library functions. Unfortunately, to receive documentation on what these functions actually do, you'll need to buy either Visual Basic or a good book on the Windows API.

Using these tools is straightforward; the ODE creates appropriate entries for the utilities on your Start menu, and adequate help is provided for all of them. The Setup Wizard runs from within Access; the Replication Manager, Help Workshop, and Win32 API Viewer are applications unto themselves. If you're writing databases for others to use, the ODE is a must-have.

Getting Help

There's much more to Access than can be covered in any one book. Writing database applications, like writing programs in general, becomes easier and more effective with practice. There's no substitute to working in the Access environment for learning to write efficient, comprehensive applications, but there are several resources that you should keep at your fingertips as you work. These include (but are certainly not limited to):

- The Microsoft Knowledge Base (**http://www.microsoft.com/kb/default.asp**). Thousands of technical notes and tips are cataloged here (in several Microsoft SQL Server databases) and are searchable using the search engine provided. Searching the entire site (or just the Access portion of it) when you get an error message that doesn't seem to make sense, or need to know how to do something unusual (like installing two versions of Access on the same machine) will often reveal time-saving hints and step-by-step procedures.

- Access online help (\Program Files\Microsoft Office\Office\Acmain80.hlp) is a great reference for the syntax of programming elements (like functions) and for top-level information on the workings of those parts of Access you're not sure of. It's surprisingly comprehensive regarding the day-to-day operation of Access and Access databases.

- *Microsoft Access 97 Developer's Handbook* (Microsoft Press, 1997) is widely recognized as the authoritative guide to Access 97 programming. It contains nearly 600 pages of programming notes and tips geared to the intermediate-to-advanced Access programmer. Despite some pretty esoteric sample applications (a room area calculator and an ATM example), the code examples in this book often give you the boost you need to figure out how to do similar things in your own code.

- Microsoft TechNet is a fully searchable CD mailed monthly to subscribers. It contains the entire Knowledge Base, plus examples, code samples, feature articles, and techniques serious developers may find useful. In many cases, if a problem doesn't show up in a search of the Knowledge Base, it can be found on TechNet. TechNet is not inexpensive, but it may be worth the cost if you depend on Microsoft products for mission-critical applications.

- The Microsoft Access Developer Forum (**http://www.microsoft.com/accessdev/**) contains frequently updated techniques for using Access, as well as the latest patches and fixes for Access and Office software. It also includes a browsable library of tips, a job forum, and case studies concerning the integration of Access into the workplace.

- *ACCESS-OFFICE-VB Advisor* magazine (home page at **http://www.advisor.com/av.html**) contains hints and tips from basic interface design to advanced programming, and is updated monthly. The latest tools are previewed here and you can often learn more from reading other reader's questions than you can by browsing the Knowledge Base. Although the focus of this magazine has recently shifted away from Access and more toward general VBA programming, Access is still a focal point for most articles.

- *Access 97 Expert Solutions* (**http://www.mcp.com/que/developer_expert/access97es/**) (Que, 1996) is 1,200 pages of detailed, insightful information about using Access 97 to develop custom applications, and the entire text is available online at Que's Office 97 Resource Center (**http://www.mcp.com/que/msoffice/**). If you can't read this whole book, at least read Chapter 6, "Leszynski Naming Conventions for Access" to streamline your debugging efforts and improve the maintainability of your code.

- CNET's ACTIVEX.COM (**http://www.activex.com**) contains hundreds of custom (ActiveX) controls that you can use in your forms and reports. Many are trial versions or require a nominal registration fee, but many are free. Using these controls in Access often requires some experience manipulating control properties and some knowledge of how the operating system registers controls.

Finally, don't be afraid to ask the experts for help. As you progress in your experience with Access, you'll find more and more people coming to you for help. There's nothing like the feeling you get when you recognize someone else's problem as one that once afflicted you, and you know how to solve it. ●

Appendix

Access Control
Descriptions

This appendix covers most of the Access controls, and
concentrates on how they might be used in a typical application. All of the controls in Access are documented in the
online help, which has examples of their use. Check the
help whenever you use a control at which you're not an
expert. The controls are presented in order of usefulness,
which isn't how they appear on the Toolbox; you'll also
find the associated icon, properties, and some typical uses
of the control in a form. ■

The Label Control

The label control (see Figure A.1) is used to place text on a form without affecting data in the underlying table. A full range of text formatting tools are available, including alignment, fonts, and colors.

FIG. A.1
Customers

Label control —

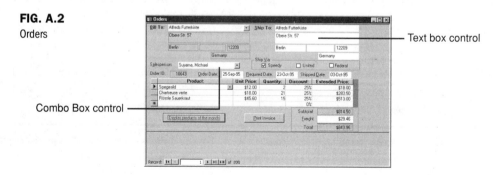

Key properties for the Label control:

Property	Comments
Caption	Controls the text that appears on the screen.
Back Style	Set to Transparent to make the background show through behind the text.
Hyperlink Address	Enter a URL and click the label. This activates the URL.

The Text Box Control

The Text Box control (see Figure A.2) is used to show and edit data in a related table. Text boxes serve as "windows" to underlying fields in the form's Record Source. If the underlying table permits the editing or addition of records, data typed in a Text box will be entered in the table as soon as the user moves to a different record.

FIG. A.2
Orders

Text box control

Combo Box control —

Key properties for the Text Box control:

Property	Comments
Control Source	The name of the field in the underlying table containing the data shown in this control.
Input Mask	A string specifying that text entered in this control should be formatted specially; for example, a mask might force the entry of a phone number with the hyphen placed correctly.
Enabled	When set to Yes, users can select this control. Depending on the value of "Locked," they may or may not be able to change data in it.
Locked	When set to No, users can change the contents of this control. If Enabled is set to No and Locked to Yes, users cannot select or change data in this control.
Status Bar Text	Text entered in this property appears at the bottom of the screen when this control is selected.

The Combo Box and List Box Controls

  When a field has a finite list of possible values, a combo box or list box will display them for the user when he clicks the control. Combo boxes and list boxes differ only in their appearance; the values in combo boxes only appear when the user clicks a pulldown arrow at the right end of the field, where list boxes show several of their values all the time.

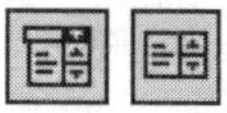

Both combo and list boxes (see Figure A.3) can get their list of possible values from a data source (such as a table or query), the contents of other controls, or from a static list of values, separated by semicolons. They share most properties with text boxes. Both combo and list boxes can display values from more than one field in the underlying data source, but only one of the values in the list can be "bound" to the underlying field.

FIG. A.3

These two controls share the same row source, but display differently.

Combo Box

List Box

Key properties for Combo and List Box controls:

Property	Comments
Row Source	Either an expression specifying the source of the data for the list of valid entries, or the list itself.
Column Count	The number of columns to show for each value in the combo or list box.
Column Heads	When set to Yes, Access shows a title over each column of values in the control.

The Command Button Control

Command buttons (see Figure A.4) look and act like push buttons on the form. When clicked, they appear to depress and then pop back out. They can contain text or images, can be of any size, and usually activate some underlying VBA code attached to the OnClick property of the control. The Command Button Wizard makes the creation of command buttons for common tasks (opening and closing forms, running macros, traversing records, and printing forms and reports) practically foolproof.

▶ **See** "Events," **p. 200**

FIG. A.4
Products

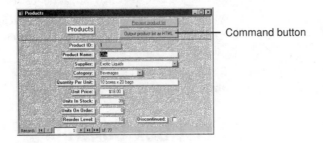

Command button

Key properties for the Command Button control:

Property	Comments
Picture	A wizard helps specify an icon to appear on the button from Access' internal list of several dozen, or you can choose a bitmap or icon file from the local disk.
Default	Setting this to Yes makes this button the one that's activated if the user presses the Enter key. You still must write the code that the button executes when pressed.
Cancel	Setting this to Yes makes this button the button selected when a user presses the Esc key. You still must write the code that the button executes when pressed.
Transparent	Setting this to Yes makes the button active, but invisible. It's useful for placing a command button on top of another control. Note that if you use the Visible property to make a command button invisible, the button cannot be activated.

The Tab Control

The Tab Control (see Figure A.5) provides an intuitive way to switch among several forms. This is useful when there's just too much information about a single entity (a person, a project, an office) to effectively display on one screen. Tab controls have their own properties, and each tab in a tab control has its own separate property sheet. Clicking a tab in Form view displays that tab's "page" which takes up most of the rest of the area of the tab control beneath the tabs.

To place controls on a page, select the appropriate tab in Design view and draw or paste the controls in the desired position on the page. Individual pages inherit the properties of the parent Tab control unless they're specifically changed for each particular page. Because most users seem to understand how to use them, the use of tab controls can add a lot of power to an application. You also can increase the amount of data that can be placed on a page. Furthermore, the contents of an entire tab control are loaded into memory when the control is first displayed, making switching between controls very fast.

The Tab Control, unlike most controls, includes some properties that are only accessible by right-clicking the control after it's created. These properties include the settings for the number of tabs in the control, their order, and methods to insert and delete tab pages.

FIG. A.5

Employees

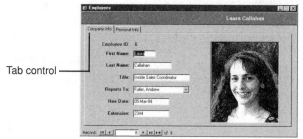

Tab control

Key properties for the Tab control:

Property	Comments
Multi Row	If set to Yes, tabs can "stack" in several rows when their combined width exceeds the width of the tab control itself. If set to No, navigation arrows appear to scroll through the single row of tabs if necessary.
Picture	You can choose a picture, instead of text, to appear on the tab to describe the contents of the associated tab page.
Page Index	0-based count of the number of tabs on a page. If you have more than one tab control, the numbering continues across all of the controls. These numbers are generally used by VBA code written to manipulate the tabs.

The Option Group, Toggle Button, Option Button, and Check Box Controls

When an underlying data element only can accept a certain set of values, and the legal values are known at the time the form is designed, an Option Group is an effective control to use to show the user all of the available options, while only permitting selection of one.

When an Option Group is used, it is bound to the underlying data field and then it is filled with one or more of the following types of controls:

- Toggle buttons (these look like raised and depressed squares)
- Option buttons (sometimes called "radio buttons," that look like filled and unfilled circles)
- Check boxes (depressed squares that appear either blank or are filled with a check box)

The controls within the Option Group (see Figure A.6) are not bound to a Control Source, so they do not directly impact data in the underlying table. Instead, each control within the Option Group is assigned a number, usually beginning with 1. These numbers are maintained in each control's OptionValue property. When the record is saved, the value of the OptionValue property of the selected control is saved. Only one control within an Option Group can be selected at a time (the other will automatically deselect when another is selected), and the value returned must be a number (no strings, etc.).

If the data in the underlying table or query is not Null, the appropriate control within the Option Group appears selected as you move from record to record.

Toggle Buttons, Check Boxes, and Option Buttons also can be used outside an Option Group. In this context, the buttons should be bound to a data field of type Yes/No; the control appears selected if the value of the data field is Yes. When used in this way, the value of any one of these controls does not affect the values of any others.

The properties of Toggle Buttons are similar to Command Buttons, and they can be used in much the same way. Check Boxes and Option Buttons have nearly identical properties, differing primarily in appearance.

FIG. A.6

Orders

Option group

Check box control

Key properties for Option Group, Toggle Button, Option Button, and Check Box controls:

Property	Comments
Special Effect	For an Option Group, choosing a clear demarcation line for its borders is key to helping users understand which controls are contained within it. There are several border styles available under this property that make it clear where the Option Group ends.
Picture Type	Toggle buttons can contain pictures, rather than labels.

The Unbound Object Frame, Bound Object Frame, and Image Controls

 These three controls are used to display binary objects on a form. These objects typically include, but are not limited to, word processor documents, pictures, sounds, spreadsheets, and so on. Most Windows programs can export native objects using Windows Object Linking and Embedding (OLE) ability, and Access can display those objects and use the application in which they were created to edit them.

For example, you can use an Unbound Object Frame to embed an Excel spreadsheet into a form. Because the object frame is "unbound," the spreadsheet has no relationship to the data underlying the form and is not stored in the database. As records change on the form, the spreadsheet remains the same. A user double-clicking the spreadsheet can start Excel to edit the spreadsheet.

If you included a field of type "OLE Object" in the table your form represents, and stored a spreadsheet in the OLE Object field, you could use a Bound Object Frame (see Figure A.7) to display the spreadsheet. Because the frame is "bound," it will load a different spreadsheet with every different record displayed. Additionally, because the object is OLE-compliant, double-clicking it will start Excel to edit it, and the changes will be stored in your Access database.

The Image control is always "unbound," and contains a simple, static bitmap. You cannot store the image in a table in the database (although it is stored with the form in most cases), and you cannot double-click it to edit it. In return for this limited functionality, the image loads relatively quickly. Use the Image control for decorative graphics on forms, but use it sparingly to preserve system memory.

FIG. A.7
Categories

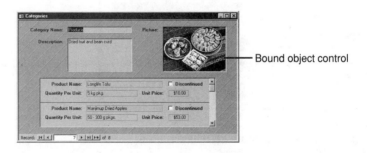

Bound object control

Key properties for Unbound Object Frame, Bound Object Frame, and Image controls:

Property	Comments
Display Type	If set to "Content," Access displays the OLE Object specified in its native format. If set to Icon, Access displays an appropriate icon (which can be double-clicked to start the native application). Icon loads much faster.

continues

continued

Property	Comments
OLE Class	Different applications on your system are "registered" with Windows to edit objects of different types. The OLE Class property contains the standard name for the object you embedded.
OLE Type Allowed	You specify whether an OLE Object will be "Linked" or "Embedded" when you insert it into your form or table. An Embedded object is stored in the database and its representation elsewhere on the disk is no longer required. A Linked object sets up a reference within the database to the object itself, which must remain stored in a file on a disk drive.
Size Mode	If set to Clip, the image or object is cropped to fit the size of the control. If set to Zoom, the image resizes to fit the window, maintaining its proportions. If set to Stretch, the object resizes to fill the window, even if this causes distortion.

The Line and Rectangle Controls

For graphic impact within a form, you may want to place rectangles and/or lines (see Figure A.8) around and behind other controls on the form. This technique is useful to delimit a group of related controls to ease navigation.

FIG. A.8
Startup

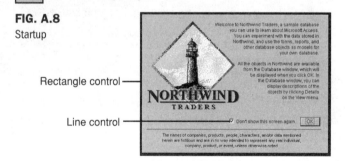

Rectangle control ——

Line control ——

Key properties for Line and Rectangle controls:

Property	Comments
Back Style	A rectangle with the Back Style set to Transparent, but with a colored border, effectively sets a region of a form apart.

The Page Break Control

When a form is long, you may want to mark a point at which the page should seem to "break" if the Page Up and Page Down keys are used. If the form is longer vertically than the window in which it is displayed (as is often the case with Subforms), Access will automatically display a vertical scroll bar to traverse it (see Figure A.9). If a Page Break Control ( ) is present, the Page Down key will redraw the form so the top of the form appears to be the point immediately after the Page Break.

Page Break controls are not visible in Form view.

The real value of Page Break Controls is when they're used in reports. Because reports can use almost all of the same controls as forms, this control is included for both types of objects.

FIG. A.9
Employees (Page Break), in Design view.

Page Break control

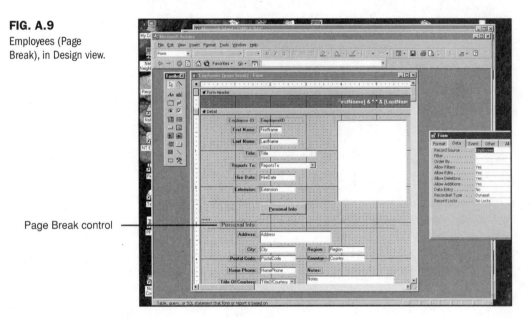

▶ **See** "Choosing Data Sources and Controls for Your Report," **p. 113**

There are no key properties for the Page Break Control. ●

Index

Symbols

* (asterisk), query wildcards, 76

\ (backslash), passwords, 229
Delete queries, 85

^ (caret), macros, 138

: (colon), VBA labels, 195

, (comma), default thousands separator, 29

{ } (curly braces), macros, 138

. (period), default decimal separator, 29

+ (plus sign), macros, 138

? (question mark), printing code, 211

_ (underscore character), code, 179

A

Access 97
Access Developers Toolkit, *see* ODE (Office 97 Developer's Edition)
Basic, converting to VBA, 223-225
  entirely, 224-225
  errors, 225
  partially, 224
case-sensitivity, 76
functions, 203-204
help, 257-259
  keywords, 186
new features, 3-4

Access 97 Expert Solutions, **258**

access permissions, 230
Administer permission, 230
setting/removing, 234-235
  new objects, 234

ACCESS-OFFICE-VB Advisor magazine, 258

actions
events comparison, 200
macros, 133-135
  arguments, 134-135
methods comparison, 199

Active Server Pages (ASP), 143
creating, 158-161
  forms, 160-161
  specifying data sources, 159
  tables, 159-160
  timeout values, 159

ActiveX, CNET ACTIVEX.COM Web site, 259

Add Watch command (Debug menu), 209-210

Admin user, 231
changing password, 231, 236
removing permissions, 236

Administer permission, 230

aggregate functions
reports, 117-119
  creating, 118
  headers/footers, 118
Select queries, 79-82
  Avg, 81-82
  conditional usage, 80-81
  QBE grid Totals row, 79-80

aligning controls
forms, 62
reports, 120

Allow Zero Length attribute, data types, 30

Analyze command (Tools menu), 47
Documenter command, 254
Performance command, 166

analyzing
databases, Documenter, 254-255
tables, Table Analyzer Wizard, 46-47

Append queries, 90-91

arguments, macros, 134-135

ASPs (Active Server Pages), 143
creating, 158-161
  forms, 160-161
  specifying data sources, 159
  tables, 159-160
  timeout values, 159

assigning
access permissions, *see* access permissions
users to groups, 233

asterisk (*), query wildcards, 76
Delete queries, 85

attributes (data types), 28-31
Field Size, 28-29
Format, 29-30

Auto Data Tips, testing code, 208-209

Complete and Return this Card
for a *FREE* Computer Book Catalog

Thank you for purchasing this book! You have purchased a superior computer book written expressly for your needs. To continue to provide the kind of up-to-date, pertinent coverage you've come to expect from us, we need to hear from you. Please take a minute to complete and return this self-addressed, postage-paid form. In return, we'll send you a free catalog of all our computer books on topics ranging from word processing to programming and the internet.

Mr. ☐   Mrs. ☐   Ms. ☐   Dr. ☐

Name (first) ☐☐☐☐☐☐☐☐☐☐☐☐ (M.I.) ☐ (last) ☐☐☐☐☐☐☐☐☐☐☐☐☐☐☐

Address ☐☐☐☐☐☐☐☐☐☐☐☐☐☐☐☐☐☐☐☐☐☐☐☐☐☐☐☐☐☐☐☐☐

☐☐☐☐☐☐☐☐☐☐☐☐☐☐☐☐☐☐☐☐☐☐☐☐☐☐☐☐☐☐☐☐☐

City ☐☐☐☐☐☐☐☐☐☐☐☐☐☐☐☐ State ☐☐ Zip ☐☐☐☐☐☐☐☐☐

Phone ☐☐☐ ☐☐☐ ☐☐☐☐ Fax ☐☐☐ ☐☐☐ ☐☐☐☐

Company Name ☐☐☐☐☐☐☐☐☐☐☐☐☐☐☐☐☐☐☐☐☐☐☐☐

E-mail address ☐☐☐☐☐☐☐☐☐☐☐☐☐☐☐☐☐☐☐☐☐☐☐☐

1. Please check at least (3) influencing factors for purchasing this book.

Front or back cover information on book .... ☐
Special approach to the content .... ☐
Completeness of content .... ☐
Author's reputation .... ☐
Publisher's reputation .... ☐
Book cover design or layout .... ☐
Index or table of contents of book .... ☐
Price of book .... ☐
Special effects, graphics, illustrations .... ☐
Other (Please specify): _____ ☐

2. How did you first learn about this book?

Saw in Macmillan Computer Publishing catalog .... ☐
Recommended by store personnel .... ☐
Saw the book on bookshelf at store .... ☐
Recommended by a friend .... ☐
Received advertisement in the mail .... ☐
Saw an advertisement in: _____ ☐
Read book review in: _____ ☐
Other (Please specify): _____ ☐

3. How many computer books have you purchased in the last six months?

This book only .... ☐   3 to 5 books .... ☐
books .... ☐   More than 5 .... ☐

4. Where did you purchase this book?

Bookstore .... ☐
Computer Store .... ☐
Consumer Electronics Store .... ☐
Department Store .... ☐
Office Club .... ☐
Warehouse Club .... ☐
Mail Order .... ☐
Direct from Publisher .... ☐
Internet site .... ☐
Other (Please specify): _____ ☐

5. How long have you been using a computer?

☐ Less than 6 months   ☐ 6 months to a year
☐ 1 to 3 years   ☐ More than 3 years

6. What is your level of experience with personal computers and with the subject of this book?

	With PCs	With subject of book
New	☐	☐
Casual	☐	☐
Accomplished	☐	☐
Expert	☐	☐

Source Code ISBN: 0-7897-1439-6

7. Which of the following best describes your job title?

Administrative Assistant .... ☐
Coordinator .... ☐
Manager/Supervisor .... ☐
Director .... ☐
Vice President .... ☐
President/CEO/COO .... ☐
Lawyer/Doctor/Medical Professional .... ☐
Teacher/Educator/Trainer .... ☐
Engineer/Technician .... ☐
Consultant .... ☐
Not employed/Student/Retired .... ☐
Other (Please specify): _____ ☐

8. Which of the following best describes the area of the company your job title falls under?

Accounting .... ☐
Engineering .... ☐
Manufacturing .... ☐
Operations .... ☐
Marketing .... ☐
Sales .... ☐
Other (Please specify): _____ ☐

9. What is your age?

Under 20 .... ☐
21-29 .... ☐
30-39 .... ☐
40-49 .... ☐
50-59 .... ☐
60-over .... ☐

10. Are you:

Male .... ☐
Female .... ☐

11. Which computer publications do you read regularly? (Please list)

_____
_____
_____
_____
_____
_____
_____
_____
_____

Comments: _____
_____
_____

Fold here and tape to ma[il]

BUSINESS REPLY MAIL
FIRST-CLASS MAIL PERMIT NO. 9918 INDIANAPOLIS IN

POSTAGE WILL BE PAID BY THE ADDRESSEE

ATTN MARKETING
MACMILLAN COMPUTER PUBLISHING
MACMILLAN PUBLISHING USA
201 W 103RD ST
INDIANAPOLIS IN 46290-9042

NO POSTAGE
NECESSARY
IF MAILED
IN THE
UNITED STATES

Check out Que® Books
on the World Wide Web
http://www.quecorp.com

As the biggest software release in computer history, Windows 95 continues to redefine the computer industry. Click here for the latest info on our Windows 95 books

Make computing quick and easy with these products designed exclusively for new and casual users

Examine the latest releases in word processing, spreadsheets, operating systems, and suites

The Internet, The World Wide Web, CompuServe®, America Online®, Prodigy®—it's a world of ever-changing information. Don't get left behind!

Find out about new additions to our site, new bestsellers and hot topics

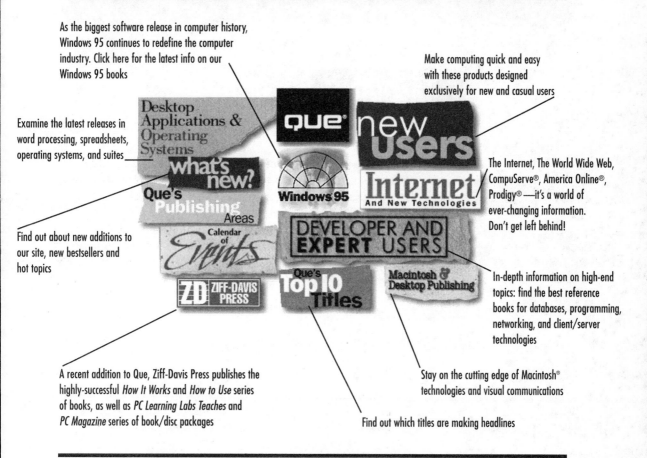

In-depth information on high-end topics: find the best reference books for databases, programming, networking, and client/server technologies

A recent addition to Que, Ziff-Davis Press publishes the highly-successful *How It Works* and *How to Use* series of books, as well as *PC Learning Labs Teaches* and *PC Magazine* series of book/disc packages

Stay on the cutting edge of Macintosh® technologies and visual communications

Find out which titles are making headlines

With 6 separate publishing groups, Que develops products for many specific market segments and areas of computer technology. Explore our Web Site and you'll find information on best-selling titles, newly published titles, upcoming products, authors, and much more.

- Stay informed on the latest industry trends and products available
- Visit our online bookstore for the latest information and editions
- Download software from Que's library of the best shareware and freeware

MACMILLAN COMPUTER PUBLISHING USA

A VIACOM COMPANY

Technical Support:

If you need assistance with the information in this book or with a CD/Disk accompanying the book, please access the Knowledge Base on our Web site at **http://www.superlibrary.com/general/support**. Our most Frequently Asked Questions are answered there. If you do not find the answer to your questions on our Web site, you may contact Macmillan Technical Support **(317) 581-3833** or e-mail us at **support@mcp.com**.